'Education for adulthood finally comes of age at the hands of Finger and Asún. A brilliantly incisive critique of adult education's fall from grace and an inspiring practical plan for its re-enchantment. They return adult educators to their original moral tasks and agenda of democratic political action, collective creativity and critical social change. These are uncompromising scholars who refuse to let adult education compromise itself.'

John Broughton, Teachers College, Columbia University

'In *Learning Our Way Out*, Finger and Asún cogently analyse the important role that adult education has to play in building a sustainable human community, which is increasingly threatened by turbocapitalism, the decay of politics, postmodernism, and the ecological crisis. Their call to link learning with issues of power and organization needs to be on the agenda of all adult educators.'

Ron Cervero, University of Georgia

'Finger and Asún bring a critical and multi-disciplinary eye to the challenge of deepening our theory at a time of globalization.'

Budd L. Hall, vice-president,
International Council for Adult Education

'This book captured my interest, not because I agree entirely with Finger and Asún's analysis, but because I appreciate the breadth and direction of their writing. They propose a social learning and structural change theory that challenges the hegemony of psychological explanations while navigating between rationality and postmodern standpoints. It is more than a text; it is a "must read" for any serious adult educator.'

Phyllis Cunningham, Northern Illinois University

About the Authors

Matthias Finger holds doctorates in both Political Science and Adult Education from the University of Geneva. He was Associate Professor of Adult and Continuing Education at Columbia University, New York, in 1992–94. He is a Member of the Commission on Environmental Strategy and Planning of the IUCN (the World Conservation Union). He has published widely in English, French and German on social issues including ecology, development, management, adult education and the peace movement. For several years he edited the magazine *Eco-currents*. His books include (with Pratap Chatterjee) *The Earth Brokers: Power, Politics and Development* (London, 1994) and (with Thomas Princen) *Environmental NGOs in World Politics: Linking the Global and the Local* (London, 1994). He is currently Professor of Management of Public Enterprises at the Graduate Institute of Public Administration (IDHEAP) in Lausanne.

José Manuel Asún is a Spanish adult educator who for many years (1984–92) was Director of the Ministry of Education's Adult Education Territorial Centre in Zaragoza. His original university education was at the universities of Zaragoza, Salamanca and the Universidad Pontifica de Salamanca. In 1993 he went to Teachers College, Columbia University, where he spent the following three years. When writing this book, he was a research fellow at the University of Barcelona's Centre for Research on the Education of Adults. His professional experience has included a spell as a resident specialist at the UNESCO Institute of Education (Hamburg). He has also served as the Spanish government's representative on the IFOMA Programme of UNESCO's regional bureau in Dakar, Senegal. He currently works for the Regional Ministry of Education of Aragon.

Adult Education at the Crossroads

Learning Our Way Out

——————

**MATTHIAS FINGER &
JOSÉ MANUEL ASÚN**

ZED BOOKS
London & New York

NIACE
Leicester

To Yann Finger, Pablo López-Herranz

And those of their generation.
May they, when adults,
Encounter a world where
Learning the way out
Will be easier.

Adult Education at the Crossroads was first published in 2001 by
Zed Books Ltd, 7 Cynthia Street, London N1 9JF, UK,
and Room 400, 175 Fifth Avenue, New York, NY 10010, USA

Published in paperback in the United Kingdom by NIACE,
the National Organization for Adult Learning, 21 De Montfort Street,
Leicester LE1 7GE, UK

Distributed in the USA exclusively by Palgrave, a division of St. Martin's
Press, LLC, 175 Fifth Avenue, New York, NY 10010, USA

Copyright © Matthias Finger and José Manuel Asún 2001

The right of Matthias Finger and José Manuel Asún to be identified as the
authors of this work has been asserted by them in accordance with the
Copyright, Designs and Patents Act, 1988

Designed and typeset in Monotype Baskerville
by Illuminati, Grosmont.
Cover designed by Lee Robinson/Ad Lib Designs
Printed and bound in the United Kingdom by Biddles Ltd,
Guildford and King's Lynn

A catalogue record for this book is available from the British Library

Library of Congress Cataloging-in-Publication Data applied for

ISBN 1 85649 750 X (Hb)
ISBN 1 85649 751 8 (Pb)

NIACE ISBN 1 86201 108 7

Global Perspectives
on Adult Education and Training

Series Editors: Budd Hall with Carol Medel-Anonuevo
and Griff Foley.

Series Advisors: Peggy Antrobus, Phyllis Cunningham,
Chris Duke, Patricia Ellis, Matthias Finger, Heribert Hinzen,
Agneta Lind, Peter Mayo, Derek Mulenga, Jorge Osorio, Lalita
Ramdas, Te Rippowe, Nelly P. Stromquist, Rajesh Tandon,
Carlos Alberto Torres, Alan Tuckett, Shirley Walters, Makoto
Yamaguchi, Karen Yarmol-Franko, Frank Youngman
and Abdelwahid Yousif.

This new series is designed to provide for the first time a genuinely
global basis to the theory and practice of adult education and
learning worldwide. A key goal is to introduce readers to issues,
debates and understandings related to centrally important areas
in adult education and training, particularly but not exclusively in
the majority (or 'third') world, and to provide a forum where practitioners from the South, women, and other social groups
historically underrepresented in AET, can find a voice. To this
end, the new series will contribute to redressing an imbalance in
the literature whereby our understanding and debates in adult
education and training in the English-speaking world have been
unduly dominated by bodies of knowledge and theoretical perspectives drawn from experience in the USA and Britain and relatively unrepresentative of class, race and gender.

Among the issues of immediate and vital interest to adult educators throughout the world which new titles in this series will
address are: popular education, adult learning and civil society,
post-colonial perspectives, women's perspectives, informal learning
in peoples' struggles, worker education, environmental adult
education, participatory research, the political economy of adult
education, indigenous knowledge and adult learning, and the
impact on them of globalization and other social trends.

Titles already available

Shirley Walters (ed.), *Globalisation, Adult Education and Training: Impacts and Issues*

Peter Mayo, *Gramsci, Freire and Adult Education: Possibilities for Transformative Action*

Griff Foley, *Learning in Social Action: A Contribution to Understanding Informal Education*

Frank Youngman, *The Political Economy of Adult Education and Development*

Matthias Finger and José Manuel Asún, *Adult Education at the Crossroads: Learning Our Way Out*

For full details of this list and Zed's other subject and general catalogues, please write to: The Marketing Department, Zed Books, 7 Cynthia Street, London N1 9JF, UK or email Sales@zedbooks.demon.co.uk Visit our website at: http://www.zedbooks.demon.co.uk

Contents

List of Figures and Tables

List of Acronyms

AAAE	American Association for Adult Education
ACE	Adult and Continuing Education
AEA	Adult Education Association (USA)
AEGIS	Adult Education Guided Independent Study
AERA	American Educational Research Association
AERC	Adult Education Research Conference
CAME	Conference of Allied Ministers of Education
CIDOC	Center for Intercultural Documentation
ECOSOC	Economic and Social Council
ERIC	Educational Resources Information Clearinghouse
EU	European Union
FAO	Food and Agriculture Organization
HRD	Human Resource Development
ICAE	International Council for Adult Education
IFDA	International Foundation for Development Alternatives
ILO	International Labor Organization
ISO	International Standardization Organization
IUCN	International Union for the Conservation of Nature
MIT	Massachusetts Institute of Technology
NGO	Non-Governmental Organization

NSM	New Social Movements
NTL	National Training Laboratory
OD	Organizational Development
OECD	Organization for Economic Co-operation and Development
PAR	Participatory Action Research
SDL	Self-Directed Learning
TC	Teachers College Columbia University
UCLA	University of California at Los Angeles
UNDP	United Nations Development Programme
UNEP	United Nations Environment Programme
UNESCO	United Nations Educational, Scientific and Cultural Organization
UNRISD	United Nations Research Institute for Social Development
USAID	United States Agency for International Development
UTS	Union Theological Seminary
WCEFA	World Conference on Education for All
WTO	World Trade Organization
WWF	World Wide Fund for Nature

Introduction

'Learning Our Way Out', the key concept of this book, has a double meaning: on the one hand, we think, industrial civilisation has to learn its way out of a process which inevitably leads to a dead end. On the other hand – and because it is so closely tied to this process of industrial development – adult education also has to learn its way out of a process which leads both to its unprecedented success in terms of practice and to its demise as a field and an intellectual discipline.

Adult education is, indeed, burgeoning. Never before has there been so much talk about 'learning' – and not only about learning by children, but learning by all members of society, organisational units, business, and even society as a whole. This is not to say that it has never happened before, but now such learning – which hitherto has been informal – is being measured, quantified, certified, recognised, and actively promoted. At the same time, learning is being customised, adapted to the needs of individuals and organisations, computerised, marketed, and sold worldwide like any other commodity. Soon, refusing to learn will become a crime. The survival of our economy, our entire civilisation, it is argued, now depends on learning. We need only to look at the business literature, where, since the mid-1990s, every other book has at least a chapter about the wonders of learning. We have become a society of learning individuals – not least because our individual attractiveness and competitiveness on the market now depend on whether or not we are permanently learning. In other words, UNESCO's dream of the early 1970s, which had inspired the entire field of adult education, has now become true: a 'learning society'!

Yet adult education, as a field and an intellectual discipline, seems to be overwhelmed by its very success. Not only was it not prepared for it, but this explosion of learning appears to go hand in hand with the crisis of industrial civilisation, of which it is an expression, and which it should help to solve. Yet adult education has nothing to say about this crisis, since it has always considered industrial development to be profoundly beneficial, simply in need of humanisation, which adult education should provide. In other words, the explosion of learning as practice goes hand in hand with the implosion of adult education as a discipline. In our analysis, there are two reasons for this evolution, both of which will be discussed in detail in our book.

The first reason is that adult education has never been an intellectually coherent and unified field. It has very diverse theoretical foundations, which have never been integrated, either theoretically or conceptually. As we will show in Part I, adult education has never had a coherent practice or a coherent discourse when it comes to learning. Indeed, at times learning is considered purely individual, contributing to personal growth. In this case, adult education refers, in essence, to humanistic psychology. Then, learning is considered to be a cognitive development process, leading to awareness and intellectual competencies. Here, adult education refers to Enlightenment pedagogy and critical theory, an approach which is especially widespread in Europe. Finally, learning is a process of individual and even collective problem-solving, which is in particular the American approach. Here, adult education refers to pragmatism, which, as a matter of fact, has shaped most of adult education conceptualisation. Today, as learning explodes, adult education's theoretical and conceptual incoherences are clearly visible.

The second reason is that, simultaneously, the reality which historically has held adult education as an intellectual discipline together has substantially changed. All three of the schools of thought listed above, differently as they conceptualise (adult) learning, have one thing in common: the idea that it is adult education's mission to humanise industrial development. In other words, adult education's *raison d'être* is to give development a human face.

This mission, clearly articulated by UNESCO at the beginning of the 1970s, has given adult education an apparent coherence it had never had before. Yet the intellectual foundation of this mission was and remains shallow; it is grounded in a political opposition between learning and participation in development on the one hand, and schooling and domination by experts on the other. Ever since – and this is a positive result – adult education has become synonymous with democracy and human development. On the negative side, however, adult education has never questioned industrial development but has, rather, legitimised it by actively contributing to its humanisation – a task of quasi-religious dimensions. Who but Ivan Illich, a former priest, could question this mission? This is why we will present Illich's views on adult education in the very first chapter of our book. Illich was and remains the only thinker in the field of adult education who has dared to question its very foundational assumption. He will therefore be our guiding light throughout. More than ever before, his thinking is relevant today, as the very idea of 'sustainable' industrial development goes up in smoke, while all its sustaining institutions try to survive … and make things worse in doing so.

In Part II, we will argue that the process of industrial development has progressed and been distorted to a point where it no longer has much to do with 'development'. We think that in the age of 'turbo-capitalism' – a term coined by Edward Luttwak (1999) – with its irreversible destruction of nature, society and cultures, industrial development is no longer 'humanisable'. Consequently, adult education, whose role was to humanise development, enters a profound intellectual and conceptual crisis. Interestingly, when turbo-capitalism leads to a dead end, creative and collective learning appears to be the only resource available in the search for a way out. Permanent and ever-accelerating learning by individuals and organisations becomes a necessity if industrial development is to survive; as a result, learning now emerges as the miracle solution to all problems. The prominence of learning makes the role that adult education can play all the more relevant, while at the same time adult education is being instrumentalised to help industrial civilisation to continue. In other words, the success or explosion of adult education goes hand in hand with its implosion: the loss of all its ideals and the mission it once stood for.

How can adult education find a way out of the dead end into which it has manoeuvred itself alongside industrial development – that is, precisely because it was not critical enough of the very process of industrial development? We think that adult education cannot learn its way out without critically questioning industrial development, and asking whether this process is still humanisable. It must ask what adult education for social action, to which it was once committed as a field, would look like today. Apparently, today's challenges have something to do with learning. But what kind of learning are we talking about? Who should learn what? Is it learning to give industrial development an additional lease of life, or is it learning to find a way out of the dead end to which this development leads? If it is the latter – as we will argue – adult education must critically question its own concepts, theories and practice. It must analyse where such 'learning our way out' already takes place today. It must uncover the theoretical and conceptual foundations of such learning our way out, and translate them into corresponding adult education practices. This is what we set out to do in Part III.

If adult education is capable of creatively addressing these two challenges – its success or explosion, and its identity crisis or implosion – then, we think, it does have a future as an intellectual discipline. Thanks to such adult education, it might then become possible to imagine and to engage practically in ways out of the current dead end of industrial development.

This book is the result of long reflection and a long-term collaboration: we know the theory of adult education and most of the facets of its practices, from grassroots activism to top management training. We also strongly sympathise with a social change agenda. Yet many activist adult educators will probably miss a systematic presentation of the various adult education activities for social change, in the areas of gender and race relations, environment and labour. Much has been written over the last years on adult education for social justice (Newman, 1994; Atweh, Kemmis and Weeks, 1998), the rights of indigenous peoples (Beetson, 1996) or against racism (Hayes and Colin, 1994; Haymes, 1995; Peterson, 1996), sexism (Hart, 1992; Gore, 1993), or ecological destruction

(Follen, Clover and Hall, 1997). Nevertheless, while we find that all such adult education endeavours are certainly a step in the right direction, we want to go deeper. We are basically concerned with the epistemological aspects of such social and political aware-ness-raising in the new context of a 'dead-end industrial civilisa-tion'. Rather than asking how and on what kind of issues awareness should be raised, we ask what it means to raise awareness within an overall societal context in which inequalities can no longer simply be compensated or 'bought off'. In other words, we ask ourselves whether adult education as awareness-raising on social and environmental issues is still enough, given the perspective of a 'dead-end industrial civilisation'. Furthermore, we ask whether (adult) learning should not be approached in a different way al-together, and this is the type of reflection we have in mind when we use the phrase 'Learning Our Way Out'.

Chapter 1

Ivan Illich: Learning Webs,
Not One-way Streets

Ivan Illich will accompany us throughout this book. Although he wrote in the 1970s, Illich still offers a fresh alternative to the main paths on which adult education was embarking at that time, and has remained firmly upon. Among all adult education theorists and most practitioners, Illich certainly has the broadest, the most critical, and also a quite 'Southern' perspective. His idea of building 'Learning webs for a convivial society' (Illich, 1970a: 103–50) has, we believe, enduring value.

It was in the context of the 1970s that – on philosophical, epistemological and theoretical levels – adult education took the form it still has today. Most adult education theorists and practitioners saw themselves as part of the countercultural movement, the New Left, and/or participatory development. In the North, adult education set out to build a new field of practice, research and study, carving out a niche in academia and creating a profession. In the South, popular and non-formal adult education practices were emerging at the same time. Illich shared most of the ideas of the practitioners and thinkers of that time, yet differed because of his much broader intellectual framework. He was among the very rare thinkers in the field also to address ecological concerns, to reflect on technology in a constructive way, and really to think about pedagogical issues.

This is not to say that Illich did not reflect the spirit of the time, probably best captured by Marcuse's (1964) 'philosophy of the no' and by the countercultural movement more generally. Both in the North and in the South, people were rallying on campuses and streets, shouting no to the 'system', which was seen as perpetuating an oppressive social order. In the North, universities, the Vietnam War, the psychiatric hospitals, and many other constitutions, and in the South the imperialism of the North – exemplified by US military and foreign policy and by multinational corporations – were all viewed as representations of the very 'system' it was imperative to fight against. Yet Illich went beyond this – from today's perspective – quite simplistic view. As an anarchist with a long-term historical perspective and solid anthropological knowledge and experience, he was able to give his critique of the 'system' a much deeper intellectual grounding. His critique of dominant education and the alternatives he proposed in terms of collective learning received much attention at the time, but were perhaps too radical even for the radicals.

During that time, Illich set up his headquarters in the South (Mexico) but he deliberately did not build a school of followers, which is certainly one reason why he – and especially his contribution to adult education – has been more or less forgotten. In this first chapter we would therefore like to recall who Ivan Illich is, what he stood for intellectually both in general terms and in the field of education, and what – in our view – Illich's contribution to adult education constitutes today.

Ivan Illich: the person

Ivan Illich was born in Vienna in 1926 of a Croatian Catholic father and a Sephardic Jewish mother who left Germany during World War I. At 24 he earned a PhD in History from the University of Salzburg with a dissertation on Toynbee's philosophy of history. As a Catholic, he then studied Philosophy and Theology at the Gregorian University in Rome, and was subsequently ordained a priest. Undoubtedly, Illich's education occurred in the midst of the tension between the pre-Vatican II Council scholastic thinking on the one hand, and the Church Left on the other. As a German-speaking Catholic, Illich was particularly sensitive to neo-Marxist Critical Theory.

Illich's first assignment in 1951 as an assistant pastor perfectly reflected his political sensitivities. He went to a Puerto Rican (and Irish) parish in Manhattan's Washington Heights – a 'vanguard' post where he worked essentially with disenfranchised immigrants. There, he came in touch with issues of adult education and community development. Between 1956 and 1960 Illich was sent to work at the Catholic University of Puerto Rico in Ponce, where some still remember his lucidity and his 'heterodox' pastoral manner. There, he set up an intensive training centre for US priests practising in Latin American cultures and in Spanish. After some confrontations with the local bishops around political issues, Ivan Illich returned to New York, where he taught at Fordham University.

Because of his preoccupation with the training of missionaries, he went in 1963 to Cuernavaca, Mexico, where he started the Centre for Intercultural Formation, later called Centre for Inter-cultural Documentation, CIDOC (Centro Intercultural de Docu-mentación). The centre still exists today as a language school.[1] At CIDOC Illich put his ideas about adult education into practice. In his own words:

> CIDOC was meant to be the inverse of a university: a library-centred place for advanced learning where courses grew out of self-organized reading, and all readers were equally empowered to organize their own seminars.... There was no administration at CIDOC that could im-pose a curriculum or theme: only the library, the money-making school for spoken Spanish and the housekeeping activities were 'managed.' By statute any participant could organize the seminar of his fancy by describing it in the periodic catalogue or on the bulletin board. (Illich, 1979: 2)

CIDOC worked in the way Illich had envisioned for approxi-mately ten years, until 'success' undermined its very purpose – that is, until university professors went there to organise credit courses. During those ten years CIDOC was a 'free island, an oasis for the free exchange of knowledge and experience' (Ohliger and McCarthy, 1971: 5), a refuge for countercultural people and, later, also for indigenous Latin American peoples. It was during these years, and through debates and convivial reflection, that Illich developed his radical proposals. Many famous adult educa-tors visited CIDOC and came into contact with Illich and his ideas – for example, Paulo Freire, who published a book with Illich (Freire, Illich and Furter, 1974), Gaston Pineau (1977) and

Everett Reimer (1971). In the field of adult education, however, and even in other fields, Illich has not produced any disciples except, perhaps, for John Ohliger (1991), who is among the very few people still to echo Illich's ideas today.[2]

It was during the 1970s, in the context of the social movements, that Ivan Illich became widely known through his books and articles (Illich, 1970a, 1970b, 1970c, 1973a, 1973b, 1974a, 1974b, 1975, 1976, 1977). His *Deschooling Society* – published in 1970, and translated into many languages[3] – was heavily debated among educators. This was also the time of A.S. Neill's *Summerhill* and Freire's *Pedagogy of the Oppressed*, among many other famous educational experiences and authors. Illich continues to publish books (1978b, 1978c, 1981, 1983, 1985, 1988, 1991, 1993a, 1993b, 1996), and writes in widely read journals and newspapers such as *Esprit*, *Kursbuch*, *America*, *Siempre*, *Le Monde*, and many others. He has also been guest lecturer at many universities, including the University of Kassel (1979–82); the University of California at Berkeley (1982); the University of Marburg (1983–84); Pennsylvania State University (Professor of Humanities and Sciences, 1986–87); the University of Oldenburg, Federal Republic of Germany (Karl Jaspers Professor, 1990–91); the University of Bremen, Federal Republic of Germany (1991–95); and the University of Pennsylvania, Doctoral Program in Architecture (Visiting Professor, since 1990). Illich has been published in Spanish, French, German, Japanese, and other languages, and is also well known in the fields of social ecology, history, and anarchist thinking.[4] He lives in Germany, and continues his commitment to ecology.[5]

Ivan Illich: the theory

At the time of the Club of Rome's report on the limits to growth (Meadows et al., 1972), and several years before ecology emerged as a full-fledged social and political issue, Ivan Illich was already strongly criticising the consequences of industrial development, yet from an *anti-institutional* perspective. He denounced the monopolisation of core societal functions such as education and health by institutions. Furthermore, he condemned the way people were increasingly living in artefacts and, moreover, becoming artefacts themselves; how industrial development was destroying the environment; and how this process was undermining simple native abilities, making people dependent on objects. He had apparently developed this anti-institutional approach and perspective by reflecting on his experience in the highly institutionalised Catholic Church (cf. Illich, 1970d). The Church institutionalised charity at the time when it became politically recognised, and this institutionalisation is, according to Illich, at the very root of the Church's idea of 'services' and its 'service economy' (see We The People Organization, 1996). Once social functions are monopolised by institutions, social relationships and life more generally become degraded. In other words, institutions create the needs and control their satisfaction, and, by so doing, turn the human being and her or his creativity into objects.

Although it was developed in a political context, Illich's argumentation is basically organisational – or, rather, anti-organisational. We can distinguish four aspects:

- First, there is a critique of the *process of institutionalisation*: here Illich criticises the way modern society creates more and more institutions. In other words, as modern society unfolds, more or less everything becomes institutionalised. This process undermines people – it diminishes their confidence in themselves, and in their capacity to solve problems. This process also destroys what he calls 'conviviality'; that is, it kills convivial relationships. Finally it colonises life like a parasite or a cancer that kills creativity.
- Second, there is a critique of *experts* and *expertise*: indeed, the agents of such institutionalisation are the experts, the technocrats and the professionals. Experts and an expert culture always call for more experts. Experts also have a tendency to cartelise themselves by creating 'institutional barricades' – for example by proclaiming themselves gatekeepers, as well as self-selecting themselves. Finally, experts control knowledge production, as they decide what valid and legitimate knowledge is, and how its acquisition is sanctioned.
- Third, there is a critique of *commodification*. If the previous two argumentations seem to be heavily inspired by Max Weber's critique of rationalism and bureaucratisation, this third critique

of commodification reflects a Marxist influence. Illich applies this critique of commodification to education and learning, as we will see below:

> If the means for learning are in scarce supply, or are assumed to be scarce, then educational arrangements crop up to ensure that certain important knowledge, ideas, skills, attitudes, etc., are 'transmitted.' Education then becomes an economic commodity, which one consumes, or to use common language, which one 'gets.' (Illich 1996: ix)

• Finally, there is the *principle of counterproductivity*, which is probably Illich's most original theoretical contribution. By counter-productivity Illich means a mechanism which turns a funda-mentally good process (of institutionalisation and organisation) into a profoundly negative or 'counterproductive' one. In other words, once it reaches a certain threshold, the process of insti-tutionalisation becomes counterproductive. For example, Illich is not against schools or hospitals as such, but once a certain threshold of institutionalisation is reached, schools make people more stupid, while hospitals make them more sick. And more generally, beyond a certain threshold of institutionalised exper-tise, more experts are counterproductive – they produce the countereffect of what they set out to achieve.

Besides applying these critiques and principles to the Church and to theological expertocracy in *The Church, Change and Development* (Illich, 1970d), as well as to education, as we will see below, Illich has also applied them to other vital functions of modern society. In *Medical Nemesis: The Expropriation of Health*, where he shows how more doctors lead to a sicker society (Illich, 1975), and in *Energy and Equity* (Illich, 1974a) he applies the same argumentation to the energy system.

In response to these processes of institutionalisation, expert-ocracy, commodification and growing counterproductivity, Illich first called for 'a celebration of awareness': a consciousness of how the native – or, as he calls it, 'vernacular' – ways of living have become distorted. He then called for the disestablishment and deinstitutionalisation of a society which has turned people into accessories of bureaucracies and machines. He proposed the building of a convivial society, which fosters a different attitude towards peoples and tools:

> To the degree that [a person] masters his tools, he can invest the world with his meaning: to the degree that he is mastered by his tools, the shape of the tools determines his self-image. Convivial tools are those which give each person who uses them the greatest opportunity to enrich the environment with the fruit of his vision. Industrial tools deny this possibility to those who use them and they allow their designers to determine the meaning and expectations of others.... As an alternative to technocratic disaster, I propose the vision of a convivial society. A convivial society would be the result of social arrangements that guarantee for each member the most ample and free access to the tools of the community. (Illich, 1973a: 10–12)

Thus Illich ultimately, and through his critique of the process of institutionalisation, calls for a radical critique of the entire modern industrial development paradigm, which is based on the abuse of nature, on competition, affluence and waste.

Counterproductive education and its alternative

Illich's originality, in our view, is to apply his critique of the process of institutionalisation to education. This leads him to a much more fundamental critique than the dominant political view at that time, which criticised the instrumentalisation of education for capitalist purposes (Bourdieu and Passeron, 1977). His critique goes as follows (Illich, 1970): the school, and schooling more generally, have acquired, or been granted by the state, an *institutional monopoly* over education. As a result, they have managed to make everybody believe that learning can result only from schooling. This devalues all other forms of learning, in particular learning by means of native or vernacular tools. Knowledge and education then become an economic commodity which one consumes or is administered. Moreover, in the area of education – as opposed to the other areas to which Illich has applied his critique – this process of institutionalisation is particularly *perverse*: indeed, on the one hand, the more sophisticated the educational system becomes, the more people recognise themselves as being unable to learn and in need of formal education. As a result, they will no longer be able to learn outside the school system. On the other hand, teachers are a particularly vicious form of experts, as they reinforce this process on an ideological level by making everyone believe that they are the only ones entitled to define and certify knowledge and learning. As a result, people are supposed to learn only from teachers and within their conceptual and institutional framework.

According to Illich, adult education is the alternative to this state of affairs. In other words, adult education is *not* the portion of traditional education which caters for adults. Rather, it is an alternative to the very processes of institutionalisation, commodification and expertocracy. Adult education is thus synonymous with learning, as opposed to formal education. In adult education, knowledge is created *by* the people, not *for* the people; and it presupposes free and 'unhampered participation', and abundant access to learning tools (Illich, 1973a). Although Illich thinks from the perspective of adult learners, and actually reacts against the newly emerging discourse on education for all, lifelong learning, and learning needs (see Chapter 2 below), adult education, as he defines it, is not just for adults. Rather, it is an alternative to the entire field of education, as neither institutions nor society can tell people what they need and what they have to learn. This alternative can be characterised by the following four oppositions, which at the same time summarise Illich's philosophy of adult education:

- *learning*, as opposed to schooling;
- *conviviality*, as opposed to manipulation;
- *responsibilisation*, as opposed to deresponsibilisation; and
- *participation*, as opposed to control.

Learning through participation and responsibilisation is therefore a key element for the necessary alternative to the industrial society, which Illich calls the convivial society. A convivial society is made up of learning webs, where people have free access to their own learning tools (e.g. his idea of 'tools for conviviality'), where (adult) education is the equivalent of collectively and actively participating in the understanding of the world so that more responsible decisions are made. In this sense, Illich anticipated the very issue of our book: 'The alternative to the dependence of a society on its schools is not the creation of new devices to make people learn what experts have decided they need to know; rather, it is the creation of a radically new relationship between human beings and their environment' (Illich, 1978a: 80).

Illich's significance for adult education and this book

Illich did not create a school of thought – neither in the field of adult education nor elsewhere. Rather, he dismantled CIDOC and pursued his anthropological critique of the development paradigm and its consequences. Nevertheless, Illich's considerations were introduced into mainstream adult education in a distorted form: his call for deschooling society was translated by the adult education establishment into the need for education throughout the whole of life. Moreover, today's competitive economy is about to convert society into a 'global class-room', while putting experts in charge of controlling the access to 'valuable' – that is, officially recognised – knowledge. Illich's critique of development and his call for 'the creation of a radically new relationship between human beings and their environment' were soon abandoned, and adult education chose to travel paths which, from today's standpoint, appear to be dead ends. In Part I we will present adult education's four main theoretical paths, each time presenting their features, their strengths, and their inherent weaknesses. In Part II we will see where the practices of adult education are currently taking us. We will also recall the main challenges to modern society, which we see as challenges to the practice and theory of adult education. Illich's insights, truly prophetic at the time, are today shared by some ecologists and Southern indigenous peoples, who suggest some of his 'tools for conviviality' (Borremans, 1979) as a way out of the dead end industrial civilisation is currently manoeuvring itself into. So, in Part III we will try to recover Illich's spirit in our analysis and proposals for a new adult education theory and practice.

We believe that Illich outlined an original identity for adult education. Considering today's societal problems – which in our view are not very different from the problems Illich had already identified in the 1970s – this identity is probably still very relevant today. Instead of continuing the main roads of adult education, which were all also shaped during those years, we should reactivate the forgotten Illich by building for adult education an epistemological and a political grounding which respects and furthers the convivial relationship among peoples themselves, as well as among peoples and nature.

Notes

1. See http://www.cuernavaca.infosel.com.mx/cls/cls.html.
2. John Ohliger publishes on adult education outside the regular circuits from his Basic Choices Inc., PO Box 9598, Madison, WI 53715, USA.
3. *Une société sans école*, in French; *La sociedad desescolarizada*, in Spanish. Even Illich himself claims that his editor misrepresented his thoughts in the English title: 'the book advocates the disestablishment of schools' (Illich, 1996: vii).
4. See: http://www.spunk.org/library/pubs/anarchiv/sp001193.txt.
5. On Illich, see: http://www.cogsci.ed.ac.uk/~ira/illich/.

Part I

The Main Historical Traditions
in Adult Education

In Part I we will present the main conceptualisations of adult education. In so doing, we view the entire field of adult education theory as a complex map on which it is possible to distinguish three roads. Thus we identify the highway of pragmatism (Chapter 3), the freeway of humanism for lonely travellers (Chapter 4), and the multiple trails of Marxism, which all lead to the same destination (Chapter 5). Since the 1970s, UNESCO has been able to articulate a synthesis of three tracks that might be called scientific humanism; this we consider in Chapter 2. Along these main roads adult education has travelled and still rolls today. Adult education theorists refer to them explicitly, while adult education practitioners often do so in a more incoherent and more implicit way.

The purpose here is not one of taxonomy. Rather, by drawing this map we want to locate adult education developments in their historical and sociocultural contexts. We consider the changing social contexts in which adult education has flourished, and continues to flourish, to be the overall framework in which adult education practices and conceptualisations really make sense. Also, we do not want to write a history of adult education ideas. We propose a concise yet comprehensive and engaged look at the conceptual field.

Our approach is based on three foundational ideas: first, that adult education developments are inextricably linked to particular historical and sociocultural contexts, are being shaped by them, and collaborate in shaping them. Second – and because of this historical and sociocultural embeddedness – that adult education is closely tied to what we call the 'development paradigm' – that is, with Gilbert Rist, 'a set of practices ... which require – for the production of society – the general transformation and destruction of the natural environment and of social relations. Its aim is to increase the production of commodities (goods and services) geared, by way of exchange, to effective demand' (1997: 13). It is this development paradigm which has shaped modern and modernising societies at least since the Industrial Revolution. As we will show, it has also substantially shaped the various paths of adult education, which can be understood as attempts to humanise precisely this development process. Third, we claim that the social responsibility dimension of adult education can be recovered from beneath this all-encompassing development paradigm. This is what we ultimately set out to do here by critically surveying adult education's main historical traditions.

Chapter 2

UNESCO: Humanising Development through Permanent Education

UNESCO – the United Nations Educational, Scientific and Cultural Organization – has played a foundational role in adult education. One can say that it has constructed the intellectual infrastructure, at least on its most general level. Not that the three main schools of thought in adult education – humanism, pragmatism and Marxism – did not exist before UNESCO, but UNESCO has managed to assemble them into a parallel three-lane highway – that is, a more or less coherent framework according to which adult education is actively put into the service of development. In doing this, UNESCO has actually recuperated adult education for its own institutional purposes; and Illich's critique of education cannot be separated from UNESCO's institutionalising role.

In this chapter, we present and critically discuss this intellectual framework, which still underlies much of adult education thinking. In order to do so, we will first briefly recall what UNESCO is and where it comes from. We will then present UNESCO's core concept – the French *éducation permanente* or, in English, life-long education – in order finally to criticise it from both our and Illich's perspective.

The context and history of UNESCO

On 4 May 1945 the fifty-one founding members signed the UN Charter in San Francisco. Its very first words, 'We the peoples of the United Nations', had been written by the leaders of the Allied governments, and actually echoed the US Constitution, since the founding fathers of the USA, the politicians, attributed to themselves a universalising moral mandate. These governments wanted the UN primarily to maintain international peace and security, while simultaneously promoting the Western model of civilisation. This was to be achieved through both direct (e.g. Security Council resolutions, diplomacy and missions) and indirect ways, such as promoting human rights and especially development, Western style (e.g. ECOSOC, the Economic and Social Council, which co-ordinates the corresponding specialised development agencies). UNESCO, part and parcel of this somewhat ethnocentric promotion of peace through development, was set up a year later as a specialised agency of ECOSOC. Three periods of its half-century of existence will be mentioned here: its origins, its heyday in the 1970s – which is also the birth of *éducation permanente* – and the current era.

From its very inception UNESCO was a battlefield for divergent political interests, leading to diplomatic compromises. Thus its Constitution was a compromise between the desires of the Conference of Allied Ministers of Education (CAME) on the one hand, and French government interests on the other. The former suggested actions to rebuild the educational infrastructure, which had been destroyed by the war. The French government instead wanted the organisation to be based in Paris and rooted in a rhetoric of intellectual co-operation and moral solidarity. The resulting compromise led to the establishment of the headquarters in Paris, and a discourse on the promotion of intellectual co-operation. CAME, led by the USA[1] and the UK, had its way in so far as governments were put entirely in charge of UNESCO's decision-making processes, science was included in the agency's title and functions, and communication was also to be part of its agenda. Not surprisingly, the compromise failed to make clear what UNESCO's purposes and functions really were, other than 'to contribute to peace and security by promoting collaboration among the nations through education, science and culture' (UNESCO Constitution).

With the independence of the former colonies in the 1960s, UNESCO membership grew rapidly and the political influence of the 'developing' countries increased. This was also the time when 'development' came to the fore: the 1960s, for example, were declared the first 'Development Decade', and UNDP, the United Nations Development Programme, was started in 1965. With the support of the newly independent countries, UNESCO clarified its vision: education, science and culture were now clearly to be put into the (political) service of development for (developing) countries and peoples. UNESCO's role now was to guide, to encourage and to assist development activities funded by governments or by multilateral organisations, such as the World Bank, the International Monetary Fund, and UNDP. This was also the time of UNDP's 'Capacity Study', the so-called Jackson Report (1969), and the World Bank's 'Partners in Development' document, the so-called Pearson Report (1969). UNESCO's equivalent was the book *Learning to Be*, the so-called Faure Report (Faure et al., 1972). This heyday of UNESCO goes hand in hand with a growing (political) educational role played by social movements and non-governmental organisations (NGOs). For example, the International Council for Adult Education (ICAE) was created at the same time by a close collaborator of UNESCO,[2] and shared the same philosophical framework.

After the end of the Cold War, the UN reframed its discourse somewhat – also in the light of growing environmental concerns, as well as growing trade. The dominant discourse changed from 'development' to 'sustainable development', as enshrined in the 1992 Rio 'Earth Summit': meaning both environmental sustainability and sustainable growth. The UNESCO science programme was the first to adapt to the 'new paradigm' of sustainability. The agency's concern for environmental conservation had started as early as 1968, when it convened the so-called Biosphere Conference. Later, UNESCO participated in the 'World Conservation Strategy', which was launched in 1980 jointly with the International Union for the Conservation of Nature (IUCN), the World Wide Fund for Nature (WWF), the UN Environment Programme (UNEP), and the Food and Agriculture Organization (FAO). In the 1990s, the 'sustainable development' discourse permeated all major UNESCO programmes, and its mission was reframed as '[to] lay the foundations for lasting peace and equitable development' (UNESCO, 1995: 3). Priority was now given to the 'least developed' and 'countries undergoing the transition to market economies' with a strategy centred on 'catalytic' actions and on building 'partnerships' with other UN agencies, especially with NGOs.[3] But this reorientation is also the result of both UNESCO budgetary constraints and the growing erosion of nation-states and intergovernmental institutions, especially in the educational implementation of (sustainable) development objectives. Accordingly – and not surprisingly – one reads in the Final Declaration of the Hamburg 1997 Adult Education Conference: '[we] reaffirm that only human-centred development and a participatory society based on the full respect of human rights will lead to sustainable and equitable development.'

In short, UNESCO's discourse and philosophy on adult and popular education, to which we now turn, are typical products of the Development Decades, along with a social action agenda of liberation and empowerment through education, both scientific and cultural.

'Lifelong education', or how to humanise development

Adult education has been a very important concern for UNESCO since its inception, and its contribution to the field can be called historical, especially when it comes to adult literacy and basic education. The UN agency has organised five International Conferences on Adult Education: Elsinore in 1949, Montreal in 1960, Tokyo in 1972, Paris in 1985, and Hamburg in 1997. Through its three subsidiaries[4] and five regional offices[5] UNESCO has promoted the mobilisation of resources and the transfer of knowledge worldwide, and it has become a clearing house for data and documents, alongside its own publications. Particularly important for adult education were initiatives such as the 'Experimental World Programme' (1966–74) (UNESCO, 1979), the 'World Conference on Education for All' held in 1990 in Jomtien (WCEFA, 1990), and the '1990 International Year of Literacy'. On the conceptual level, one must recall the core contribution of biologist and first director-general Julian Huxley, who clearly positioned UNESCO in the context of 'scientific humanism'.[6] In adult education the foundational ideas crystallised in the works of Edgar Faure et al. (1972), Paul Lengrand (1975), and R.H. Dave (1976). More recently, the works of Paul Bélanger and Ettore Gelpi (1994) and Jacques Delors et al. (1997) elaborate on the same line of thought. Since its foundation, UNESCO had been searching for a specific identity within the UN system, and it is no exaggeration to say that in *éducation permanente*[7] it finally found one.

Yet the core idea of *éducation permanente* is quite simple: to create a society where everybody is learning all the time. *Éducation permanente* has to be placed in the context outlined above: it must be understood as an institutional movement, a politico-institutional project, and perhaps as a discourse on social change, but not as a pedagogy. Philosophically, *éducation permanente* combines a Marxist analysis of history with a humanistic vision. UNESCO conceived it as an answer to four societal challenges:

- *Cultural reproduction*: The question here is how society can face the acceleration of development and growing change, while at the same time ensuring cultural continuity. *Éducation permanente*'s answer is: through more education and, more precisely, not only by learning, but by *'Learning to learn'*. Note that for UNESCO change is basically a good thing; education's task is to help society keep up with change.
- *Science and technology* are the engines of change and its acceleration, and as such they are also unquestionably good. The question here is how to use them, how to integrate them into society, and how to profit from them, while making sure that experts and technocrats do not control the change. Again, *éducation permanente*'s answer is: through more education. Not surprisingly, it champions the popularisation and demystification of science, since the whole of society has to understand, and ultimately master, scientific and technological progress.
- At that time, the *information explosion* was already seen as a societal challenge. Of course, information was fundamentally good, but again the question was how to ensure that people were able to make sense of such quantities of information, and how to integrate information in some coherent and meaningful way. Yet again, *éducation permanente*'s answer is: through more education. Education and learning help to 'humanise' information in the same way as they humanise science and technology.
- *Political control* is the fourth and probably the most important challenge foreseen by UNESCO: the question here is how to

take advantage (politically) of (scientific and technological) development. In the 1960s the newly acquired independence of mainly African countries offered great potential for development, but – as in the North – people were considered incapable of taking advantage of this vast developmental potential, unable as they were to control science, technology and change. *Éducation permanente*'s answer, yet again, is 'more education': both people and entire societies need more (civic and political) education, empowering them to be the actors rather than the victims of change and development.

In other words, *éducation permanente* is, above all, a political project: people and societies will again be able to keep up with the process of development, and eventually take control of it. Thus *éducation permanente* is a means of humanising the process of development, which is otherwise in danger of being run and controlled by experts, technocrats and other oppressors. As such, it is the ultimate incarnation of the development ideology shared by both Marxists and liberals: (scientific, technological and industrial) development is neither good nor bad; it is simply a tool. In order for such development to be 'of use', it has to be humanised, and this humanisation takes place through education and learning. And since there has been much progress on the science, technology and industrial front, there has to be a corresponding effort on the educational level. This, at least, is UNESCO's argumentation, which has underlain most adult education thinking ever since.

Éducation permanente therefore differs from 'traditional education' in three ways. First, it considers traditional education elitist, theoretical, abstract, and removed from experience (i.e. artificially divided into distinct subjects). In contrast, *éducation permanente* proposes 'education for all', education which is popular, without selection or barriers, and close to reality and experience (e.g. transdisciplinary education). Second, traditional education is also criticised for its conservatism, which perpetuates inequalities and is reflected in the authoritarian teacher–student relationship. *Éducation permanente* proposes a democratic teaching relationship which starts with the learner and helps him or her to become aware of the responsibilities in mastering development. Lastly, *éducation permanente* quite logically criticises the dehumanising split between rationality and creativity – between science and the so-called 'humanities' – perpetuated by traditional education. This split must be overcome, as a humanised development will not be realised unless art and technology are truly integrated. Hence *éducation permanente* is basically a modernised version of Huxley's scientific humanism.

We can itemise the key philosophical ideas of *éducation permanente* as follows:

- education is *permanent* – no longer limited to a particular period of one's life;
- education is *everywhere* – it encompasses formal, non-formal and informal educational activities;
- *life* is the main source of learning. Any (life) situation has the potential to be educative, and the whole of a person's life provides opportunities for learning;
- education is *for all*. As such, it must be democratised, and declared a basic universal right;
- *éducation permanente* is a *flexible* and *dynamic* approach to education: learning has no limits; all that counts is the will to learn. So flexibility and dynamism must permeate educational methodologies, techniques and contents;
- the learning *process* is more important than the subject matter. This idea stems from the fact that the ability to learn ('learning to learn') is more important than any particular content;
- *éducation permanente* aims to improve the *quality of life* – to humanise development – both by adapting to change (i.e. keeping up with it) and by actively participating in change (i.e. controlling the process); finally,
- *éducation permanente* is a badly needed (social) *movement*, as opposed to traditional education, which is said to perpetuate the status quo.

But *éducation permanente* is not limited to philosophical ideas – it has also given rise to some practical educational principles. For example, in *éducation permanente* people are considered to have an intrinsic motivation to learn; there is therefore no need for coercion or control. In other words, *éducation permanente* is a non-authoritarian and non-directive approach to education. Learning is an *individual* activity; thus the stress in *éducation permanente* on individualised content, pace and methodology. Also, building a democratic society necessitates democratic and participatory education – hence the importance of group learning in *éducation permanente*. Finally, lifelong education must include life experiences and other learning situations, which – according to *éducation permanente* – must be recognised and credited.

The key concept in *éducation permanente* is the so-called 'learning society', but note that this does not mean a society which learns. Rather, it is *a society of individual lifelong learners*. It is therefore important for a learning society that all its members have the right to education. This right must be guaranteed, and learning must be possible throughout the lifespan. There are neither exclusive periods of life, nor exclusive contents. The same remark is valid geographically and institutionally, as there are neither exclusive places nor exclusive institutions for *éducation permanente*. What a programme for an agency in search of universal recognition and permanent funding!

Critique of *éducation permanente*

The lifelong education discourse remains general, philosophical and theoretical. *Éducation permanente* is a quasi-political and thus ideological movement which claims to define itself in opposition to traditional education, yet merely perpetuates the very process of which traditional education was also a part. At best, it counterbalances the failures and problems of conventional education. We have four main criticisms of this lifelong education movement and ideology:

- *Éducation permanente* set out to humanise development without questioning it. Moreover, it set out to humanise it in a very Western (and Northern) way, as neither (Western) science and technology, nor the very Enlightenment idea of mastering matter by means of the mind, were questioned. So *éducation permanente* is clearly a step backwards from Ivan Illich's more anthropological perspective, and his much more fundamental critique of development.
- Unlike Illich, *éducation permanente* does not criticise institutions. While it presents itself as a non-institutional discourse and

accepts non-formal – non-institutional – experiences as significant learning experiences, it feeds them right into a formal, and
ultimately institutional, structure: a process which has led Illich
disciple Pineau to warn against this trend to institutionalise,
rationalise, and ultimately bureaucratise the entire lifespan of
the adult learner (Pineau, 1977). *Éducation permanente* and
UNESCO certainly legitimised and actively contributed to this
movement towards 'credits-for-life-experiences' and certification,
a process which has proved particularly counterproductive.

• As a politico-institutional discourse, *éducation permanente* is particularly weak when it comes to epistemology and pedagogy. As
strange as it is for an institution which claims to be the international spokesperson for science, the idea of lifelong education
is not rooted in psychology, or in pedagogy, or in any other
social science. It is basically a set of philosophical principles
grounded in some ideological (Western) assumptions. This is
certainly where the three schools of thought which we will
discuss below go considerably further than UNESCO.

• It is therefore not surprising that *éducation permanente* confuses
education and learning, in the same way as it mixes individual
and collective learning (e.g. the learning society). On the one
hand *éducation permanente* emphasises the individualisation of
learning (i.e. adaptation to personal rhythms, age, needs, etc.),
while on the other hand it stresses group work, democracy,
participation and societal change. Again, *éducation permanente* is
not very sound intellectually; it simply echoes the modernist
credo that the sum of enlightened individuals will automatically
lead to a better society. In this sense, UNESCO's philosophy of
adult education is not much different from the Western idea of
education in general.

Despite these criticisms, it is important to stress that *éducation
permanente* was certainly the federating moment of adult education.
It offered a coherent discourse on adult education with which
both learners and educators, from both North and South, could
identify. Moreover, *éducation permanente* gave adult education a
political – and, more importantly, an international and institutional – identity, while making it part of an overall humanising
movement. In the history of adult education there has never been

such a moment since: after the early years of *éducation permanente*, adult education's discourse split into its three constitutent parts – pragmatism, humanism and Marxism.

Notes

1. It is possible to trace US animosity towards UNESCO back to that time, as the USA decided to fund postwar educational reconstruction bilaterally rather than through the agency. During the Cold War there was continuous confrontation between the US government and UNESCO, which led in 1984 to US withdrawal from its membership.
2. J. Robbins (Roby) Kidd (1915–82), a Canadian adult educator, received his Ed.D in adult education from Teachers College, Columbia University, in 1947 with Eduard Lindeman (see Chapter 4 below). He worked with UNESCO in Canada and India, and after 1966 taught at OISE (the Ontario Institute for Studies in Education), where ICAE was set up (Thomas, 1987).
3. UNESCO maintains consultative and associate relations with 587 NGOs and 28 foundations (UNESCO, 1995: 77).
4. The International Bureau of Education (IBE, Geneva), the International Institute for Educational Planning (IIEP, Paris), and the UNESCO Institute for Education (UIE, Hamburg).
5. Corresponding to the five UNESCO 'regions' – Africa (BREDA, Dakar), Arab States (UNEDBAS, Amman), Asia/Pacific (PROAP, Bangkok), Europe/OECD countries (Headquarters, Paris), and Latin America/Caribbean (OREALC, Santiago).
6. 'UNESCO, I wrote, must work in the context of what I called Scientific Humanism, based on the established facts of biological adaptation and advance, brought about by means of Darwinian selection, continued into the human sphere by psycho-social pressures, and leading to some kind of advance, even progress, with increased human control and conservation of the environment and of natural forces. So far as UNESCO was concerned, the process should be guided by humanistic ideas, and by cultural interchange.' From Huxley (1973) 'Memoirs II': 15, recalling his 1947 pamphlet 'UNESCO: Its Purpose and its Philosophy'.
7. *Éducation permanente* is the French concept that best captures UNESCO's views. Generally, also, the French terminology is even used in English. Roughly, *éducation permanente* might be translated as 'lifelong education'. Often, however, especially American adult educators confuse *éducation permanente* with 'lifelong learning'. As we will see in Chapter 3, the idea of lifelong learning is rooted solely in the American pragmatist tradition, and must not be confused with the much broader and much more European concept of *éducation permanente*.

Chapter 3

Pragmatism: A Genuine
American Highway

After discussing the political or ideological foundations of adult education with *éducation permanente*, we now turn to its theoretical and intellectual foundations. This is where pragmatism, an American intellectual concept, comes into play. Pragmatism is adult education's intellectual core, at least for the overwhelming proportion of adult education literature, which is – not surprisingly – American. In other words, adult education is pragmatism.

In this chapter, we will present the pragmatist approach to adult education by critically discussing the main authors in the field. We will start with the roots of American pragmatist education – with John Dewey's ideas. As we will see, Dewey is the father of American adult education. His ideas were officially applied to adult education by his contemporary and Columbia University fellow Eduard Lindeman, the 'real' father of adult education. As Brookfield (1987) rightly says: '[Lindeman] articulated and implemented a vision of adult education that still constitutes the conceptual underpinnings of the field of theory and practice in the United States' (120). Since Lindeman, pragmatism has permeated the work of more or less all adult education writers, at least in the United States, but more generally in all other English-speaking countries. We will distinguish here between two pragmatist approaches to adult education: first the 'experiential learning' approach, of which Kurt Lewin, David Kolb, Chris Argyris and Donald Schön are the most typical representatives. This has to be distinguished from our second approach, symbolic interactionism, another version of American pragmatism, which has influenced Peter Jarvis and Jack Mezirow, two of the most quoted authors.

John Dewey (1859–1952)

John Dewey's thinking is at the core of American pragmatism, just as pragmatism is at the core of adult education. This is why we consider it important to offer a quite detailed presentation of the key elements of his theory. All these elements can be found throughout adult education, up to our own time. Two of Dewey's numerous books are particularly important in this context: *Democracy and Education* (first published 1916) and *Experience and Education* (first published 1938).[1] If we are to understand Dewey's intellectual evolution, we should briefly enumerate four phases of his life:

1. Let us mention, to begin with, his rural origins in pre-industrial Vermont and his psychological – or, rather, philosophical – studies at Johns Hopkins University[2] in Baltimore, where he earned his PhD in 1884 with a dissertation on Kant's psychology.
2. A second phase of Dewey's life (1889–94) can be characterised as 'organic democracy': still under the influence of the rural environment, Dewey thought in pre-industrial and religious terms. His idea of 'organic democracy' must therefore mainly be related to American communitarianism – it must refer to the countryside and to rural communities.
3. Dewey's third phase covers basically his time spent in Chicago (1894–1904). Here he found the exciting intellectual context in which modern social sciences were being born. Chicago became a sort of social laboratory; subsequently, social scientists started to be interested in delinquency and social deviation. Dewey reflected upon all this and, influenced by his past, tried to figure out how modern society held together.
4. The last phase of Dewey's life covers his work at Columbia University in New York (1905–52), where he found himself among the world's leading anthropologists. As a result, he inserted his preoccupation with education stemming from his Chicago period into an anthropological framework. Therefore, education, for Dewey, is not a technique or a pedagogical relation-

ship; rather, it is a central function in the evolutive process of the human species.

This section is divided into three parts: Dewey's philosophy or anthropology of learning; his theory of education; and the relevance of both for adult education.

Dewey's anthropology of learning

Not surprisingly, Dewey's philosophy of education is anthropological in nature: it is built on the specific learning capacities of the human species, from which Dewey then derives his optimistic view of the development process, which he calls 'growth'. Democracy, as we will see, is instrumental in this process of unlimited growth.

In this anthropological perspective, there are a number of things which characterise the human species as opposed to other species. First there is the capacity to *build tools* and to transform the environment with these tools, thus shaping the environment in a way which will make it more suitable for the human species. Furthermore, there is the capacity of *language*, which enables humans to think, to relate to each other, and to co-operate. This capacity still strengthens the ability to shape the human environment. But Dewey's most original contribution is certainly what he calls the human capacity of *plasticity* – the dual capacity first to learn from experience (mistakes), and second to build on this learning and, by so doing, increase even the capacity to learn. So plasticity – and, therefore, the entire developmental process – has no limits. With such anthropologically grounded ideals, Dewey reveals his educational optimism (e.g. there are no limits to learning) and, on the other hand, his non-dualistic view: there is no split between theory and practice, spirit and reality, reason and practice. Plasticity and development are always simultaneous.

Dewey now places these capacities, especially the capacity of plasticity, into a developmental perspective: humans have the ability to shape their environment better and better according to their needs, in part because they have the ability to learn from their mistakes. By doing this, Dewey assumes, they 'humanise their environment'. Thus Dewey has a very optimistic view of human learning: indeed, learning is one element in the unlimited process of creating an ever more humanised environment. Nature and culture cannot, therefore, be separated; moreover nature 'emancipates' itself, so to speak, through human culture – it becomes ever more human. For Dewey, the humanisation of nature is a mission, since the human being is not only part of nature but the very conscience of nature. It is humanity's task to humanise nature, and this process is not, in Dewey's view, destruction, but improvement, increased plasticity and, ultimately, the equivalent of learning.

Science, of which Dewey has a very uncritical, if not idealistic, perception, is part and parcel of this process of humanisation, development, or – as Dewey often says – 'growth'. Science, on the one hand, represents the very tool for development, a practical and useful instrument for humanising nature. On the other hand, education is plasticity *per se*, the incarnation of the scientific method (learning from experience). Science, therefore, is eminently human. It corresponds to what humans do every day – reflect on and learn from their experiences – but in a more systematised way. Science, then, is applied plasticity. Not surprisingly, Dewey therefore models learning on scientific practice, and considers the role of science equivalent to the role of learning. Learning and education, as science, make sense only as part of this process of humanisation, development and growth. Moreover, learning, education and science are not goals in themselves; rather, they are functions in the overall process of humanisation, development and growth, terms which Dewey uses more or less synonymously. This process can be represented as in Figure 3.1.

This developmental process encompasses both ontogenesis and phylogenesis, thus combining the human being as an individual and as a member of a species. In other words, development and growth occur both for the individual and for the species. Let us first comment on this process and its phases from the perspective of the human species. First there is a phase of 'habituation' – or, as we would say today, socialisation. During this phase, humans become 'habituated' to their environment by having so-called 'experiences' in it. This habituation produces so-called 'habits', which are ways of looking at things through, for example, values, beliefs and world-views. Certain habits therefore go with certain environments. Habits, in turn, translate into actions, in which new

Figure 3.1   Dewey's model of the learning circle

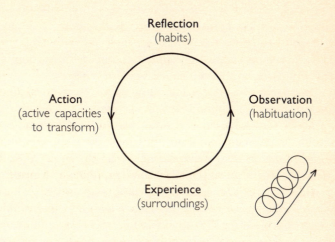

experiences are made, allowing the process – or, rather, the loop – to start over again.

Dewey distinguishes between different types of habits: fixed, static, open and dynamic habits, which correspond to different types of cultures: the more open the culture, the more open and dynamic the habits. Open cultures enhance the capacity to learn from experience, and thus the potential to transform the environment according to human needs. Cultures with fixed habits prevent development and growth. Note that this is an ideological as well as a tautological view: the more open the culture, the bigger the potential for growth, and the more humanised the environment. And a more humanised environment means more freedom for individuals, thus a more open society.

As a matter of fact, when Dewey talks about society he is in fact referring to the community – to the association of humans in a community of species. But this anthropological idea of community is quite different from the European and sociological or structural idea of society with its struggles for power, control and domination. Dewey discusses democracy in this communitarian perspective, as it means the participation of all the individuals of a community in the shaping of their own future – a truly American view. Again, this is a quite different perspective on democracy from the European one, where diversity means above all different interests and strategies, and potential conflicts. For Dewey, diversity is a richness, a creative potential for humanisation, development and growth, a unique chance to move ahead.

In short, Dewey's anthropological perspective on development and growth is not only optimistic, but also typically American. As we will show, it underlies the entire pragmatic (and at times even humanistic) philosophy of adult education, and constitutes the intellectual underpinning for most of adult education's thinking and practice. In short, this philosophy says that (1) learning is always part of a larger anthropological growth process; (2) any problems occurring during this process are learning opportunities; and (3) what is good for the individual human being is necessarily good for the human species, and vice versa. One can even say that for Dewey there is no real difference between the individual and the species, as there is no difference between learning, development and growth.

Dewey's theory of education

As we have seen, education, for Dewey, plays a key role when it comes to advancing the processes of humanisation, development and growth. But this overall anthropological role of education can be broken down into three different functions: first, there is *education as preparation*. Its role is to is to update people, to socialise them into the dominant habits in order to make them full members of the community and the process. This foundational function of education becomes ever more important and necessary as society develops and becomes more complex. Second, there is *education as potential*; its role is to instil innovation, creativity and imagination – to increase the potential to act creatively on reality. Third, there is *education as action*: its role is to increase capacities to act or, more precisely, to solve problems.

Accordingly, for Dewey, education must guarantee that all members of the community have the opportunity to have experiences, give meaning to their experiences, and ultimately learn from them.

It must also give all members equal chances to reach the same level of knowledge and habits – that is, to reach what he calls 'basic industrial intelligence'. Furthermore, it must incorporate and exploit creativity and curiosity through collective circles of inquiry and the building of communities of inquiry. This will create opportunities for everyone to have experiences from which to learn. Finally, education must make people participate in change actively, through learning-by-doing. All four aspects are necessary if the process of development and growth is to advance at optimum capacity and speed. Again, equity and diversity are crucial: the more diverse the community, the bigger the innovative potential. And the more equitable the chances to participate, the bigger the potential for development and growth.

So far we have mentioned only the anthropological dimension of education (phylogenesis). But it has an ontological or individual dimension as well: just as the human species learns from experience, so does the individual. More concretely, individuals, like the entire species, have experiences, become aware of these experiences, reflect upon the observations made, and act accordingly. Experiential learning as conceptualised by Dewey and his followers is therefore modelled on the scientific experiment: scientists have an idea (theory), carry out an experiment in reality, receive a feedback, and consequently modify their idea, model or theory. This 'learning circle' does not function unless all four elements or steps are there. According to Dewey – and the pragmatists more generally – it is not possible to learn by reflection only; it is the full circle that constitutes learning. Complexity increases as the learning spiral advances, inasmuch as new theories (individual) or habits (species) are developed each time. Similarly, reflecting on an experience becomes ever more complex, as such reflection is always also shaped by all previous experiences. Nevertheless, it must be said that for Dewey even the individual learning ultimately has to be a collective (community) endeavour: indeed, it is necessary to open individual learning to the collective, in order not to incur the danger of interpreting feedback subjectively. In other words, individual learning does exist for Dewey, but without the relationship to the community it is incomplete; it creates an impasse, and ultimately hinders the phylogenetic process of development and growth.

Relevance and critique of Dewey

Although Dewey had no specific theory of adult education, we have put a particular emphasis on his thinking because it has influenced the entire field of adult education, not to mention American education more generally (Apple, 1996). Indeed, pragmatism – and to a certain extent even humanism – in adult education have closely followed his ideas.

There are several aspects of Dewey's thinking which are worth highlighting here. Dewey offers a very broad and long-term view of education which suits adult education particularly well: education is for everybody, everywhere and all the time. Every human being has in principle the capacity to participate in this process. Dewey also makes the link between education and democracy, as education is not simply a technique, nor a content; rather, it is a means to further the process of humanisation in a democratic way – by respecting the individual learner. Dewey is also the founding father of *experiential learning*, as we shall see below: not only are experiences the key building blocks of learning, but action is an intrinsic part of the learning cycle; this implies learning by doing as well as a practical understanding of the world. Finally, Dewey integrates the subject matter and the method, as the entire learning cycle is in fact a process of problem-solving.

Nevertheless, some very serious criticisms can be made of Dewey, both from an adult educational and from a more philosophical perspective. His ultimate ideal – development and growth – is highly unspecific, abstract, and never clearly defined. Moreover, this ideal is in fact a process which has become an end in itself, while learning, education, diversity, even democracy are simply means to further this process. It is the process itself that is good; democracy, diversity, and so on, are just functions. In other words, Dewey has an almost religious belief in growth and development. Similarly, he also has a quite mystical view of science, which is not only an instrument for development and growth but also a model for learning more generally. Moreover, his views on democracy remain pre-industrial and agricultural, shaped as they are by his childhood in rural Vermont. Finally, Dewey is not very specific about education, as education encompasses almost all functions of furthering the development process. It is not exactly clear what education is *not*. In any case, his approach to education is asociological, astructural, apolitical and non-institutional. It is essentially a philosophical perspective.

Eduard Lindeman (1895–1953)

Eduard Christian Lindeman was one of ten children of Danish immigrants to the United States. After a hard childhood – he was orphaned at a very early age – in a rural environment, and with no formal schooling, he graduated from Michigan State University in agricultural science. In 1924 he joined the faculty of the New York School of Social Work (later the Columbia University School of Social Work), where he spent his professional career. As a professor of social philosophy, he mainly reflected on the social phenomena he observed around him. Lindeman's main adult education work, *The Meaning of Adult Education* (1926), therefore deals with the social problems of his time (e.g. labour issues, urban poverty, unemployment), but he clearly does not utilise a Marxist analysis.

Lindeman's main contribution is to have introduced the work of Dewey, with slight modifications, into the field of adult education. As a result, he is considered the founding father of adult education in North America (Brookfield, 1987: 120). In essence, Lindeman is Dewey: they share the same philosophy of learning, but Lindeman makes it more concrete and locates learning in a more social context. This concretisation is in part due to his Danish influence.[3] Since he had Danish ancestry, he visited the country several times and became particularly interested in the so-called 'study circles' (which had started in 1845) and the 'folk high schools' (1868). Thanks to Lindeman and others, Danish adult education methods came to play an important role.

Philosophically, Lindeman is very similar, if not identical, to Dewey. The following lines could easily have been written by Dewey:

> Adult education is a co-operative venture in non-authoritarian, informal learning, the chief purpose of which is to discover the meaning of experience; … a technique of learning for adults which makes education coterminous with life, and hence elevates living itself to the level of an experiment. (Lindeman 1925: 3)[4]

For Lindeman, as for Dewey, (adult) education is some sort of non-authoritarian co-operation among learners, whose main goal is to ascertain the meaning of experience. Yet meaning for Lindeman has a slightly different connotation than for Dewey. Unlike Dewey, who uses meaning in an anthropological sense, Lindeman uses it in a more sociological perspective: meaning is the attempt to give coherence to the fractured life of people who live in an industrial environment. Consequently, Lindeman looks for learning techniques capable of linking education to life. Adult educators intervene in this process of giving meaning to life experiences by facilitating it and by creating the optimal conditions for its functioning.

But Lindeman is also more focused than Dewey: unlike Dewey, who does not differentiate between work and leisure, Lindeman makes a clear distinction between vocational education (related to work) and non-vocational education (related to life). This focus is probably his most original contribution to adult education: for Lindeman, adult education's role is not to improve the world of work, but to incorporate the world of work within life – to give meaning to work within the larger context of life. With Lindeman, therefore, adult education becomes identical to non-vocational education; in his view, it is the answer to the fractured life of the workers. This trend was further cemented in 1926 by the Carnegie-funded American Association for Adult Education (AAAE), and in 1935 by the creation of the first Graduate Program in Adult Education at Teachers College, Columbia University. This trend lasted until the late 1970s, when vocational education gradually became included in the field of adult education. Quite logically, adult education for Lindeman was a totally voluntary affair, and – influenced by Danish adult education practices – he considered it to have nothing to do with either credentials or degrees. It was viewed as a noble enterprise, which has value in itself, and does not need certification. Again, this situation lasted until the 1980s, when it became conceivable to think of adult education in terms of certificates and qualifications.

Methodologically, Lindeman derived his thinking from Dewey and from his Danish background. To begin with, he emphasised situations: adult education takes place in relation to concrete *situations*. These are always educational situations, not subjects; the

accent being on *experiences*, as was the case with Dewey. Also, the
objective of adult education is to further the process of development and growth (of individuals and the human species alike),
content being only a means to furthering this process. This pragmatic view has had significant implications for adult education,
since it has led to the development of numerous techniques to
facilitate adult learning. Also from Lindeman comes the idea –
espoused today by many adult education practitioners – that what
counts is the fact that people learn, not what they learn: an idea
which has been further reinforced by humanistic adult education.
Furthermore, Lindeman favours *discussion* as a didactic method
for adult learning. Recalling Dewey's notion of democracy – the
communitarian participation of all – discussion becomes *the*
method of learning democracy, the method which allows all to
participate. For Lindeman, discussion groups are therefore the
equivalent of (democratic) 'learning communities'. Since Lindeman, emphasis in the field of adult education has been placed on
the collaborative dimensions of learning, such as group work and
group discussions.

   In short, Lindeman translates Dewey's thinking into the field of
adult education by enriching it with some methodological tools
from the Danish Folk School movement. In this way, he played
the role of the intellectual father of American and pragmatic adult
education. Yet all our criticisms of Dewey's conception of learning
apply equally to Lindeman. This is particularly the case with his
asociological, apolitical and non-institutional view of adult learning and education, and this criticism can consistently be applied
to all pragmatic adult education thinkers. After Lindeman, the
pragmatic tradition of adult education split somewhat into two
directions: experiential learning on the one hand, and symbolic
interactionism on the other. We will now discuss the most relevant
thinkers for each of these two directions.

Experiential learning

Experiential learning has become a catch phrase in adult
education literature (Cell, 1984; Boud, Coher and Walker, 1993).
The main author generally associated with the theory of experiential learning is David Kolb, whose *Experiential Learning: Experience*

as the Source of Learning and Development (1984) became very influential. It has not only been important for American adult education thinking, but has influenced all kind of adult educational tools, such as learning tests (e.g. the Myers–Briggs Test). Donald Schön and Chris Argyris have combined experiential learning with Kurt Lewin's action-research approach and applied it to management learning. We will present the core ideas of these authors and at the end of this section critically discuss the concept of experiential learning. Some of today's key concepts in the field of adult education – 'adult learning', 'learning styles' and 'credit for life experience' – refer directly back to this tradition of experiential learning.

Kurt Lewin (1890–1947)

Kurt Lewin applies Dewey's thinking to *organisations*. In so doing he combines American pragmatism with the German phenomenological tradition. It is important to introduce Lewin here, as he has significantly influenced the field of adult education through his psycho-sociological contributions to group dynamics, as well as to action–research and action–learning.

Indeed, from the 1930s onwards there was a growing interest in the study of organisations, particularly of private corporations. Within the humanistic tradition, as we will see in Chapter 4, this interest has, for example, shaped the emerging field of 'human resources management', aimed at creating a better environment for those who work in organisations, thus ultimately increasing productivity. Lewin took a more active approach, as he aimed at improving the organisation by involving the people concerned in the solution of organisational problems. His so-called 'action–research' approach is thus primarily an instrument of organisational development which applies Dewey's learning cycle to organisational problem-solving. Action is thus a necessary step in the transformation process, just as it is necessary to reflect on the action performed. The resulting so-called 'action–reflection' learning model has significantly influenced adult education practitioners and become, for most of them, a preferred alternative to the human resources management approach.

The group is the basic unit of Lewin's action–reflection model. A typical 'training group' – or 'T-group', as Lewin called it – was composed not only of workers and managers actively analysing the results of their learning, but also of external researchers (consultants) who observed the effects of their interventions in organisations. His National Training Laboratory (NTL) basically took the State of Maine's public administration as the object of his study and his model: at NTL, then, the results of organisational interventions, development and training were analysed with the group members, yet outside the organisation. Lewin assumed that taking some distance from the organisation made people more free to reflect, to critique, and ultimately to learn. So Lewin put into place a practical application of Dewey's learning cycle, generating a process which ultimately helped an organisation develop and grow.

Lewin's idea that this type of intervention (action–reflection–action) would help an organisation to grow has been adopted by many organisational development consultants who have perfected sophisticated instruments of intervention in organisations. Among the different organisational development practices which subsequently emerged, one can distinguish between a more interventionist and a more intellectually oriented model, which stresses the consultants' inputs (see Ventriss and Luke, 1988), and a more 'experiential' approach, in which the members of the organisation take charge of their own development process (see Senge, 1990). But more generally, Lewin's approach has influenced organisational change and development practices to the present day. For example, his action–reflection model is at the core of the recent literature on learning organisations (see Watkins and Marsick, 1993).

David Kolb (1939–)

Building on Dewey's work, David Kolb has made a significant contribution to the field of adult learning, mostly in the area of diagnostic tools – that is, so-called learning styles[5] (Price, 1983; Smith, 1982; Sims and Sims, 1995; Sternberg, 1997). Here we will briefly outline his concretisation of Dewey's learning cycle, and show how Kolb derives his learning styles from it. Kolb claims that the 'learning cycle' is rooted simultaneously in Dewey, Lewin and Piaget, all three having laid the foundations of experiential learning. Although this mixing of American pragmatism (Dewey

Figure 3.2 Kolb's experiential learning

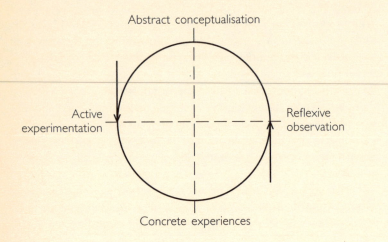

and Lewin) with European cognitivism (Piaget) is highly debatable, let us simply present Kolb's view of experiential learning. Such learning is basically a mechanism by which individuals structure reality. It encompasses four steps: (1) concrete experience; (2) reflective observation; (3) abstract conceptualisation; and (4) active experimentation. Figure 3.2 summarises his view.

Kolb attempts to combine an action–reflection mechanism (Lewin), a philosophy (Dewey), and a psychological model of learning (Piaget), in a not entirely coherent manner. Six features characterise Kolb's experiential learning cycle:

- Learning must always be seen in terms of *process*, not in terms of outcomes. This is both a Deweyan and a Piagetian concept, as ideas are never fixed but always formulated and reformulated in their confrontation with reality. In other words, there is no 'absolute' knowledge, as there is, for example, in the behaviourist perspective.
- Learning is an *experiential* process, as knowledge advances only through continuous experiences. Hence education – for Piaget, for example – is not about inculcating new ideas, but about

Figure 3.3   Kolb's learning styles

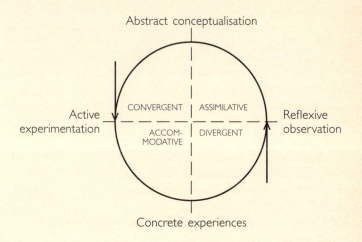

transforming the ideas received. Lewin also shares this view when he says that the objective is not to create a new model in an organisation, but to modify the old ones.

- Along the experiential process, there are four *capacities* or modes of adapting to the world: (1) the capacity of having concrete experiences; (2) the capacity of making reflective observations; (3) the capacity of making abstract conceptualisations; and (4) the capacity of making active experimentations. Learning – and this is the originality of Kolb's contribution – is the result of the combination of these four capacities, structured into two axes (see Figure 3.3).
- Learning is thus a holistic process of *adapting* to the world. All four capacities are necessary in order to learn.
- Learning therefore implies a series of *transactions* between the person and his or her environment. Experience occurs precisely in this transaction between the individual who learns and the environment.
- As a result of this transaction, learning leads to *knowledge creation*.

Two underlying axes structure the four capacities or modes of adapting to the world, leading to the definition of Kolb's learning styles: (1) the axis of the tension between what Kolb calls 'extension' and 'intension' – between active experimentation and reflective observation – and (2) the axis of the tension between what he calls 'apprehension' and 'comprehension' – that is, between concrete experiencing and abstract conceptualisation. This structure then defines four different sectors of knowledge and corresponding *learning styles*:

- convergence (i.e. convergent knowledge or convergent learning style), characterised by a combination of abstract conceptualisation and active experimentation;
- divergence, characterised by a combination of concrete experience and reflective observation;
- assimilation, characterised by a combination of abstract conceptualisation and reflective observation; and
- accommodation, characterised by a combination of active experimentation and concrete experience.

Through corresponding surveys, Kolb manages to classify individuals according to their learning styles. They therefore tend to be 'convergers', 'divergers', 'assimilators' or 'accommodators', depending on their specific mode of adapting to the world. Kolb's learning styles, a way of categorising people, has had a number of applications in learning counselling, professional consultancy, and team-building. Kolb's learning styles are therefore one example – albeit quite a simplistic one – of an application of pragmatism to the management of individual learning. Another example can be found in the conceptualisation of so-called 'double-loop learning', as proposed by MIT professors Chris Argyris and Donald Schön.

Chris Argyris (1923–) and Donald Schön (1931–1997)

We will simply focus here on Argyris and Schön's contribution to experiential learning through the concept of 'double-loop learning' (1974), not on Argyris's extensive work in the area of management, nor on Schön's work on planning. Both Argyris and Schön have their roots in organisational development, though

Argyris (1983, 1985, 1992) is more concerned with management training, whereas Schön (1983, 1987) has had more impact in the area of continuing vocational training at lower levels in organisations. Both have become reference points for what is now called 'organisational learning' (see Chapter 13 below), and both share the pragmatic philosophy of learning which can be traced back to Dewey.

Argyris and Schön's contribution pertains mainly to further conceptualising the learning cycle and the process of experiential learning. They define what they call a 'theory-in-action'. Their basic idea is that each person has a 'theory' – that is, an action-guiding model – in his or her mind. This 'theory' is one step in the pragmatic learning cycle, the one which Kolb called 'abstract conceptualisation' and Dewey called 'habits.' Being just one step in the learning cycle, this 'theory' cannot exist without relating to practice – that is, without being constantly tried out in practice. Argyris and Schön's core idea is that through reflection upon the theory in action – by making explicit the assumptions or the world-view underlying the action through so-called double-loop learning – the person learns faster than by going through the entire learning cycle, which Argyris and Schön call 'single-loop'. In other words, it is the reflection upon how action is conceptualised – the reflection upon the theory-in-action – which makes a person learn and ultimately behave differently (see Figure 3.4).

Argyris and Schön's contribution to pragmatic learning theory is, in our view, twofold: first, they introduce the term 'theory' or 'theory-in-action', which gives the function of abstract conceptualisation (in the overall learning cycle) more structure and more coherence. Abstract conceptualisation now becomes something one can analyse and work from. Second, and because of this new structuring moment called 'learning-in-action', Argyris and Schön give a new twist to pragmatic learning theory. Unlike Dewey's, Lewin's or Kolb's learning cycle, where one had, so to speak, to make a mistake and reflect upon it – that is, learn by trial and error – it is now possible, thanks to Argyris and Schön's conceptualisation, to learn by simply reflecting critically upon the theory-in-action. In other words, it is no longer necessary to go through the entire learning circle in order to develop the theory

Figure 3.4 Argyris and Schön's double-loop learning

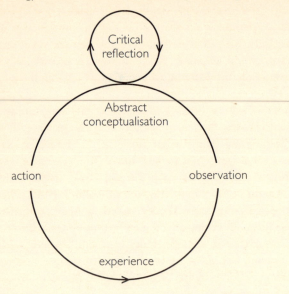

further. It is sufficient to readjust the theory through double-loop learning.

This has implications for the role of the adult educator. Instead of being a facilitator of a person's learning cycle, the adult educator becomes a coach or a mentor who helps individuals (managers, professionals, workers) to reflect upon their theories-in-action. In other words, Argyris and Schön's mentor or coach helps managers (for Argyris, especially, double-loop learning is mainly applied to managers) to make their theory explicit, and not, as Lewin would have done, to reflect upon the action and its consequences. This is done by showing an individual learner the discrepancy between what Argyris and Schön call 'espoused theory' and 'theory-in-use'. When people are asked to make their theory or theory-in-action explicit, they often come up with quite a fine model of how they think it guides their actions. This is what is called the espoused theory. But when one observes what people actually do in reality – the so-called 'theory-in-use' – there is quite a difference.

This difference between the theory-in-use and the espoused theory is used by Argyris and Schön as the trigger by which the adult educator gets a manager to reflect upon his or her espoused theory. For Argyris and Schön the role of the mentor or coach is thus crucial, as people would not otherwise spontaneously detect the discrepancies between the theory-in-use and the espoused theory, and therefore would not spontaneously engage in double-loop learning. The adult educator is thus an interventionist mentor, one who helps people to reflect upon their espoused theories. Thus Argyris and Schön contribute to a clearer conceptualisation of the role of the adult educator in the overall learning process or cycle. Unfortunately, Argyris especially has mainly limited this contribution to the area of management learning and organisational development. We should also say that Argyris and Schön have always been marginal in the field of adult education.

Symbolic interactionism and adult education

It is Jack Mezirow, especially, who has popularised in the field of adult education a very similar conceptualisation or theory of adult learning. Yet in order fully to understand his theory, as well as the theory of Peter Jarvis, we must first present yet another version of American pragmatism: 'symbolic interactionism'.

Symbolic interactionism

Like Dewey's work, symbolic interactionism can be traced back to the city of Chicago at the beginning of the twentieth century. At that time, Chicago was the cradle of social work and, more generally, sociology. Urban Chicago itself was in the making, among other things characterised by immigration, crime, poverty, and all the other ills of an urban city in the process of rapid industrialisation. For social workers, sociologists, and even philosophers like Dewey, Chicago became a sort of social laboratory, with a particular interest in delinquency and social deviation, as well as a certain social and even political sensitivity to human problems. Problems such as urban poverty and unemployment were viewed as the consequences of immigration, industrialisation and the changing organisation of work (e.g. Taylorism).

It was in this context that the so-called Chicago School of Sociology (Bulmer, 1984; Ross, 1991) emerged. Intellectually, the Chicago School was a combination of pragmatism and German phenomenology, as almost all Chicago sociologists had been trained in Germany. They were mainly interested in the social problems they saw: exclusion, marginalisation, deviation, and so on. Methodologically, the Chicago School was heavily influenced by journalism and other investigative and participatory methods. Particular importance was given to so-called biographical method- ology, whereby the researcher sought to understand the larger social reality from a single lived experience. Thomas and Znani- ecki's seminal study on *The Polish Peasant in Europe and America*, for example, was written between 1919 and 1921, and published in 1927 (Thomas and Znaniecki, 1927). George Herbert Mead (1863–1931) and Herbert Blumer (1900–87) subsequently theo- rised the Chicago School's underlying epistemology. The theory of symbolic interactionism can thus be found in Mead's *Mind, Self, & Society* (Mead, 1934), and even more clearly in Blumer's *Sym- bolic Interactionism: Perspective and Method* (Blumer, 1969). Symbolic interactionism is the foundation upon which ethnomethodology (Garfinkel, 1967; Cicourel, 1964) and so-called grounded theory (Glaser and Strauss, 1967) were developed.

Symbolic interactionism is basically the application of pragma- tism to the realm of language – that is, symbolic human interaction. It is located on the same level of abstraction as Dewey's work. It also parallels his work in that it considers that humans are funda- mentally different from other species, precisely because of their ability to manipulate symbols. Humans therefore function within a symbolic universe, which is what symbolic interactionism deals with. The following three premisses are the core ideas of symbolic interactionism, and are necessary to an understanding of Jarvis's and Mezirow's theories of adult learning (Blumer, 1969: 1–60):

- Humans act vis-à-vis things according to the *meaning* these things have for them. This is a critique of determinism, both in psy- chology and sociology: action is shaped neither by inner drives nor by social circumstances. Human behaviour is thus a func- tion of the meaning things have for people, not a function of what reality objectively is. In other words, there is no objective reality when it comes to human interaction.

- The meaning things have for humans is not personal, but is itself the result of *social interaction*. In other words, meaning gradually crystallises through human interaction in a social context. This is a critique of realism – of the idea that things have meaning in themselves – as well as a critique of relativistic psychologism, the idea that meaning is purely personal.
- Consequently, meaning can be and is constantly changed through the process of social interaction. In interacting with each other, humans always introduce slightly different meanings; this implies that collective meanings are constantly evolving.

In short, symbolic interactionism is astructural, non-institutional and apolitical: humans are said to live within a purely symbolic universe, where all their relations and interactions are ultimately a matter of symbolism and interpretation. This general view leads us straight to Herbert Mead's more specific theory of *personality*. The logical consequence of such an approach is that the human being, his or her personality, and his or her identity are the results of a purely symbolic interaction with reality and with others. In other words, a person does not have an essence; he or she is the product of social interaction. By interacting with others, the same person simultaneously contributes to the evolution of the overall meaning of a group or a society, and thus even to the evolution of the personality of its members.

The *self*, for Mead, is the identity of the person. This identity stems from the interaction between the person and their symbolic environment. At any given moment, this identity is the result of past cumulative interactions. In other words, the self is at the same time what the person takes from and what he or she contributes to the symbolic reality. This self has therefore simultaneously an individual and a social dimension: it is individual inasmuch as the accumulated history of one's interaction with the symbolic environment is always unique, but it is also social, since by being shaped by the social meaning of things, a person is always also in harmony with his or her symbolic world. In short, a person is simultaneously an individual and a social being (see Figure 3.5).

Figure 3.5   Mead's self

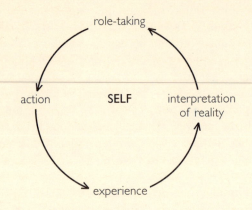

Role-taking is another key concept for Mead, as it is the means by which individual and collective meaning evolve. Role-taking refers to the human capacity or possibility of putting oneself in the place of others – of seeing oneself from the perspective of others. Mead distinguishes here between the 'I' – what one (symbolically) is at a given moment – and the 'me' – how one sees oneself from the perspective of another person. Role-taking is the movement from the 'I' to the 'me': when one tries to see oneself as others do. By taking such roles, one tries to adapt one's behaviour or actions in such a way that that they conform to what others expect. In other words, the 'me' becomes the 'I'. Here we can identify Dewey's experiential cycle adapted to a symbolic environment: a person interacts with the symbolic environment (concrete experience) and derives from this interaction the 'me perspective' (reflective observation). The person then tries to conform to the way others see him or her (abstract conceptualisation) and finally behaves accordingly (active experimentation). By going through this symbolic learning cycle, a person simultaneously builds his or her identity while contributing to shaping the symbolic world through his or her actions. Growth or development results from the continuous discrepancy between the way one sees oneself and the way society (others) see one: through role-taking, a person is constantly driven to reduce this discrepancy. This pressure never stops, as the person cannot exist outside symbolic reality. The never-ending challenge is to remain individual while at the same time being in tune with society.

Peter Jarvis (1937–)

Peter Jarvis, the British sociologist of religion, is certainly one of the most prolific and therefore also best-known authors in the field of adult education. He has written and edited numerous volumes about many relevant subjects. Most of his contributions are quite descriptive in nature, for example his *Sociology of Adult and Continuing Education* (1985), *Twentieth Century Thinkers in Adult Education* (1987b), *An International Dictionary of Adult and Continuing Education* (1990), *Training Adult Educators in Western Europe* (1991), *Perspectives on Adult Education and Training in Europe* (1992), and *Adult Education and Theological Interpretations* (1993). As editor of the adult education series first at Croom Helm and later at Routledge, he has in effect functioned as a 'gatekeeper' of the field. These books, along with his *International Journal of Lifelong Education*, have had a great impact internationally, including in the United States. His vast body of work makes him quite difficult to classify. Nevertheless, his intellectual contribution to adult education theory can clearly be located within the pragmatist, and even more precisely within the symbolic interactionist, context. As a theorist, Jarvis is thus mostly preoccupied with adult learning, or, more precisely, with *Adult Learning in the Social Context* (1987a), a book which earned him the Houle Award in 1988.

Jarvis's intellectual contribution to adult education theory is basically his translation of symbolic interactionism into a model of adult learning, combining his sociological view of the adult learner with the mechanism of pragmatic learning. According to Jarvis, experiential learning, therefore, does not lead simply to new knowledge, skills and attitudes, but to the building-up of the self, which he calls the 'person'. As we have already seen with Mead, the 'self' of symbolic interactionism is basically an 'individual without substance', the result of a process of individual adaptation to a symbolic environment. The self is thus aware,

Figure 3.6   Jarvis's model of adult learning

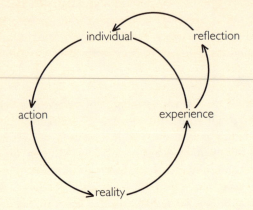

through role-taking, of being different from other individuals, yet nevertheless entirely in tune with society. 'Self-awareness' for Mead, and 'problem-solving' for Dewey, are in fact simply ways to respond and adjust to the ever-changing (symbolic) environment. Jarvis's model of adult learning is more or less identical with Mead's theory of 'self-construction'. What he calls the 'social context' of adult learning is in fact nothing other than Mead's symbolic environment, in which the self – or, for Jarvis, the person – evolves. In other words, what Jarvis calls 'adult learning in the social context' is a pragmatic experiential learning cycle placed within a symbolic context, as shown in Figure 3.6.

As we can see, the 'experience' to which Jarvis refers is always a symbolic one: one's symbolic interaction with others prompts their reaction, which in turn triggers one's 'experience'. One therefore reflects on the experience so triggered and made in this interaction with others. This experience is in fact nothing other than the feedback one gets from interacting with others. By reflecting on that feedback, one readjusts to the way the others would like one to be. In a new interaction or feedback loop, this newly acquired 'self-understanding' is again tried out with others. Through this process, the self (for Mead) or the person (for Jarvis) is gradually built. In other words, what we see here is Kolb's learning cycle applied to a symbolic environment. And unlike Argyris, who applies reflection to the 'theory-in-action' (which is the result of the analysis of previous experiences), Jarvis applies reflection to the immediate feedback received from the symbolic interaction, and thus downplays the role of abstract conceptualisation.

In addition, if for Dewey and Kolb reality was the physical reality people experienced, for Jarvis it is the symbolic reality. If for Dewey, Kolb, Lewin, and even for Argyris, the pragmatic learning cycle is basically a means of problem-solving, for Jarvis, putting the learning cycle into a symbolic context, it is a means of building the self or the person – that is, an instrument of identity construction. Adult learning, with Jarvis, thus equals identity self-development. There is problem-solving in the process, as the image one presents to others does not correspond to the image others have; or, vice versa, the image of oneself others receive does not correspond to one's image of oneself. In both cases, there is a discrepancy which, according to Jarvis, prompts (adult) learning: 'The disjunction between biography and experience lies at the start of the learning process' (Jarvis, 1987a: 87).

In short, by referring to symbolic interactionism, Jarvis develops a model of adult learning which equates learning with identity self-development. Yet this model has no solid theoretical foundation, either in psychology or in psycho-sociology: it is therefore not a theory of individual or personal development, as one cannot talk about stages or phases. There is a process, but no clear direction. By adopting this symbolic interactionist model, Jarvis thus implicitly shares all the weaknesses of symbolic interactionism when it comes to personality construction: indeed, the development of the self is a process of becoming simultaneously more individualised and more socialised – that is, more adjusted to the dominant symbolic environment. Consequently, the function of adult education becomes to help people adjust to society, while making them feel ever more individual.

Jack Mezirow (1923–)

Although he is not a sociologist by training, Jack Mezirow has a much more social orientation. Moreover, today Mezirow has acquired a status in the field of adult education comparable to that of Illich and Freire. His theory of 'perspective transformation' is certainly the most elaborate and intellectually the most solid conceptualisation of adult learning, linking such learning to social change. Yet, as we will show, the theory of perspective transformation is firmly grounded in pragmatic philosophy and, more precisely, symbolic interactionism. In this section, we briefly outline the main phases of Mezirow's intellectual life and their respective influences on his theory, present the key features of 'perspective transformation', and conclude with some critical remarks.

The intellectual and practical foundation of Mezirow's work lies in American community development – the effort to integrate people from various ethnic and social backgrounds into coherent communities, a problem quite typical for a society made up of immigrants. Since he comes from Minnesota, a state that is very much influenced by Scandinavian social-democratic and even socialist ideas, his concern with community development in a social perspective is quite natural. He started to work, as an adult educator, with communities at the grassroots level, an activity which, despite his academic achievements, has never stopped. On the advice of Malcolm Knowles – at that time Director of the National Adult Education Association (see below) – Mezirow then went to work on his Ed.D[6] in adult education with Paul Sheats at the University of California at Los Angeles (UCLA). Sheats aroused his particular interest in the relevance of group dynamics for democratic participation. After graduation he went to Pakistan, where he worked for two years with USAID (US Agency for International Development), promoting American-style community development. In retrospect, Mezirow questions this ethnocentric missionary work, particularly after his political awareness was raised by Freire's work and ideas. As a result, Mezirow became more socially aware and active. In 1970, for example, he was one of the founders of the League for Social Commitment in adult education; he also joined Miles Horton and other social activists in the North American Alliance for Popular and Adult Education (Mezirow, 1991b).

During the 1960s Mezirow did post-doctoral work in Berkeley, California – that is to say, during the heyday of social activism. He came into contact with Herbert Blumer (see above) and Glaser and Strauss (see Glaser and Strauss 1967). The interpretative

sociology of these authors also influenced Thomas Kuhn, especially his 1962 book *The Structure of Scientific Revolutions*, which was
to become a reference point for Mezirow's theory of perspective
transformation. It was at that time that Mezirow laid the ground-
work for his conceptualisation of meaning perspectives and perspective transformation. This early conceptualisation was then
applied in empirical research – first in the area of adult literacy[7]
and then particularly in that of women re-entering college.[8] Both
research projects were carried out at Teachers College, Columbia
University, where Mezirow had been recruited by Alan B. Knox
in 1968. Mezirow started to view the role of adult education as
fostering what he called *perspective transformation*.

But Mezirow, as a good pragmatist, never stopped developing
his conceptualisation of perspective transformation and adult
learning. During his sabbatical in 1980 he met and worked with
Roger Gould, a psychoanalyst and professor of clinical psychiatry
at UCLA. In his practice, Gould applied a popularised version
of psychoanalytic theory to adult development (Gould, 1978).
With this encounter, Mezirow's theory of perspective transformation became more concrete, especially with respect to adult
development. Perspective transformation was now no longer simply seen as analogous to Kuhn's paradigm shift, but in addition
as a means and significant step in the process of emancipation.
More concretely, with Gould's influence, perspective transformation is a significant step in freeing oneself from psychological
distortions acquired during infancy, as well as throughout the
whole of life. With his social action background, Mezirow saw
such personal emancipation as being very similar to Freire's
political emancipation.

The time was thus ripe when, during the 1980s, Mezirow read
the work of the German Critical Theorist Jürgen Habermas
(Habermas, 1971, 1984, 1987). From Habermas's writings Mezirow
borrowed certain concepts and tools of emancipation, but not the
overall Marxist framework. Habermas helped Mezirow to clarify
in particular the methodology of perspective transformation: that
of 'discourse analysis', including contextual awareness, a Marxist
concept which can also be found in Paolo Freire's thinking (see
below). 'Critical reflection' now became a key concept for Mezirow,
along with the attention paid to the conditions under which such

Figure 3.7 Mezirow's perspective transformation

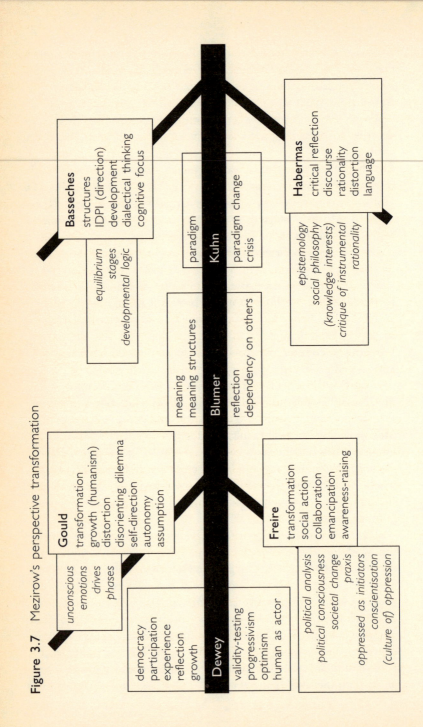

critical reflection can take place – that is, Habermas's 'ideal speech situation', in which (ideological) assumptions can be critically questioned. With Habermas, Mezirow's theory of perspective transformation now takes a linguistic turn. This, incidentally, was a critique which had already been addressed to Habermas's interpretation of Critical Theory. But with Habermas, Mezirow's conceptualisation of perspective transformation took a clear, emancipatory direction – not least because Habermas, in the tradition of Critical Theory, had himself already established a link between individual emancipation (as described in Freudian psychoanalysis) and Marxist sociopolitical emancipation. As a result, Mezirow sees perspective transformation as leading to 'more integrative, more discriminatory, more permeable, and more inclusive perspectives', a process which equals individual and collective emancipation. This idea of perspective transformation was being institutionalised when Mezirow started his famous doctoral programme, AEGIS (Adult Education Guided Independent Study), at Teachers College in 1982.[9]

After many discussions and further theorisation Mezirow published, in 1991, his seminal book *Transformative Dimensions of Adult Learning* (Mezirow, 1991a). Perspective transformation was now put back into a pragmatic adult learning, or rather development, framework, as Mezirow departed from Habermas's epistemology and returned to his Deweyan and symbolic interactionist background. Before presenting the key features of Mezirow's theory of perspective transformation, let us briefly outline graphically the various authors and concepts Mezirow has borrowed from during his intellectual journey. In so doing, we distinguish between the concepts Mezirow incorporates into his theory and the concepts which, in our view, he does not really incorporate (in italic). Figure 3.7 thus shows that Mezirow's theory of perspective transformation is basically grounded in the work of Dewey, Blumer and Kuhn.

Mezirow sees adult learning, located in the context of symbolic interactionism, as an evolving way of looking at (symbolically constructed) things. Yet he goes much further than symbolic interactionism, and than Jarvis, inasmuch as he tries to give this evolution a concrete direction, which he sees as some sort of individual and societal emancipation. His main intellectual effort is

to conceptualise the means by which such direction can be introduced into the pragmatic learning cycle. In order to do this,
Mezirow distinguishes between 'meaning schemes' and 'meaning
perspectives', somewhat in analogy to Argyris and Schön's
distinction between 'espoused theory' and 'theory-in-use'. Mezirow,
however, does not refer to them but, rather, to the distinction
made in linguistics (Chomsky) between depth and surface language structures: there is a grammar (meaning perspectives) which
generates an unlimited amount of grammatically correct sentences
(meaning schemes). In order to evolve in our way of looking at
things, it is necessary to focus critical reflection on the grammar
– i.e. the meaning perspectives – and not on the surface – i.e. the
meaning schemes, which is, unfortunately, were most learning
occurs. According to Mezirow, perspective transformation – the
transformation of meaning perspectives – occurs either because of
a 'disorienting dilemma' – for example, a huge discrepancy between experience and *meaning perspective* – or incrementally through
a series of little changes in the meaning schemes, which finally
create a significant discrepancy between a meaning scheme and a
meaning perspective. If meaning schemes are changed through
simple reflection, meaning perspectives are transformed through
what he calls 'critical reflection', that is, by questioning one's 'fundamental assumptions', 'guiding principles', or 'premisses' – a
process very similar to Kuhn's 'paradigm shift' and Argyris and
Schön's 'double-loop learning'.

According to Mezirow, true adult learning occurs when such a
perspective transformation happens. The ideal conditions for
transformative adult learning are the ones Habermas has identified as being the ideal conditions for communicative discourse. It
is at this moment of communicative learning through rational
discourse that critical reflection can actually develop its full potential and help one to question one's basic assumptions and, by
doing so, help one to transform one's perspectives. Such perspective transformation will lead towards a more 'inclusive, differentiated, permeable, and integrated perspective'. Perspective
transformation is thus viewed as identical to the process of adult
development.

Several criticisms can be made of Mezirow's theory of perspective transformation. Let us focus here on the two – in our view

– most important ones. Mezirow is at times very eclectic, mixing perhaps incompatible philosophies and epistemologies, such as pragmatism and Marxism. Such eclecticism is evident in his inconsistent use of Habermas's idea of 'knowledge interests', as well as his misuse of Habermas's concept of 'lifeworld'. Similarly, concepts borrowed from psychoanalysis and Critical Theory are equally distorted. Nevertheless, it must be said that Mezirow is one of the very few theoreticians in the field of adult education – if not the only one – who does not simply summarise these various theoretical contributions but critically analyses them, and tries to integrate them into a unified conceptual framework and theory. Given the wide range of epistemologies, it is understandable that Mezirow's theory is still not completely integrated.

The second type of criticism, however, is – in our view and from our perspective – more serious: Marxists have criticised Mezirow on the grounds that he has no theory of social action and social change (Collard and Law, 1989; Welton, 1995). In our view, this criticism should be phrased not as a question of political correctness but as an epistemological issue, as Mezirow's theory lacks a sound connection between (individual) perspective transformation and social change. We have already pointed out that Mezirow has not really integrated Freire's and Habermas's political analysis; this has led him to focus, in the typical symbolic interactionist tradition, on the way adult learners adapt to rather than criticise society. As a result, Mezirow simply assumes, like the humanists we will discuss in Chapter 4, that perspective transformation and adult learning will automatically lead to social action and social change.

Critique of pragmatic adult education

In this chapter, we have presented pragmatism as applied to the field of adult education. As we have seen, there are basically two different applications of pragmatism, both grounded in Dewey's work. On the one hand, there is the tradition of experiential learning, describing in essence learning as a problem-solving mechanism. This application of pragmatism leads to the development of diagnostic tools, as well as to defining adult education as facilitating problem-solving. In other words, adult educators become facilitators of the learning cycle. On the other hand, there is the tradition of symbolic interactionism. Here, problem-solving is applied to identity self-development. Adult learning becomes a process of constantly confronting one's (symbolically constructed) self to the (equally symbolically constructed) environment, while 'solving' the discrepancies observed. The role of adult education, in this application of pragmatism, is to facilitate such 'symbolic problem-solving' and, by so doing, contribute to self-, identity, or adult development. Lindeman and Mezirow try to break out of or enlarge this view by placing adult development in a larger societal context: adult learning is thus not only a means of self-development but also a process which simultaneously contributes to social change. Yet neither Lindeman nor Mezirow goes beyond Dewey in this respect, as adult learning does not take place in a critical relationship, and even less in opposition to societal development and growth. At best, in the case of Mezirow, perspective transformations of adult learners contribute to steering society in a direction more compatible with the 'inclusive, differentiated, permeable, and integrated perspectives' of critically reflective adult learners.

In other words, the fact that it has never problematised the parallelism between individual and societal development is certainly one of the key weaknesses of pragmatism as applied to adult education. It is one reason why the relationship between adult learning and social change cannot be thoroughly conceptualised. Another reason might stem from the fact that pragmatism – like *éducation permanente*, which we discussed in Chapter 2 – does not problematise social structures and institutions. The absence of such conceptualisation is an epistemological weakness with negative consequences for our field: none of the adult education authors who draw on pragmatism and symbolic interactionism has ultimately developed a theory of adult learning, even less so a theory of adult learning as social action. Even if it is not merely a set of techniques to diagnose or facilitate the learning cycle (as in the case of Kolb and his followers) or double-loop learning (as in the case of Argyris and Schön), pragmatic adult education is at best a discourse on adult learning as symbolic problem-solving. The relationship between such adult learning and societal change remains, even in the case of Mezirow, mainly wishful thinking. One can therefore conclude that the pragmatic tradition in adult education is not critical of societal development and growth, since ultimately human development and societal development go hand in hand; this is most perfectly illustrated in symbolic interactionism. It is very probable that pragmatic adult education, as it has been conceptualised so far in the United States and in the United Kingdom, does not even contain the potential for social change.

Notes

1. For a complete bibliography, see The Center for Dewey Studies, *The Collected Work of John Dewey 1882–1953* (37 vols), or on CD-Rom (Charlotteville, VA: Intelex Corp.). See also Cross-Durrant (1987: 95–7). On Dewey, see Barbara Levine (ed.), *Works about John Dewey 1886–1995* (1996), updated in www.sin.edu/deweyctr.

2. Although Charles Sanders Peirce (1839–1914) was teaching there, Dewey worked under the auspices of George Sylvester Morris. After graduation, invited by Morris, he went to the University of Michigan, Ann Arbor.

3. Danish adult education had also inspired Myles Horton (1905–1995), who was studying at Columbia University's affiliated Union Theological Seminary at the time when Lindeman was at the New York School of Social Work. Horton founded his Highlander Folk School in 1932.

4. Quoted in Brookfield (1987: 122).

5. See 'Learning Styles Network' at School of Education and Human Services, St. John's University NY.

6. In his dissertation *The Coordinating Council and Urban Demography in Los Angeles County*, Mezirow actually studied one hundred Los Angeles community councils.

7. See J. Mezirow, G. Darkenwald and A. Knox, *Last Gamble in Education* (Washington DC: AEA of USA, 1975), which won the Imogenes Oakes Award in 1980.

8. See J. Mezirow, *Education for Perspective Transformation: Women's Reentry Programs in Community Colleges*, with contributions by Victoria Marsick (New York: Center for Adult Education, Teachers College, Columbia University, 1978).

9. See www.tc.columbia.edu. The authors of this book should be mentioned at this stage of adult education theory development. Matthias Finger had written his PhD on the application of Habermas to adult learning, and was appointed in 1992 to replace Mezirow at Teachers College, and as director of the AEGIS programme. José Asún was then a doctoral student in this programme, and later AEGIS programme manager. Matthias Finger left Teachers College in late 1994, as the Adult Education programme was integrated, institutionally and intellectually, into corporate organisational behaviour.

Chapter 4

Humanism: The Lonely Traveller
on the Road to Heaven

Adult education humanism is not totally unrelated to pragmatism. Indeed, the chief author of humanistic adult education, Malcolm Knowles, was considerably influenced by Dewey and Lindeman, though his main influence was the humanistic psychologist Carl Rogers. After pragmatism, humanism is probably the most important school in adult education thinking and practice (Merriam, 1993). Its origin is to be found in humanistic psychology. In 1954 Abraham Maslow wrote his famous book *Motivation and Personality*, and his ideas perfectly summarise the essence of humanistic thinking: the idea that human motivation is related to the satisfaction of needs, self-actualisation being the ultimate need. But humanistic thinking itself is embedded in the larger philosophy of existentialism, developed in Germany in the interwar period (Jaspers, Barth, Heidegger) and in France after World War II (Marcel, Sartre, Camus). Existentialism, like humanism, stresses the uniqueness of human existence, in particular human freedom, and the possibility of self-development.

By referring to humanistic psychology, as opposed to any other kind of psychology, adult education also positions itself without ambiguity within the field of psychology. Humanistic psychology itself is a 'third way' – that is, an attempt to break out of the two schools that dominated psychological thinking in the early twentieth century. On the one hand, there was the behaviourist approach of Watson, Thorndike, Pavlov and Skinner, which was considered truly scientific. Its focus of study was observable and measurable behaviour, and it considered that learning mechanically changed behaviour through stimulus–response conditioning, and reinforcement. On the other hand, there was the psychoanalytic approach of Sigmund Freud, Carl G. Jung and Erik Erikson, which focused on the subconscious and irrational components of behaviour: defence mechanisms, drives and transference.

Humanistic psychology as an existentialist approach reacted against both the reductionism of behaviourism and the intellectualism of psychoanalysis. Against the idea of human behaviour being predetermined either by the environment or by the subconscious, humanistic psychology proposed a 'third way' which respected control over one's own destiny. For humanistic psychologists, people are fundamentally good, free to act and to choose, and responsible for the development of their own full potential. Carl Rogers, the key thinker of humanistic psychology, will be briefly introduced here. Rogers, along with Abraham Maslow and Gordon Allport, is the intellectual founder of humanistic psychology. He is also the one who has considerably shaped humanistic adult education and its core concept, 'andragogy'. But andragogy, and other humanistic versions of adult education, are not original theoretical contributions. Rather, they are applications of the humanistic psychology of the founding fathers, like Gestalt Therapy (Bode, Wertheimer, Kohler, Koffka) or Transactional Analysis (Eric Berne). It is in this spirit of popularising humanistic psychology that we will discuss adult education authors Malcolm Knowles and Stephen Brookfield, as well as the key concepts humanistic psychology has given birth to in our field – that is, the concepts of 'andragogy', 'facilitation' and 'self-directed learning'.

Carl Rogers (1902–1987)

Rogers's thinking can be traced back to three quite different intellectual roots: first his initial studies in agronomy, which shaped his basic idea on growth; second, his theological education (Masters) at Union Theological Seminary[1] in New York, which brought him into contact with existentialism and shaped his belief in the intrinsic value of the human being; finally, his doctoral studies in psychology at Columbia University, which determined his practice. This practice, in turn, can be divided into three phases, each corresponding to different interests, as well as to different conceptions of learning. Between 1931 and 1944 Rogers worked as a therapist in a community clinic. This phase gave rise to his reflections on the therapeutic, interpersonal relationship, best described in his 1951 book *Client-Centered Therapy*. Between 1945 and 1963 Rogers was a professor of psychology at Chicago University, another key location of adult education thinking. There he came into contact with phenomenology and symbolic interactionism, which reinforced his 'existentialist' approach. Rogers now enlarged his reflections on learning (see *Freedom to Learn*, 1969). Between 1963 and 1987 he worked as a therapist in California, in an environment shaped by alternative and New Age movements. At that time Rogers opened up his thinking to social problems, committing himself to peace and ecology issues. The book which best captures this last phase of his life is *A Way of Being* (1980).

Three basic assumptions underlie Rogers's thinking. First there is the idea that the human being is active and free – that is, fundamentally good. Rogers's existentialist and teleological perspective here is in total opposition to the psychoanalytic view which considers that humans are subject to drives which they have constantly to control. Second, there is the idea that human beings have an inner drive, an intrinsic motivation, for self-development. Rogers's reference to agricultural growth and germination, in our view, is more than a metaphor here. Third, there is the idea that while this potential resides within the human being, its activation depends heavily on the environment, which ultimately decides whether this potential for self-development can or cannot unfold. In other words, in a favourable environment all humans, like all plants and vegetables, can develop. Here Rogers is very close to pragmatic American thinking, the only difference being that the relevant unit is the individual, society being simply an environment for the individual.

Even if Rogers extended his considerations to education and social change at a later stage in his life, his framework is fundamentally therapeutic. His ultimate purpose is to help the individual grow. This is basically done by creating a favourable – that is, a non-threatening – environment, as one cannot force growth, only create the right conditions, which in turn activate the growth potential, the intrinsic energies, of every individual. Creating such an environment requires from the therapist, and more generally from any human being, a series of characteristics: empathy, comprehension, non-judgemental respect (as opposed to preconceived analytic categories, as in psychoanalysis), authenticity (which implies that the therapist accepts him- or herself), transparency, a spirit of nurturing, warmth and love. All these characteristics of such a humanistic relationship are summarised in Rogers's concept of *non-directivity*. In other words, a relationship which allows a person to grow is a non-directive relationship.

Technically, the process of personal growth and development is characterised by the continuous reduction of the discrepancy or 'incongruence' between an 'experience' and its 'meaning' for a person. Unlike the pragmatic school, where 'experience' is in essence an experiment with reality, for Rogers and humanistic psychology 'experience' is existential in nature. It cannot be separated from the (inner) 'meaning' of the experience. Incongruence results from the discrepancy between the true meaning of an experience for a person and the socially constructed meaning ascribed through verbalisation. The greater the role of the environment in this meaning-giving process, the greater the possibility of incongruence. Therapy aims to reduce this incongruence – to rediscover the inner meaning of an experience. In other words, it aims to reduce the gap between what society wants one to be and what one is, and might become. Thus Rogers's therapy is client-centred and non-directive: development occurs when the interpretation of the experience corresponds to its true meaning.[2] Such development is synonymous with increased freedom; while freedom, in turn, is also a condition for such development to take place.

Some of the key ideas of Rogerian psychology can be found today in humanistic adult education, while others have deliberately been cast aside: for example, humanistic adult education seeks to 'facilitate the learning process', as opposed to teach. Facilitating the learning process in adult education is the equivalent, in humanistic psychology, of creating the optimal conditions for human development. Adult learning is thus equated to personal growth and adult development – that is, self-actualisation. The role of the adult educator is therefore focused mainly on the learning environment, where he or she has to create the optimal conditions for self-development. Like in humanistic psychology, humanistic adult education believes that a person does not grow – that is, learn – if the learning experience is not meaningful for him or her. Both in humanistic psychology and in humanistic adult education, the role of the so-called 'facilitator' is crucial. His or her role is in particular to create an optimal climate or environment for learning, to help a person to clarify his or her interpretations of experiences and, by so doing, to help him or her to grow and develop. The facilitator has to minimise his or her judgements, accept the intellectual and emotional attitudes of each person, to pay attention to hidden feelings and make them explicit, and be aware of his or her own limits in fostering such learning and growth.

There are other key ideas, however, which humanistic adult education does not adopt. These pertain in particular to the *therapeutic nature of the relationship* between the facilitator and his or her client. Indeed, this therapeutic relationship can be painful, as there is resistance to change, development and growth. Such resistance materialises in the form of denial, distortion and symbolising (a way of rationalising), and results in an inability to connect with one's experience. Unfortunately, humanistic adult education never refers to such resistance. Nor does it refer much to the role of the environment in fostering learning in growth – a factor Rogers stressed especially later in his life. Given that the structure of the self tends to be more rigid under threat, the goal of therapy is to free the environment of such threats. In other words, an environment that favours and differentiates perception (i.e. helps to explore alternative interpretations of experiences) increases the opportunity of decreasing the incongruence between meaning and experience. If the role of the environment in personal growth and development is not adequately taken into account, there is indeed the danger that humanistic adult education will become purely individualistic. And this is unfortunately what happened when Rogerian humanistic psychology got translated into the field of adult education, as we will now see.

Malcolm Knowles (1913–1997)

Malcolm Knowles is generally known as a populariser of humanistic psychology, translating it into the field of adult education. In this field, however, Knowles was considered a founding father, the so-called 'apostle of andragogy'. Indeed, triggered by Knowles, especially by his concept of andragogy, some 200 articles and studies were produced between 1970 and 1980 alone. Knowles himself is the author of numerous articles and books, his most important contributions to adult education being *The Modern Practice of Adult Education: Andragogy versus Pedagogy* (1970), *The Adult Learner: A Neglected Species* (1973), and *Andragogy in Action: Applying Modern Principles of Adult Education* (1984).

Knowles was born in a rural area of Montana, studied political science at Harvard University, and wanted to enter the diplomatic service. In the midst of the Depression, which followed the collapse of the stock market in the autumn of 1929, he joined the National Youth Administration, where he worked as training director of unemployed young people. This experience shifted his earlier professional interests towards adult education. Subsequently, he came into contact with Lindeman and enrolled at the adult education graduate programme under the auspices of Cyril O. Houle at the University of Chicago. At Chicago he came into contact with Carl Rogers's thinking, through Arthur Shedlin, a Rogers associate. In 1960 Knowles became a professor at Boston University, where he set up a graduate programme based on his ideas on informal and self-directed learning. After retirement in 1979, he successfully continued his career through his very influential adult education company 'Knowles Enterprises'.

In Knowles's work it is possible to distinguish two components: his contribution to the institutionalisation of the field on the one hand, and his conceptual contributions on the other. With reference to the former, we must say that Knowles was an extremely successful salesman and promoter of adult education. During the 1970s he managed to carve out a niche for adult education by packaging his products – andragogy and self-directed learning – for an expanding market of adult learners in search of self-development. In the 1980s he repackaged the same products, but this time targeted them towards the management development market. Throughout his career, he had a non-critical view of society and organisations, and he managed to conceptualise adult learning in such a way that it did not challenge the status quo and middle-class American norms and values. Here, however, we will present and critically discuss Knowles's successful combination of pragmatism and humanistic psychology, as well as his key concepts, 'facilitation' and 'andragogy'.

Mixing humanism and pragmatism

Knowles takes ideas from both the pragmatic and the humanistic traditions, though humanism is dominant. Like Dewey and Lindeman, he focuses on problems and situations, which are the real challenges for learning. But, like Rogers, he stresses the role of the environment, as it is the environment which either favours or hinders adult learning. From both, Knowles takes the concept of 'experience'. Even though this concept has different meanings in the pragmatic and the humanistic traditions, Knowles manages to combine these two approaches. Experiences are, on the one hand, a source of learning (pragmatism), especially when one reflects upon them; but, on the other hand, they are also the outcome of the learning process; this contributes to making these experiences more congruent with their inner meaning, and thus more meaningful (humanistic psychology).

Nevertheless, for Knowles the influence of humanistic psychology prevails. From Rogers he takes not only the key role of the environment in learning, but the motivation and the goal. Indeed, like Rogers, Knowles starts with the assumption that there is an intrinsic motivation for growth, development and learning. This intrinsic motivation has to be put into a relationship with the ultimate goal of such a process, which is 'self-actualisation'. Learning, which is synonymous with growth, is the means for self-actualisation – that is, the mechanism by which congruence can be established between one's experiences and their inner meaning. Facilitating such (adult) learning, for Knowles, is called 'andragogy' (see below). Let us recall that, for Rogers, the establishment of such congruence is a fundamentally therapeutic process. This is no longer the case for Knowles, for whom it has become a pedagogical, or rather andragogical, process.

Yet one can also detect a pragmatic influence: indeed, Knowles's other key concept of 'self-directedness' or 'self-directed learning' has a double meaning. On the one hand, self-directedness is the movement of an individual from dependence to maturation, to autonomy, and to independence (Rogers); while on the other hand, it is also a process which leads towards more control over

the environment in which the person lives (Dewey). Knowles combines the two: he sees 'growth' as a process of self-actualisation as
well as as a process of accumulation of experiences (Dewey), which
then become 'resources for learning.' Through such a process of
growth the person becomes more open to society, and society
'grows' in turn (Rogers); while simultaneously, the person becomes
more capable of solving problems, which increases a society's
capacity to master its environment (Dewey's 'plasticity').

The concept of 'facilitation'

The concept of facilitation pertains precisely to this ambiguous
definition of growth, called self-directed learning. It is the role of
the facilitator to foster growth, development and self-directed
learning, both in Rogers's and in Dewey's sense. The learner feels
the intrinsic need to grow, and the facilitator clarifies his or her
needs, motivation and goals. In addition, the facilitator helps the
person to take control of this process, by creating a favourable
climate and environment. Finally, by blending the person's experiences with concrete situations, the facilitator also contributes to
solving problems, thus shaping the environment in a way that is
conducive to further growth.

For Knowles, an ideal *facilitator* can be characterised as someone
who:

- considers the learner as a human being capable of self-direction,
  able to take care of her own growth process;
- considers adult learning as a process of self-development;
- considers the role of facilitator to be a resource-person for the
  self-directed learner;
- believes that learning is more significant if it is driven by
  intrinsic motivation;
- stresses the creation of a facilitating learning climate, characterised by warmth, mutual trust and respect, concern and attention
  for others, and informality, – that is, non directivity;
- involves the learner in setting the learning objectives, always
  within the goal that these objectives must be meaningful for the
  learner him/herself, for example through so-called 'learning
  contracts';
- develops sequential learning experiences which take into
  account the group's similarities (e.g. shared concerns) and the

individual's differences as organising principles of learning projects; and

- selects techniques and materials that involve the learners actively in the process of self-inquiry.

Andragogy, not pedagogy

As we said above, Knowles is considered to be the 'apostle of andragogy', understood as 'the art and science of helping adults learn' (Knowles, 1970: 43).[3] Nevertheless, it is necessary to mention his evolving use of the term. Indeed, in 1968, in the counter-cultural context, Knowles saw andragogy as antithetical to pedagogy, which was the dominant way of practising education. Significantly, he wrote: 'Andragogy, not pedagogy' (Knowles, 1968). Two years later, in the context of a developing niche for adult education, Knowles wrote *The Modern Practice of Adult Education: Andragogy versus Pedagogy* (1970). But by 1980, especially in the light of numerous critiques addressed to this opposition, Knowles changed the subtitle of the second edition of the same book to *From Pedagogy to Andragogy*.

Since then, it has become standard practice in adult education to oppose – or at least to compare – pedagogy and andragogy. Many authors have contributed to this opposition by declaring andragogy a unique perspective on adult education and learning, different from, and at times even incompatible with, pedagogy (e.g. Jarvis, 1987a: 176–7; Merriam and Caffarella, 1991: 250–51). Let us briefly summarise the six key points of this opposition, as it is defined by Knowles and his disciples:

- the *learner*: if in pedagogy the learner is defined in relation to the teacher, in andragogy the learner has an independent status, and the role of the teacher is precisely to make him or her ever more independent;
- the *need to know*: similarly, while in pedagogy the needs are defined by the teacher, in andragogy, instead, the facilitator helps the learner to articulate his or her own needs, and contributes to satisfying them;
- the *role of experience*: while in pedagogy, according to Knowles, experience does not play a significant role in learning, in andragogy experience is the basic resource and foundation for learning;

- *learning*: if in pedagogy learning is induced by the teacher, in andragogy learning stems from the person's intrinsic need for growth and self-actualisation;
- learning *content*: if in pedagogy what is being learnt is defined through programmes and standardised curricula, in andragogy the starting point of learning is life problems. In other words, if in andragogy learning makes sense in relation to the person, in pedagogy learning is related to the teacher, the curriculum or the establishment; and finally
- *motivation*: if in pedagogy motivation is external and imposed, in andragogy it is intrinsic to the learner him- or herself.

It is necessary to contextualise this artificial and quite ideological opposition made by Knowles, which reminds us, at times, of Illich's opposition between teaching and learning. Indeed, this opposition has to be placed in the context of the 1970s, when adult educa-tion – or, rather, andragogy – was seen as a social and political alternative to conventional top-down education. But unfortunately, the opposition made here between andragogy and pedagogy is not a political one, but an opposition between two schools of thought in psychology. If pedagogy reflects cognitivist psychology, andragogy is merely a popularisation of some concepts of human-istic psychology. Both approaches are individualistic in nature, and contain hardly any social or political dimensions. In other words, the concept of andragogy appears above all to be an ideological statement, some sort of wishful thinking, which mixes concepts from humanistic psychology with elements of pragmatic educa-tional practice.

Stephen Brookfield

Stephen D. Brookfield, a distinguished professor at the University of St Thomas in St Paul, Minnesota, has taken the field of adult education further along this humanistic and individualistic road, enriching it with some politically more correct vocabulary. Having previously taught at Teachers College, Columbia University, with Jack Mezirow, today Brookfield is one of the most successful and prolific adult education authors (see Brookfield, 1987, 1988, 1990, 1995; Brookfield and Preskill, 1999). Like Knowles, he referred back to Lindeman (Brookfield, 1983, 1984a, 1984b, 1987), and has became an excellent salesman and promoter of adult education.

Intellectually, Brookfield does not make any significant contribution to the field of adult education beyond that of Malcolm Knowles. However, he has played an important role in defining the specificity of the field by crystallising a series of key principles of adult education (Finger, 1990: 24–30). Even though the wording of some of these principles suggests a comprehensive understanding of the theory and practice of adult education, they are essentially humanistic. The six key principles of adult education according to Brookfield are:

- First, adult education is characterised by *voluntary participation*. Indeed, in line with humanistic psychology, it is the learner who defines his or her own needs, learning pace, and learning process.
- The second principle of adult education is *mutual respect*: this idea, again, is rooted in humanistic psychology, which states that the facilitator must respect the (adult) learner, who has to be taken seriously in his or her individual learning process. There is therefore no possibility of standardisation, and adult education is basically a process of facilitating individual learning.
- The third principle is the profoundly *collaborative spirit* between learner and facilitator. In a Rogerian spirit, it is up to the facilitator to adapt her or his behaviour to the expectations of the adult learner. Facilitator and learner together engage in a 'collaborative inquiry' – that is, some sort of therapeutic (personal) problem-solving adventure.
- The fourth principle of adult education is *action and reflection*, a typically pragmatic concept. For Brookfield, however, reflection pertains primarily to psychological, not social or political experiences, which brings action and reflection close to therapy.
- The fifth principle of adult education is what Brookfield calls *critical thinking*, a concept he has borrowed from Jack Mezirow's Habermasian phase. As we have seen, already for Mezirow the concept had nothing to do with its original definition in Critical Theory. But Brookfield changes the concept beyond recognition, and manages to translate it into a device for personal growth

and development in a humanistic perspective. In other words, by reflecting on one's personal experiences one can grow, become more self-actualised, and actually become a 'critical thinker'.

• The sixth and final principle of adult education is *self-directed learning*, which is synonymous with the process by which adult learners develop, grow, and become more self-actualised.

Critique of humanistic adult education

With Brookfield self-directed learning emerges as the very essence of humanistic adult education (Brookfield, 1985; Caffarella and O'Donnell, 1989). This concept – and, more generally, the whole reduction of humanistic psychology to self-directed learning – has led to its operationalisation. Since Brookfield, we now have, for example, self-directed learning schemes, self-directed training centres, self-directed learning contracts, self-directed readiness learning typologies, and many other devices.

Yet one should not forget that this quantitatively important tradition in the field of adult education is no more than a popularised second-generation version of humanistic psychology. As such, it is above all a therapeutic and individualistic approach to personal development, with a risk for adult education of further promoting individualism. It is also an ideological approach in the sense that facilitation and self-directed learning are automatically said to lead to self-actualisation. In addition, humanistic psychology, and therefore andragogy, confuse learning and growth, a confusion we have already identified with Deweyan pragmatism. Finally, andragogy, like humanistic psychology, is ahistorical, astructural, apolitical and non-institutional. Indeed, once the optimal environmental conditions have been created, the process of personal growth unfolds almost by itself, helped only by the skilful facilitator (Brookfield 1990). Andragogy, like humanistic psychology, simply assumes that self-actualised individuals lead automatically to a better society – that is, a better environment which, in turn, will further facilitate self-actualisation among individuals. This sociologically naive view is certainly andragogy's biggest weakness.

Notes

1. It is interesting to note that Union Theological Seminary (UTS), Columbia University, and Teachers College (TC), three sister organisations located on the same campus on the Upper West Side of Manhattan, have played a key role in shaping adult education, as many thinkers in the field have passed through one of these institutions. Let us mention here, besides Rogers, Miles Horton (UTS; see below), Dewey (Columbia), Lindeman (TC) and Mezirow (TC).

2. The role of reflection and verbalisation in this process of meaning-seeking remains unclear in the case of Rogers and humanistic psychology more generally: there is indeed a danger that reflection takes a person further away from the true meaning of their experience. It is therefore legitimate to question the translation of such a therapeutic model into the realm of education.

3. According to Jarvis (1987: 174, 169–70), the term 'andragogy' was first coined by the German philosopher Alexander Kapp in 1833. Having being criticised by Herbart, it was abandoned until it was recovered in 1921 by Rosenstock, achieving some notoriety in Central and Eastern Europe. Lindeman used the term in 1927, but Knowles claims to have learned it from the Yugoslav adult educator Dusan Savicevic in the late 1960s. For a longer historical view, see Van Gent, 'Andragogy', in Tuijman, 1996: 114 ff.

Chapter 5

Marxist Adult Education:
Democratic Centralism or Multiple Paths
to the Right Solution?

Marxism is the third major school of thought in the field of adult education. Like pragmatism and humanism, Marxism in adult education has its specific authors and literature, and here we will present the most pertinent elements. Marxist adult education has also had an influence on some other figures we have already presented: Illich and UNESCO.

Nevertheless, one must not confuse Marxism with *radicalism*, a term often used in the United States. Indeed, we will focus here on Marxist adult education, not on radical adult education, which includes in particular some pragmatic perspectives, such as Mezirow's[1] (Evans et al., 1987; Thompson, 1980). We are not, of course, underestimating or downplaying the social and political commitment of many adult educators who call themselves radical, nor are we minimising their Marxist inspiration, but often their intellectual foundation is not Marxist. In other words, the utilisation of terminology such as 'critical' (Brookfield), 'transformative' (Mezirow), 'emancipatory' (Collins), 'internationalist' (Gelpi), and others, is not in itself an indication of Marxist thinking.

This chapter is structured as follows: in the first section we will briefly present the line of descent which leads from Marxism to so-called 'critical pedagogy', a school of thought which has inspired adult educators mainly in Germany and the United States. We will then present the person and thinking of Paulo Freire, one of the leading figures, if not the leading figure, in Marxist adult education. Finally, we will present and critically discuss Participatory Action Research (PAR), an adult education approach – and now a school of thought – which has become particularly prominent in the South.

From Marxism to critical pedagogy

We cannot present the entire richness and diversity of Marxist thinking here. Rather, we will focus on those aspects which are particularly relevant to adult education, or constitute a Marxist discourse on education. After introducing some general elements of Marxism pertaining to education, we will briefly present so-called 'Critical Theory', as it is Critical Theory which has inspired critical pedagogy.

Marxism and education

Marxism can be viewed as two different things, both of which are highly relevant for education: on the one hand, Marxism offers a *scientific analysis of social reality* – in Marxist macro-sociology, for example, the theory of the capitalist mode of production, the critique of ideology, the materialist interpretation of history, and so forth. The implicit educational philosophy here is plain cognitive development– in other words, a rational understanding of social reality. On the other hand, Marxism is a *political programme*, aiming at social transformation through class struggle. Here, education is something quite different: part and parcel of a political struggle. Both these apparently contradictory perspectives on education are linked in a conception of the way human history progresses.

Indeed, from a Marxist perspective human progress is the result of a dialectical relationship between the evolution of the *infrastructure* – the means of production, economic development and techno-scientific progress – on the one hand; and the evolution of the *superstructure* – the (power) relations of production, institutions, ideologies and cultural norms – on the other. There is a deterministic element in Marxist thinking which leads to the assumption that the infrastructure is always more advanced than the superstructure. In other words, the superstructure's political reality (vested interests, power relations, domination, etc.) is holding back the liberating potentialities of infrastructural development. The gap so created is proportional to the domination of the ruling class, as well as to the alienation of the oppressed masses. But the class struggle brought about by political education of the masses, led by an enlightened elite, will move society forward.

Marxist thinking on education criticises both the traditional scholastic understanding of education as the purposeful improvement of human potentialities and the Rousseauian naturalistic view, which considers that society blocks human development (see Bowles and Gintis, 1976; Bourdieu and Passéron, 1977; Freinet, 1966; Makarenko, 1967; Suchodolsky, 1966). Marxism considers that education is part and parcel of the superstructure. As such, it is shaped by vested interests, not by the search for human emancipation. In other words, education is not exempt from the critique of ideology. This means that there is no such thing as 'neutral' education. Education either reproduces inequities – and, as such, is an instrument of domination – or critically analyses the forces perpetuating such inequities, and contributes to fighting against them. As such, it will be an instrument of emancipation and liberation.

Among all the different Marxist schools of thought, it is Critical Theory which has most directly contributed to a Marxist discourse on education. Critical Theory also led, at a later stage, to so-called critical pedagogy, Marxism's most direct contribution to education (Finger, 1991).

Critical Theory

Critical Theory is represented by at least two generations of authors, both of which are directly relevant for education (Jay, 1973). The first generation comprised German Marxist intellectuals – for example, Theodor Adorno, Walter Benjamin, Erich Fromm, Max Horkheimer and Herbert Marcuse – who gathered in the 1920s around the Institute for Social Research at the University of Frankfurt. They were basically concerned with a politico-cultural understanding of fascism. 'How was it possible that fascism happened?' was their question, and they interpreted fascism not as an accident of history but, rather, as a perversion of the entire Enlightenment project (Adorno and Horkheimer, 1944). They also asked how it was possible that the proletariat (the subject of revolution) supported Hitler. Again, they did not answer by simply saying that the masses were alienated and manipulated. Instead, they embarked on a complete revision of Marxism, trying to update it through a new analysis of contemporary society involving the emergence of mass culture as well as the commodification of art and culture (Fromm, 1941; Marcuse, 1964). The basic idea was that there were now new, much more subtle and culturally deeply embedded forms of domination at play, from which humanity had again to emancipate itself. These forms of domination further cemented economic domination. Consequently, a much more radical negation of the dominant system, and a much deeper form of critical reflection, were needed in order to free humanity from these new forms of domination – such a reflection would even question something the system presented as a fact: instrumental rationality. The only direct pedagogical contribution from these early days of Critical Theory comes from Adorno and is formulated in his book *Erziehung zur Mündigkeit* (Adorno, 1970).

The second generation of the Frankfurt School consisted of Fromm and Marcuse in the United States, but also of the German philosopher Jürgen Habermas (born 1929). All three wrote under the very optimistic umbrella of the New Left (Europe) and the countercultural movement (USA). Habermas especially tried to locate the emancipatory potential within language and discourse, particularly in his seminal work *The Theory of Communicative Action* (1984). In a nutshell, Habermas tries to reaffirm the possibility of a critical reason against what he calls the 'colonisation of the lifeworld' by instrumental reason (McCarthy, 1978). His is an attempt to outline a rational theory of emancipation, conceived as a cognitive consciousness-raising process among socially interacting individuals. Not surprisingly, this is the theory which has been picked up by educational philosophers and turned into 'critical pedagogy'.

Critical pedagogy

In the field of education it is Habermas's Critical Theory which has been translated into (critical) pedagogy. This is especially the case in Germany, where many authors have adopted his ideas and translated them into educational consciousness-raising tools or theories (Bühner and Birnmeyer, 1982; Friesenhahn, 1985; Hoffmann, 1978; Oelkers, 1983; Puekart, 1983; Witschel, 1983). In the English-speaking world the translation of Habermas into critical pedagogy was more indirect – through his disciples Bernstein (1985), Fay (1987), and others, mainly during the 1970s. Particularly well-known promoters of critical pedagogy are Michael Apple (1996), Stanley Aronowitz (1993), Wilfred Carr and Stephen Kemmis (1986), Henry Giroux (1997), Peter McLaren (1993) and Ira Shor (1992). During the late 1980s and 1990s, critical pedagogy evolved into what is now known as 'critical adult education'. Again, critical adult educators – or, rather, adult education theorists – were mainly influenced by Habermas, yet many of them base their thinking on classical Marxism. Well-known adult education authors inspired by Marxism and Critical Theory are Susan Collard, Phyllis Cunningham (1993), Ramon Flecha (1997, 1999), Mechtild Hart (1992), Michael Collins (1991), Carlos Torres (1997), Robin Usher (1997), Michael Welton (1995), and Jeff Zacharakis-Jutz (1988).

The main problem with both critical adult education and critical pedagogy is that there is little practice but a lot of theory – not to mention the fact that most of these authors rarely discuss, simply profess. Critical pedagogy and critical adult education therefore mainly constitute a discourse about the importance and necessity of 'becoming critical' (Carr and Kemmis, 1986). It is a discourse which leaves practitioners frustrated, and this is why, from a practical point of view, we now have to turn to Paulo Freire, who is still the intellectual father of any form of emancipatory adult education practice.

Paulo Freire (1921–1997)

The Brazilian philosopher and educator Paulo Reglus Neves Freire was born in Recife on 19 September 1921, and died in São Paulo on 2 May 1997. Undoubtedly, Freire is the most widely known and acknowledged author in adult education. When he died, tribute was paid all over the world. For example, the Fifth UNESCO International Conference on Adult Education organised a 'Freire memorial' presided over by the former UN secretary-general Boutros Boutros-Ghali. Freire had received scores of *honoris causa* doctorates and prizes, including the 1987 UNESCO Peace Prize and, in 1985, the Association of Christian Educators of the US Outstanding Christian Educator's Prize. Death came as he was preparing for a trip to Cuba to collect an award from Fidel Castro.

It has been said that 'we can stay with Freire or against Freire, but not without Freire' (Carlos Alberto Torres). Cornell West said: 'Freire is the exemplary organic intellectual of our time. If Gramsci had not coined this term, we would have to invent it to describe the revolutionary character and moral content of the work and life of Paulo Freire'. Moacir Gadotti (Director of the Paulo Freire Institute of São Paulo[2]) and Carlos Alberto Torres remembered, in their 1997 AERA (Adult Education Research Conference) homage:

> Paulo enchanted us with his tenderness, his sweetness, his charisma, his coherence, his commitment and his seriousness. His words and actions were words and actions of struggle for a world 'menos feio, menos malvado, menos desumano' (less ugly, less cruel, and less inhumane), as he always used to tell us. He always challenged us to 're-invent' the world, pursue the truth, and refrain from copying ideas. Paulo Freire leaves us with roots, wings, and dreams.

In this section, we will briefly recall the main stages of Freire's life, outline the philosophical foundation of his thinking, present his pedagogy, and finally make some personal yet critical remarks.

Freire's context and life

We will distinguish three periods in the life of Paulo Freire, linked to his thinking (Torres, 1997). The first period (1921–70) leads up to his most significant intellectual contributions; the second (1970–80) is a period of transition during his stay in Geneva, and the third (1980–97) follows his return to Brazil.

Born in 1921, the son of a middle-class family stricken by the Great Depression, Freire enrolled in Law School, and also studied philosophy and linguistic psychology. Until 1964, he lived and worked in Brazil – first as a lawyer, later as a language teacher in secondary schools (1941–47); he finally became an adult educator in different institutions – worker training; director of the Department of Cultural Extension at the University of Recife (1961–64); literacy training in the northeast; and president of the National Commission of Popular Education (1963). The military coup soon put him in jail and subsequently forced him into exile. After a brief stay in Bolivia, he went to Chile, where he worked for the Institute for Training in Agrarian Reform. In 1970 Allende's *Unidad Popular* came into power in Chile, but this hope for the Left was abruptly ended by Pinochet's military coup in 1973. In 1970 Freire was offered a job at the World Council of Churches in Geneva, but he had already travelled often to the United States.

The period between 1960 and 1970 was a historic one for Latin America, marked on the one hand by political events such as the Cuban Socialist Revolution (1959–62), and the emergence of popular socialist unions and parties throughout the continent; and on the other by economic and developmentalist policies which translated into agrarian reform, industrialisation and penetration by multinational corporations. In other words, the period was characterised by a strong tension between the attempts to set up US-inspired capitalist regimes and the resistance of popular USSR-backed revolutionary movements. Freire's proposals for a pedagogy of the oppressed fitted well into this overall context, and were listened to by the progressives of the continent, including the Catholic Church, which, in 1968, adopted so-called 'Liberation Theology' at its Medellín regional Latin American Bishops' Assembly.[3] Freire's chief intellectual contributions – *Pedagogy of the Oppressed* (1968 in Portuguese and Spanish) and *Education as the Practice of Freedom*[4] (1969) – were published during this period.

Between 1970 and 1980 Freire worked for the education department of the World Council of Churches in Geneva. In his own words, however, his 'heart was not there'. Under his supervision, his ideas were being implemented in Latin America (Uruguay, Argentina, Mexico, Chile, Ecuador) and Africa (Tanzania, Guinea-Bissau, Cape Verde, São Tomé e Principe, Angola, Mozambique). Post-colonial Africa in particular lived, during this period, through similar developments as those in Latin America, characterised by the tension between capitalist regimes and popular resistance movements, leading, at times, to socialist regimes. Later, when they came to power, some of these regimes tried to implement Freire's proposals, with varied success (Nyerere in Tanzania; Cabral in Guinea-Bissau). As a result, Freire's ideas evolved – for example, in *Pedagogy in Process: Letters to Guinea-Bissau* (1976).

In 1980 Freire returned to Brazil, where he worked as Professor of Education in the Catholic University of São Paulo and the

State University of Campinhas. He also created the 'Vereda' adult education centre, collaborated with the Commission of Education of the Partido dos Trabalhadores (Workers' Party), and become honorary President of Fundaçao Wilson Pinheiro, the Workers' University of São Paulo. When the Workers' Party won the municipal elections in São Paulo in 1988, Freire was appointed Secretary of Education. He promoted fundamental school reform, and developed a bold adult education programme called 'Mova São Paulo' (Move São Paulo). After his resignation in 1991, Freire continued to devote his time and energy to popular education, lecturing and writing. During this period of his life Freire wrote several books (1994, 1998a, 1998b), among them many 'dialogue' books – for example, with the Brazilian theologian Frei Betto, *E esta escola da vida* (1985); with Moacir Gadotti, current general director of the Freire Institute, and Sergio Guimaraes, *Pedagogia: Dialogo e conflito* (1986); with Ira Shor, *A Pedagogy for Liberation: Dialogues on Transforming Education* (1987); with Donaldo Macedo, *Literacy: Reading the Word and the World* (1987); and with Myles Horton of Highlander,[5] *We Make the Road by Walking: Conversations on Education and Social Change* (1990).[6]

The philosophical foundations of Freire's thinking

Freire's thinking can be traced back to four different intellectual roots: Catholic humanism, Marxism, German philosophy, and development theory. Freire combines them in an original way in order to build his own 'liberation pedagogy'.

The origin of Freire's thinking is Christian Personalism (Maritain, Bernanos, Marcel, Mounier, and the Brazilian Ataide), into which he later incorporated Critical Theory (Marcuse, Fromm). This combination fitted perfectly into the emerging intellectual movement in Latin America called Liberation Theology, which was also a translation of German political theology (Metz, 1970; Moltmann, 1971) into the Latin American context of the 1960s and 1970s. During those years the most important works of Liberation Theology (Boff, 1974; Ellacurría, 1973; Galilea, 1976; Gutiérrez, 1974; Segundo, 1975; Sobrino, 1976) were produced, along with the emergence of the Iglesia Popular de Comunidades de Base (Popular Church from the Base), which sided with the 'oppressed' and led many Catholics (e.g. Camilo Torres) to get involved in guerrilla activities and 'martyrdom'. Freire combined the Movement of Education from the Base and the intellectual dimensions of Liberation Theology, and thus rapidly became a key figure in Latin America.

The writings of the young Marx form another basis of Freire's analysis, especially after his experiences in Bolivia and Chile. As we have said, *Pedagogy of the Oppressed* draws directly on these experiences of exile. As a result, he conceives of pedagogy as the 'cultural action for liberation [that is] a process through which the oppressor consciousness "living" in the oppressed consciousness can be extracted' (Freire, 1980: 85). 'Banking education' is now opposed to 'problem-posing' or 'liberatory education': of these, the former 'attempts to maintain the submersion of consciousness; the latter strives for the emergence of consciousness and critical intervention in reality' (Freire, 1971: 5). For Freire, critical consciousness, or *concientizaçao* (conscientisation), is basically the critique of false consciousness – or, in Marxist terms, the critique of ideology – which will lead to collective emancipation, and Critical Theory's analysis of (cultural) alienation added more Marxist arguments to Freire's liberation pedagogy.

It was via Marxism that Freire came in contact with the German tradition of existentialism, and especially *phenomenology*, sharpening his thinking about *language*. Language, according to this tradition, is not neutral but rather conveys a certain culturally transmitted world-view. As such, language is much more than a simple means of communication; rather, it is directly linked to culture. Through language, one can both question and strengthen culture. Freire incorporated this view into his liberation pedagogy, which might also be seen as a way of becoming aware of and transforming the dominant and oppressive culture through questioning the language it imposes upon us.

Finally, one must not forget to locate Paulo Freire both within the South and within the context of the Cold War. Especially in Latin America, this context gave rise to so-called Dependency Theory, a Marxist and political version of development theory. One of its authors, Fernando H. Cardoso, for example, in *Dependency and Development in Latin America* (1979), considers (South–North or, rather, periphery–centre) dependency as a sociopolitical phenomenon that is harmful to development. So Freire does not question development. Rather, what is in question is the cultural domination exercised by the core countries (the North) over the peripheral countries (the South). Thus liberation pedagogy was thus also conceived as a contribution to a Brazilian development path.

As a result of Marxism, Liberation Theology and Dependency Theory combined, Freire's liberation pedagogy takes place in a situation of oppression. Yet Freire, influenced by Critical Theory and phenomenology, is less interested in physical or institutional oppression than in cultural and internalised oppression. Following Marcuse and Fromm, he pays particular attention to language and world-views, which are both manipulated and manipulative, leading to the internalisation of oppression – ultimately, to the oppressed identifying themselves with the oppressors. Freire's liberation pedagogy is therefore a cultural action or process towards liberation. It has two phases: critical consciousness (conscientisation) and critical praxis. Conscientisation is the process by which a group (class) become aware of their cultural oppression, of their 'colonised mentality', and by so doing discover that they have a popular culture, a political identity and a societal role. Conscientisation is in itself a liberatory process, as one is freed from self-deprecation. It is important to mention that for Freire, the oppressors must also be considered, as they too must become aware of their dehumanising situation, which maintains injustice. But as a second phase, conscientisation requires *critical praxis*. Such praxis is not a revolutionary seizure of power from the oppressors. Rather, it is a peaceful intervention in order to develop alternatives. Developing such alternatives must include the oppressors, by transforming unjust power relations through dialogue.

Freire's pedagogical practice

Freire implemented his ideas through adult literacy programmes with the rural populations which had migrated to the northeast of Brazil from the newly industrialised cities. But for him, literacy work was embedded in a much broader political programme, aimed at addressing issues of rural development and migration. Freire's literacy programmes taught people to read and to write, and at the same time to become aware of their internalised cultural oppression. This was done through the selection of literacy subjects, pertinent to the people and related to their existential issues. There was therefore a political intention, conscientisation being the hidden agenda of literacy.

Freire's pedagogical model takes people from a situation of 'magical consciousness' – where they are not able to analyse their situation (they are 'voiceless') – to a stage of 'naive consciousness' – they recognise their oppressors, but are afraid of them – to 'critical consciousness'. This is the stage where people envision the possibility of acting upon the situation, and ultimately take concrete steps towards such action. Critical consciousness therefore encompasses two elements: first, a critical understanding of society and culture within which people live. The relevant question here is: *What is our oppressive situation?* Second, critical consciousness also implies a comprehension of people's capacity to change the situation. The relevant question here is: *What is our capacity to influence this situation?*

According to Freire, there are four distinct steps in leading a group of people from naive consciousness to critical consciousness:

- The *investigation of the thematic universe*. In this first step, external researchers investigate the language and culture of the people, in order to understand their cultural universe.
- The *identification of the generative themes*. In this second step, this thematic universe is structured collectively by the people, distinguishing between the root causes and the symptoms, which are simply the expressions of the root causes.
- The *codification of generative themes*. In this third step, particularly relevant root causes are selected and translated into meaningful themes. For each of these so-called generative themes, a collection of relevant expressions or sentences is developed. This is done through role play, drawings, posters, theatre, and other activities.
- The *dialogue within the cultural circle*. This is the final, yet most important step of Freire's liberation pedagogy. Here, the previously developed expressions or sentences are codified. In other words, they are decomposed into their basic elements. Their pronunciation and ways of being written are identified, the goal being to get at the most meaningful words for that particular group of people. The cultural circle is where literacy and critical consciousness are actually manifested.

Let us once more recall Freire's underlying *epistemology*. Freire believed that culture integrates people and their daily life – it is a reflection of what people do every day. Furthermore, he believed that popular culture is an artificial construct, and people are its victims. Finally, Freire's aim was to make people become aware of their culture's artificiality (false consciousness). An emancipation process thereby takes place – from internalised oppression towards a more objective consciousness. From being victims, they become subjects, a typical Enlightenment model of education. Ultimately, Freire's liberation pedagogy aims at changing society. Indeed, even though his pedagogical model has been applied in totally different contexts and sometimes been reduced to mere techniques, Freire's aim was never to make people function better within any given system. Instead, he wanted them to become aware of injustices and to act in order to change them.

Critical appreciation of liberation pedagogy

Without doubt, Freire is one of the most important adult education writers. In addition to his life, committed to the cause of the disenfranchised, he has left an important body of work, which has become the object of numerous dissertations, books and critical discussions. Freire and his work have underscored, reinforced, and perhaps even combined the basic assumptions of the field of adult education: the Enlightenment ideas of rational understanding leading to emancipation and, more generally, of the transformative power of education; the humanistic ideas of respect for the learner and his or her growth; and the pragmatic idea of addressing problems collectively. But, more than the dominant pragmatic approach, Freire stresses the collective dimension of learning, especially in his cultural circle: it is collectively that people not only solve problems but, moreover, transform their sociopolitical conditions. Also, Freire differs significantly from all the schools and authors discussed hitherto, in so far as the adult educator is not just a facilitator. Rather, he or she is an animator, committed to the cause of the people he or she works with. As such, the *animator* cannot be neutral – he or she has to take sides.

At the same time, this is one of the key ambiguities of Freire's liberation pedagogy: his approach is anti-authoritarian, yet politically and ideologically oriented. Even if he does change the phraseology over time – for example, from 'conscientisation' to 'dialogical critical consciousness'; or from 'revolution' to 'radical democracy' – ultimately, the 'true' path is known by the animator. It is the animator who knows the 'overall vision which has to be always retained' (Freire and Faundez, 1989: 123). To be fair, this is the problem of the entire Enlightenment education project. Nevertheless, it is possible today to challenge the assumption of class coherence, a common oppressor, and cultural coherence – which are the pedagogical instruments with which Freire works. More generally, one can argue that Freire confuses epistemology – that is, learning – and politics – that is, freedom from oppression. In Freire's theory and praxis, epistemology and politics (learning to be free from oppression) mix – this is simultaneously adult education's greatest strength and identity, and its greatest conceptual weakness.

This is all the more true because Freire remains unspecific about the concrete action or result of the pedagogical praxis. On the one hand, he clearly rejects revolution and violence – a violent revolt in order to seize power from the oppressors and to establish a proletarian dictatorship; convinced as he is that the oppressors must also undergo a learning process. But on the other hand, his suggestions for alternatives remain unspecific beyond acknowledging that they have to be political. This can be viewed as a strength – there is no 'one' solution, and the solution has to be invented by the people, given their particular situations – but it might also be seen as a weakness, where liberation pedagogy can simply not be able to live up to people's expectations.

It is precisely this lack of specificity which involves the risk that Freire's pedagogy could become instrumentalised and mainstream, especially when it is integrated into the overall adult education framework of facilitation and process-orientation. This risk is compounded by the fact that Freire, unlike Illich, remains uncritical of institutions, as well as of the overall development process. This is all the more surprising, given that Illich also adopts an anthropological (cultural) conceptual framework, but – unlike Freire, and uninfluenced by Critical Theory – does not make a 'linguistic turn', which is both the basis of Freire's original pedagogical practice and the source of its potential instrumentalisation.

Participatory Action Research

Participatory Action Research (PAR) is another practical approach to social change through learning inspired by Marxism, which developed in the late 1970s and throughout the 1980s.[7] Like Paulo Freire's ideas, PAR flourished in the South, but unlike Freire's philosophy – which relies on Northern concepts (derived from Marxism, phenomenology and Catholic humanism) – PAR has been created in the South, and is more rooted in a Southern perspective. The key actors here are Anisur Rahman in Bangladesh, Rajesh Tandon in India, Orlando Fals-Borda in Colombia, Francisco Vio Grossi in Chile, Kemal Mustafa in Tanzania, and many others (see Fernandes and Tandon, 1981; Kassam and Mustafa, 1982; Fals-Borda and Rahman, 1991; Rahman, 1993, 1994). There have also been followers of PAR in the North – for example, John Gaventa, who has also been working at the Highlander Research and Education Center in the United States (Gaventa, 1988), and Marja-Liisa Swantz. In Australia, PAR has been used with Aboriginal adult education (Foley and Flowers, 1990, 1992), as well as more generally (McTaggart, 1991). The International Council for Adult Education (ICAE) in Toronto – whose first president, significantly, was Julius Nyerere – promoted PAR throughout the 1980s through its journal *Convergence*,[8] and has actually linked PAR to Freire's liberation pedagogy.[9] The United Nations Research Institute for Social Development still uses a PAR approach in its War-Torn Societies Project (Stiefel and Wolfe, 1994). But it was Budd Hall, the former secretary-general of the International Council for Adult Education in Toronto, who, during the late 1970s and throughout the 1980s, played a key role in promoting PAR worldwide (Hall, 1998). Indeed, building on the ICAE, Hall has set up an International Participatory Action Research Network, which still promotes PAR practices and thinking.

Yet PAR should not be confused with so-called Action Research, an epistemological critique of mainstream social science practice, which developed in Germany and France, also during the late 1970s (Moser, 1975; Touraine, 1978). While it is somewhat similar in its epistemological claim, Action Research 'Northern style' differs significantly from PAR inasmuch as it makes no reference to the Southern development environment, and focuses solely on epistemological and methodological questions.

In this section, we briefly present the political and social context of PAR: the context of 1970s self-reliant development. We then move on to discuss PAR philosophy and epistemology. Comparing PAR to Freire's liberation pedagogy, we finally highlight and appreciate the basic differences and relevant contributions of PAR.

The context of PAR

The specificity of PAR becomes particularly understandable when it is put into a historical and societal context, and compared to the ideas of Paulo Freire (Rist, 1997). Freire was a typical product of 1960s Latin America. As such, he was substantially influenced by the Dependency Theory developed by Raúl Prebisch, Fernando Cardoso, Celso Furtado, Rodolfo Stavenhagen, and others. This is a context of so-called 'Third-Worldism': basically, national liberation from Northern dependency. The underlying perspective is modernising, and the conceptual framework is shaped by the theory of international political economy.

PAR, however, is a product of the 1970s, developed both in Africa (Tanzania: Kassam, Mustafa) and Southeast Asia (India: Tandon, Fernandes; Bangladesh: Rahman) in the context of a certain disillusionment with the results of the UN's first 'Development Decade', the 1960s. Tanzanian president Julius Nyerere was probably the first to outline a new view concerning the escape from underdevelopment and poverty, characterised by the concepts of 'self-reliance', 'autonomy', and 'auto-centred development'. Self-reliance, in Tanzania, is a bottom-up approach by which so-called *ujamaa* villages take their development into their own hands. In India, self-reliance can be traced back to Gandhi and his principles of *swadeshi* (endogenousness) and *sarvodaya* (improving one's living conditions), also at the village level. Conceptually and theoretically, self-reliant development and *ujamaa* found an international voice in the 1975 Dag Hammarskjöld Foundation Report entitled *What Now*, and in the International Foundation for Development Alternatives (IFDA). From the 1970s until 1990 the Report, and IFDA through its 'Dossiers', promoted the idea of 'another development', characterised by 'needs satisfaction, self-reliance, harmony with nature, and structural change' (Rist, 1997: 156).

Since many former promoters of 'another development' – in particular Mahbub ul-Haq (UNDP), Juan Somavia (ILO), Jan Pronk, Sonny Ramphal, Maurice Strong, Dharam Ghai and M. Zammit-Cutajar – have become mainstream over the years, it is useful to recall the core ideas of self-reliant development as they can be traced back to *ujamaa*, and other authors who have kept a clear line of thinking (see Kothari, 1989, 1993; Sachs, 1992). Four ideas are particularly worth recalling here. First, self-reliance is above all about people, not money. It builds on people – their capacities, their strengths and their self-confidence. Quite logically, then, this leads, second, to self-reliance as opposed to aid from outside, which is seen as a danger to independence. Third, self-reliant development starts at the local level, and is therefore bottom-up, not top-down. Although this idea has been substantially distorted through a state-centric view, this is the idea of 'subsidiarity', not (national) autarky. Finally, self-reliance refers to 'appropriate technology', as opposed to high technology imported from the North and the West. In short, self-reliant development unfolds bottom-up through the people and with the technology appropriate to the corresponding needs. On a critical note, one can highlight the fact that neither ecological nor cultural aspects are particularly emphasised.

Korten (1990) has tried to conceptualise the (political) action that goes along with this new conception of self-reliant or alternative development. He defines 'second-generation non-governmental organisations' (NGOs), which he opposes to first-generation NGOs, concerned with aid and help to cover basic needs (health, food, shelter, literacy). Second-generation NGOs are more sensitive to peoples' participation in their own development, especially in the areas of agriculture, reproductive health, and small-industries development. Consequently, they are more locally and community-orientated, and increasingly see their role as catalysing and facilitating people-centred development efforts. Quite logically, it is with such second-generation NGOs that pedagogy and PAR become important. Nevertheless, it should also be said that these numerous NGOs engaged in self-reliant development do not (yet) form a social movement in themselves. To see self-reliant development as a social movement of the South, as many authors did and still do (Korten, 1990; Wignaraja, 1993; IFDA dossiers), is in our view misleading. Rather, self-reliant or alternative development should be seen as an intellectual current, and it is this current which – along with the numerous self-reliant practices – constitutes the context of PAR.

PAR's philosophy, epistemology and practice

It is important to stress that PAR's reference is primarily a *rural* context of the South, upon which Northern-style development is being imposed in its technological, cultural and political dimensions. Through this fundamentally colonial process, peoples' endogenous knowledge is being or has already been destroyed, and replaced by Northern expert knowledge and corresponding Northern technologies, world-views, power structures, and so on. PAR assumes that peoples and communities are capable of recovering their endogenous knowledge, thus engaging in an autonomous or self-reliant development process.

In other words – and unlike Freire – PAR seeks to go *deeper*: it is not enough to make peoples aware of their oppression. Rather, PAR wants (1) to help them understand how the entire oppressive process of colonisation has destroyed – or, at least, evacuated – their endogenous knowledge, and by so doing (2) help them to recover this knowledge so that they can take control of their own development again. For PAR, poverty and 'underdevelopment' are therefore not problems of oppression but, rather, problems of the marginalisation of endogenous and indigenous knowledge. In other words, PAR adds an epistemological dimension to the political dimension already identified by Freire. This collective process of uncovering, recovering and activating endogenous knowledge has to take place within concrete and geographically rooted communities. So PAR not only adds a community dimension to the relatively abstract political struggle identified by Freire, it also adds a more local, more pragmatic, and more cultural aspect to liberatory politics.

PAR, therefore, has a strong *epistemological dimension*, which is lacking in Marxist and critical pedagogy – with the exception of Illich. Inspired by the 1970s movement towards small and human-scale development through appropriate technologies (Schumacher,

1974), and influenced by the intellectual current of the same period on the sociology of science and technology, PAR is particularly critical of Western and Northern knowledge and its technological manifestations. Thus, if a hospital or a school, for instance, is built in a given community, it brings with it an underlying philosophy (its cultural world-view, values, rationality, etc.); this means that it is more than simply a problem-solving tool. Another example, the tractor, is not just an instrument; it brings with it a new relationship to nature. Such considerations, interestingly, bring us very close to Illich's thinking. Simply to seek the control of the means of production, therefore, is not enough. One also needs to 'control' the various societal, cultural and ecological consequences of these means of production, and the only way to do so is to reappropriate these instruments and tools within the context of endogenous knowledge. This knowledge, however, first has to be recovered. In short, PAR goes significantly beyond Freire, as it questions the epistemological issue of knowledge production and knowledge appropriation. More precisely, people have to recover not only control over their means of production but, more profoundly, the *control over the means of knowledge production*. The pedagogical practice of PAR helps them to do this.

In its practice, PAR proposes to recover endogenous knowledge, and bring it to bear upon self-reliant development efforts. Hall, for example, summarises PAR practice: (1) it involves a whole range of powerless groups of people; (2) it implies the full and active participation of the community in problem definition, analysis and resolution; (3) it has as its main focus the radical transformation of social reality, as well as the improvement of the lives of the peoples themselves (Hall, 1978: 5). But this is not simply a process of going back to traditional knowledge, idealising indigenous peoples and their way of life, as does the New Age movement (Norberg-Hodge, 1991). Of course, in a first step, PAR identifies traditional techniques – for example, of spinning or sewing – which have been eliminated by imported Northern technologies, but at the same time it evaluates what Northern technologies have done to the community in economic, political, social, cultural and ecological terms. The tractor, for instance, makes work in the fields easier and generally increases production, yet it needs roads, fuel, and so on, thus increasing dependency. PAR then crystallises the various societal, cultural and ecological functions fulfilled by these traditional techniques, and assesses their relevance and importance for the local community and its sustainable livelihood. Third, PAR highlights the main problems faced by a given community, for example poverty, some of which result precisely from imposed Northern development. Finally, PAR seeks to recover some of the endogenous knowledge in order to address the problems identified, while simultaneously appropriating some of the newly imported elements. So PAR is thus not opposed to development and modernisation, but wants to bring development back to the human and local scale of the communities, allowing them to master and manage their own (self-reliant) development process. These four steps are conceptualised by PAR as a collective (and community) learning process, which either can or need not be facilitated by an external actor. In any case, this external actor is only a facilitator, not – as is the case for Freire – a political awareness-raiser, someone who already knows the solution. The 'solution', in the case of PAR, is practical and concrete in nature, and can be developed only by the people themselves through a collective learning process (for practical examples, see Fals-Borda and Rahman, 1991: part II, 'Vivencias'; Wignaraja, Sethi and Wignaraja, 1990; Fals-Borda, 1993).

PAR: A critical appreciation

As we can see, PAR goes significantly further than critical pedagogy and Paulo Freire, especially in four dimensions:

- Unlike Freire and critical pedagogy, PAR is particularly critical of development, even though the ideal of development is not entirely abandoned. Nevertheless, PAR advocates an alternative form of development on a much smaller and more human scale, and with tools appropriate to that scale.
- PAR also has an *epistemological* dimension, concerned as it is with the endogenous production of knowledge. Critical pedagogy remains in fact on a purely cognitive level, while Freire adds some linguistic aspects. Yet Freire and critical pedagogy do not really see knowledge production as a social process.
- PAR is much more *grounded*, as it links adult learning to very concrete processes of community development, and to very

concrete problems in the areas of agriculture, health, sanitation, and so on. Ultimately, for PAR, adult learning through participatory action is a problem-solving approach, not – as for Freire – a pretext for political awareness-raising, with the nation-state as the relevant political entity. This actually brings PAR into the vicinity of pragmatism.

- Finally, PAR reflects on tools and *technology* by putting them into a social context. Unlike Freire and critical pedagogy, for which the tools and technologies of development are simple instruments to be cognitively mastered, PAR sees them as playing a significant role when it comes to learning, either fostering or preventing it. In this respect, PAR is very similar to Illich's anthropological view.

On the other hand, PAR has some significant weaknesses. First – and despite its criticism – PAR still believes in the development process, albeit a bottom-up, human-scale development process. We have no problem with this view of the development process, but we think that PAR is not sufficiently critical of the overall process of industrial development and trade, and its ability to recuperate local development efforts, as advocated by PAR itself. In other words, we find PAR quite naive in the context of the overall global development picture. Similarly, PAR does not really place the development problems it highlights into today's context, which is characterised by an increasingly global economy. Many local problems – for example, drought – have global root causes, which the PAR approach can neither analyse, nor find solutions to. Finally, PAR is grounded in the idea that endogenous knowledge can be recovered and activated, and actually serve as the fertile ground on which an alternative development path can be constructed. While this assumption may still be reasonable in some not yet entirely destroyed societies and cultures, it is certainly no longer true in highly industrialised societies. The question, therefore, remains: can PAR be applied in contexts other than agricultural and developing societies? Despite all these reservations, however, we think that PAR can serve as the starting point for what we call 'Learning Our Way Out'. We will therefore come back to PAR in Part III of this book.

Notes

1. In 1995 Mezirow wrote: 'As an adult educator from the United States, inspired by ideas of John Dewey, Eduard Lindeman, and Myles Horton, I read Welton's introductory chapter on the history and nature of Critical Theory with its many references to contemporary European social theorists with a feeling of being far from home' (Mezirow, in Welton, 1995: 213).

2. For a complete bibliography on Freire, his work and his legacy, see the extraordinarily valuable website: http://www.ppbr.com/ipf/.

3. The 1968 *Final Document of Medellín* says: 'This education is called education for liberation; that is, education that allows the learner to be the subject of his own development' (IV.8).

4. The English translation is entitled *Education for Critical Consciousness.*

5. We do not specifically discuss here the work and intellectual contributions of Myles Horton (1905–1990) and Highlander. Though it is very important in the history of the adult education for social action movement, on the purely intellectual and conceptual levels, Horton's contribution is entirely covered by Freire and by Participatory Action Research (see below). For more thorough information on Myles Horton, see http://nlu.nl.edu/ace/Resources/Horton.html; M. Horton with J. and H. Kohl, *The Long Haul: An Autobiography* (New York: Doubleday, 1990); A. Horton. *The Highlander Folk School: A History of its Major Programs. 1932–1961* (Brooklyn, N.Y.: Carlson, 1989).

6. For a complete biobibliography of Paulo Freire's writings, see M. Gadotti et al., *Paulo Freire: Uma biobibliografia* (São Paulo: Cortez Editora, 1996). See also the special issue of *Convergence* dedicated to Paulo Freire, vol. 31, no. 1–2, 1998.

7. See: PARnet, http://www.parnet.org.

8. See *Convergence*'s special issues on PAR, in particular vol. 8, no. 2 (1975) and vol. 14, no. 3, 1981.

9. See the ICAE website: http://www.web.net/icae/.

Chapter 6

Conclusion: Adult Education
and Development

In Part I we identified and critically analysed the main roads on which adult education travels today. We have also shown that all these roads have the same foundations. Be it the track of scientific humanism, the highway of pragmatism, the freeway of humanism for lonely travellers, or the multiple trails of Marxism, all are built on the same crushed stone: the foundation of modern industrial development. And in one way or another, all these conceptualisations and approaches of adult education aspire to the same thing: to humanise this development process by involving the people in shaping its tracks.

In this conclusion to Part I we would like to substantiate our argument by outlining the main characteristics of adult education practices as they took shape and have developed geographically. Aware that we are looking at adult education through our Northern and Western lenses, we distinguish between adult education developments in the North and in the South. Within the North we will refer to the North American and European traditions. These distinctions are on the one hand rather artificial. In addition to Australia and New Zealand, there are also elites in the South. None of the geographical developments is discretely independent. For example, 'America' has been, since its inception, an Enlightenment project, and so is the idea of the 'independence' of Southern peoples and cultures. Nevertheless, we believe that it is possible to distinguish between the different adult education projects in Europe, the United States, and the South.

Adult education in Europe: emancipation and compensation

The sociocultural context within which European adult education emerged and developed was shaped by the transformations brought about by the Enlightenment and, later, by industrial modernisation. Rationality replaced religion and scientific epistemology underpinned the building of a modern – that is, rational – society. There was a firm belief in Europe that through education it was possible to build a modern society of enlightened, responsible and rational citizens. Education became the privileged tool of modernisation, and individuals – evolving emancipated subjects – were its vehicles.

These ideas were – and probably still are – at the heart of European adult education. The origins of its practice, in fact, go back to the first negative consequences of industrial development at the beginning of the twentieth century – emerging social problems, proletarianisation, the growth of urban centres, and many more. Be it, for example, the British workers' education movement, the Folk School movement in Scandinavia, the *Volkshochschulen* movement in Germany, or the Spanish *Misiones Pedagógicas* – all have their intellectual roots in the ideas of the Enlightenment applied to repairing some of the first negative effects of industrialisation.

European adult education therefore has two core ideas: *emancipation* and *compensation*. Adult education practices were, above all, varied and contrasted responses to the struggles of social groups and social classes aspiring to emancipation on the expectation of a better, more just, more free and more democratic society. Both liberal and Marxist adult educators shared the basic belief that education would bring about a better world – first for the social group concerned, the workers, and later for everyone. Most adult education practices – literacy, workers' education, and basic adult education – also had a 'compensatory' component, the main aim being to make education available to adults without schooling – a clearly modernist idea which aspires to education for all, not only for the elites. Implicitly we also find, in Europe, the modernist optimism which believes that 'l'éducation peut faire tout' (Helvetius). These two ideas are present throughout the European developments in adult education. From the postwar period to the

1960s and the 1970s, along with the creation of the welfare state, adult education in Europe continued to promote these ideas while enjoying growing support from public education administrations. Also, new labour and political environments created the need for further adult education in order to help people to be able to cope with the new requirements, both as workers and as citizens.

It was during the 1960s and the 1970s that adult education really grew in Europe. Educational programmes boomed. Basic and vocational education activities were organised and funded or subsidised by the state in most countries. At the same time, various social organisations, associations and movements carried out all kinds of liberal or social-change-oriented adult education activities, including literacy and basic adult education: Deutscher Volks-hochschul Verband (DVV), ATD Quart Monde, Federación de Asociaciones de Educación de Adultos (FAEA), and so on. In terms of conceptualisation, it was during this period that adult education in Europe acquired a coherent theory in the form of *éducation permanente* (see Chapter 2).

The last and most recent stage in the development of European adult education, from the 1970s onwards, was the growing importance of corporations and work-related adult education and training schemes (see Part II).

North America: Utilitarian, liberal and radical trends

Not only education but also adult education were and still are essential components of the 'American experience'. The founding fathers, especially those on the east coast, early on established so-called 'discussion groups' for mutual and self-improvement (e.g. Franklin's Junto), and libraries (see Stubblefield and Keane, 1994; Cremin, 1970). Later in the nineteenth century one could mention, for example, the 'Lyceum movement' or Chautauqua (Kett, 1994), which were mainly institutions for the 'diffusion of useful knowledge'. And until very recently, most characteristics of American adult education could be traced back to these early days. We will distinguish five such characteristics.

First, we must recall that America, unlike Europe, has been built by settlers who were often denied opportunities in their own countries, and who at times espoused a missionary perspective. Education – and especially adult education – looked like a practical means of 'Americanising', or at least homogenising, the different peoples, while at the same time creating a 'New World'. This also explains, at least in part, the important role played by civil society and communitarian initiatives in promoting adult education. In other words, adult education in America is a non-ideological and basically non-political endeavour, an instrument for creating a coherent country.

Second, there is an Enlightenment belief in the power of education, in particular when it comes to transmitting the practical knowledge required in order to make 'wild nature' habitable. This belief – along with the typically American values of democracy, freedom, property and individualism, and combined with the Puritan concern for schooling to redress inequities, to enhance opportunities, and to favour social mobility – created a distinctively American adult education approach. This is an adult education which focuses both on pragmatism and on usefulness.

Third, the same pragmatic approach also applies to academic adult education. Indeed, in the United States – unlike Europe – its usefulness was perceived early on. Let us mention here the role played by the Carnegie Foundation, as well as later on by other philanthropies such as the Kellogg Foundation, which funded the American Association for Adult Education (AAAE). AAAE, in turn, was instrumental in creating the very profession of adult educator, as well as a corresponding interest in adult education as a field of study and research. In 1928 Thorndike published his *Adult Learning*; in 1926, as we have seen, Lindeman, the follower of John Dewey, wrote *The Meaning of Adult Education*. In 1935 the first graduate programme of adult education was created at Teachers College, Columbia University, in New York City – again, long before any corresponding programme emerged in Europe.

Fourth, this pragmatic approach to adult education, combined with American individualism, also led to a more people-centred view. Indeed, unlike European adult education, which is more sociological and political in nature, and thus very much focused on removing inequalities, American adult education considers that inequality results from a lack of individual opportunities. Adult education must address this lack through, for example, Community

Colleges. Not surprisingly, American adult education focuses on individuals and individual learning – hence the importance in American adult education not only of pragmatism but also of humanistic psychology (see Chapters 3 and 4).

Finally, there is also in North America a more *political* adult education movement, inspired by Marxism. From the early resistance to Americanisation by the 'Natives' to the Abolitionists' fight for the rights of African-American people, to feminism and union activism (Schied, 1993), there is a substantial tradition of political adult education. Myles Horton's Highlander (Horton, 1989; Horton, 1990; see also http://nlu.nl.edu/ace/Resources/Horton.html) and other similar political adult education practices accompanying the fight for minorities' rights, sexual orientations (Brenda and Wanda Henson Camp Sister Spirit; see Harmon, 1998; Osborn, 1997), or immigrants' empowerment (farmworkers' rights activist César Chavez (1927–1993); see http://www.proactivist.com/links_peo/Cesar_Chavez/; Ferriss et al., 1998; Griswold del Castillo et al., 1997), all constitute the 'radical trend' of American adult education.

Lastly – and just as in Europe – since the late 1970s the corporate world seems to have taken a growing interest in pragmatic and humanistic adult education practices. As we will see in Parts II and III, organisational learning and many other market-related training schemes have become more and more important in American adult education.

Adult education in the South: accompanying development

Since World War II, and especially since decolonisation, education in general, and adult education in particular, have accompanied development projects and practices in the South. Whether it is conceived as adult literacy, as extension, as training, or as a post-literacy programme, the main goals of such adult education were – and to some extent still are – poverty alleviation and economic development, often seen as synonymous. More generally, education is understood as a key tool for development and the driving force of progress, an idea best summarised in the title of Ki-Zerbo's widely debated book *Educate or Perish* (Ki-Zerbo, 1990).

For the most part, adult education practices in the South are responses to development needs, identified on a national level and at times on subnational (regional, local) levels. Governments generally take the lead – often because they want to control the (national) development process, but also because they assume that people are not going to take the initiative by themselves. Consequently, adult education in the context of development is seen as an obligation, something targeted for the masses, which are assumed to constitute a homogeneous body.

This is typically the case of 'revolutionary' and other literacy campaigns, such as in Vietnam (1945–77), China (1950s–1980s), Burma (1960s–1980s), Cuba (1960), Brazil (1967–80), Tanzania (1971–81) and Nicaragua (1980) (see Bhola, 1982; Kozol, 1978; Arnove and Graff, 1987). On all these occasions, 'the campaigns … are usually associated with revolutionary upheavals and attempts by state authorities to create a new political culture and accelerate the process of economic development' (Arnove and Graff, 1987: 271). In many cases, Freire-type (see Chapter 5) approaches were put into practice. Thus, politically charged words and generative themes were chosen by the revolutionary leaders, for example *revolución*, *liberación* and *genocidio* in the case of Nicaragua (Arnove and Graff, 1987: 282). Through literacy campaigns, developmental objectives were generally transmitted, albeit subtly at times. To recall Freire and Macedo: 'Literacy programs should be tied not only to mechanical learning of skills but, additionally, to a critical understanding of the overall goals for national reconstruction' (Freire and Macedo, 1987: 157).

UNESCO, and later UNDP, actively supported similar practices of adult education in the South, again with the aim of promoting development (see Chapter 2). Good examples are the 'Experimental World Literacy Programme' (1966–74) (see Jones, 1988: 159–211) and the 'Literacy for All Programme', which aims to 'overcome the knowledge gap' (UNESCO, 1993) and 'eradicate illiteracy in the world by the year 2000' (see Cárceles, 1990). Illustratively, a 1976 UNESCO/UNDP report stated: 'The essential assumption of the [literacy] projects was that there is an integral link between literacy and the improvement of technical skills leading to increased productivity and social development' (UNESCO/UNDP, 1976: 56).

But not all adult education practices in the South are internationally or nationally organised. Many activities emerge locally or regionally, often within a Participatory Action Research framework, and some of these – as we saw in Chapter 5 – actually tend to go beyond a purely developmental framework. We will come back to such practices in Part III. Nevertheless, at the beginning of this century, much of the South is not much better off than it was at Independence. Aspiring to the ideal of Northern development, the South has sunk into huge debt, and in the 1980s became subject to blackmail by the International Monetary Fund, the World Bank and Northern governments. Corresponding Structural Adjustment Programmes led to deregulation, privatisation, and ultimately 'recolonisation', this time by Northern-based transnational corporations (Raghavan, 1990). Adult education programmes financed by the North have turned into vehicles for accompanying structural adjustment policies – that is, mainly tools for economic advance into the 'global casino' (see Chapter 7). Alternative adult education practices do emerge, but they are mainly geared at survival. Those, however, are the ones we shall conceptualise in Part III.

To conclude, we can say that, whether in the North or South, the basic ideas and practices of adult education were to help humanise development. Yet even the most critical and political practices of adult education in America (e.g. Highlander), in Europe (e.g. adult education in the social movements), and in the South (e.g. Participatory Action Research) are still generally uncritical about development – a process they take for granted, and on which they basically seek to put a human face.

Part II

Crossroads and Dead Ends

So far we have seen how the historical project of adult education, its conceptual foundations, and its practices in both North and South are heavily rooted in the development paradigm. As such, adult education pursues – at least in its self-perception – a social responsibility agenda, by which it seeks to contribute to humanising development. However, this self-perception is becoming increasingly anachronistic. Neither today's challenges nor current adult education practices any longer correspond to what adult education thinks it is all about. Therefore, if adult education wants again to become a significant actor for social change in today's context, it needs to understand the profound changes that have occurred in industrial development and society over the past twenty years. It also needs to look critically at what its dominant practices have recently become.

In Part II we want to do precisely that. In Chapter 7 we will show how the development process itself has become so distorted that there is no longer much to be humanised. In other words, the ideal of development, which has served as the reference point for adult education theory and practice, is vanishing. We will illustrate this transformation on four different levels: (1) globalisation or turbo-capitalism, which is destroying the very foundations of development by replacing it with trade; (2) postmodernism, which is removing the very cultural foundations of development, and replacing the entire project of modernity with individualism; (3) the erosion of the state and traditional politics, which means the end of the most relevant actor and unit for development; and (4) the ecological crisis, which leads the pursuit of development into an overall dead end. In other words, this chapter will present the fundamental changes that have occurred recently, and constitute many challenges to an adult education which thinks of itself as a significant vector of social change.

In Chapter 8 we will show that adult education, as a practice, has already been significantly affected by these trends. In particular, we will observe how adult education has become 'privatised', in both senses of the word – become simultaneously a more private activity, and an activity which is increasingly run by the private sector and for the benefit of private corporations. This also means that adult education is no longer an autonomous contributor to development; it is now being instrumentalised by existing forces. Again, an adult education which considers itself an agent of social transformation needs not only to acknowledge this reality but self-critically to understand how some of its practices can be traced back to certain theoretical foundations of the field itself.

In the Conclusion to Part II, and on the basis of Chapters 7 and 8, we will outline three possible – maybe even probable – scenarios for the future evolution of adult education practices. All three scenarios outline an adult education which is instrumentalised by one or more of the trends of industrial development listed above. Overall, all three describe a process by which adult education will probably contribute to solving some of society's current problems, but in none of these scenarios will adult education contribute to fundamental social change, as it originally set out to do.

Part II sets the stage for Part III, in which we will outline how adult education can once more play a significant role in social change and transformation. In order to do that, however, adult education must understand today's challenges, recognise its distorted practices, and look critically at its intellectual foundations.

Chapter 7

Roads Diverging

Once there was a development paradigm, which conferred a certain unity and coherence on the project of adult education, just as it conferred unity and direction on the social sciences more generally. This development paradigm is rapidly disappearing today, and thus puts into question the very project and identity of adult education. In this chapter, we will show how the development paradigm is being undermined and examine the consequences of this attack for world development; and briefly outline how all this is likely to affect adult education practice and theory. We will go on to distinguish four different angles of attack on the development paradigm.

First we will present the attack on the development paradigm, as well as on industrial development more generally, from within capitalism itself. What has come to be called 'turbo-capitalism' basically means the replacement of development by trade, leading to the illusion that the 'market', in particular the financial market, can be the motor and the regulator of development. Adult education is particularly affected by this trend, since most of what adult education did – at least in developing countries – was part and parcel of the idea and the process of development. With turbo-capitalism, such development is now increasingly giving way to neocolonialism.

Second, we will look at the erosion of the state, and of traditional politics more generally. We will see how the geographical unit within which development was traditionally conceptualised – the nation-state – is being undermined by globalisation and supplanted by new geographical units both above (region) and below (community) state level. This affects adult education inasmuch as it has to rethink its own development and fundraising strategy as the state withdraws more and more not only from adult education but more generally from all traditional development activities, as it turns into an instrument of global capitalism.

Third, we will look at how, in the cultural arena, 'postmodernism' has replaced modernism both as a cultural practice and as an intellectual ideal. In the field of adult education this means that the ideal of Enlightenment, which guided much of adult education's practice, has become, at best, one of the narratives one can refer to in adult education.

Finally, we will outline how the ecological crisis undermines the very bio-geo-physical foundations of industrial development, as well as the intellectual foundations of the development paradigm. This ecological crisis constitutes the most fundamental attack on adult education and, more generally, on any social-science-based activity.

The combination and mutual reinforcement of these four trends lead inevitably to what we would term a 'vicious circle' – some sort of deadly spiral by which industrial development devours itself. As a result, the paradigm of development is being put into question at its very core. Adult education, therefore, can no longer look at the development paradigm for guidance. The entire project of adult and continuing education seems to have lost much of its historical legitimation, and is surrounded by serious doubts about the direction that should or could be taken.

From 'development' to 'free trade': turbo-capitalism and the casino economy

The project of development, fuelled by the educational ideal of Enlightenment, gave adult education a purpose and a direction – as we have said, the 'humanisation of development' in both North and South. In other words, the 'development paradigm' in adult education was its overarching philosophy and programme. But this ideal is no longer sustainable, as the very idea of 'development' is coming to an end, and being replaced by an abstract model of free trade. We will highlight these fundamental changes, and from there derive the main implications for adult education.

Somewhere around the 1980s, as François Parlant announced (Parlant, 1982), a major shift occurred in the area of development – at least as it pertained to the relationship between North and South. This was the beginning of the end of development, and for some it was even the beginning of a 'recolonisation' of the South (Raghavan, 1990). However, we think that this phenomenon was not limited to North–South relations, where structural adjustment, imposed by the North upon the South, became a precondition for development (Rist, 1997), with growing poverty and societal break-up as its major consequences (Chossoudovsky, 1997). Rather, what is perceived in North–South terms as the end of development marks in reality a much more profound transformation of the whole of economic activity: in other words, the project of development is being replaced by the promotion of a free-trade model, also called trade liberalisation or economic and financial globalisation. Having been imposed upon the South, this model has also come to haunt the North, leading to a similar structural adjustment process. In short, the project of development is being replaced, both ideologically and practically, by the imposition of a new model of free trade. Such free trade, and the corresponding adjustments needed in order to participate in it, are now said to be a precondition for development in the South, as well as a necessity for prosperity in the North. It is quite symptomatic, in this respect, that the traditional development system – for the most part UN organisations – is also being replaced by a new trading system with its corresponding organisations, such as the World Trade Organization (WTO) or the International Standardization Organisation (Whalley and Hamilton, 1996). The effort and attention are therefore no longer put into development, but into fostering conditions conducive to trade. This is particularly evident in the case of basic infrastructures, which are being privatised and bought up by transnational corporations (Martin, 1993).

This process of replacing development by trade has been furthered – if not made possible – by the parallel liberalisation of the financial markets. Indeed, during the 1980s Northern countries liberalised their financial sectors, and so created multinational financial corporations, putting increasing pressure on the rest of the world to do the same (Chesnais, 1994). This process recently culminated in the WTO agreement on the liberalisation of financial services, and will be pushed further towards a so-called multilateral agreement on investment, currently under negotiation, whereby any corporation can invest anywhere and be able to repatriate its profits. Such a global free flow of capital is exactly what is desired by the financial markets and the speculators living off them. As a result of this process of disconnecting financial flows from the real world or development in the physical sense – a process paralleled by the emergence of financial holding companies — profits are made thanks to speculation, and no longer thanks to work (Rifkin, 1995). Thus it comes as no surprise that the free flow of money is seen by economists as the purest incarnation of the market (Henwod, 1997). Parallel to the physical world, the 'economy' increasingly seems to behave on another level – the level of finance; a phenomenon which is rightly called the 'casino economy' (Cavanagh and Barnett, 1994), characterised by 'predatory finance' and 'corporate cannibalism' (Korten, 1995). This process has of course been accelerated by technological advances, especially in the computer industry (Castells, 1996).

The results of such global finance and free trade combined are rather unpleasant – at least for the great majority of the peoples on this planet, not to speak of all other living beings. This 'triumph of the market' (Herman, 1995), this 'manic capitalism' (Greider, 1997), or what Luttwak calls 'turbo-capitalism' (Luttwak, 1995, 1999; see also Martin and Schumann, 1997), has, to start with, unsustainable economic consequences: economic polarisation, the depreciation of work, the rise of uncontrollable economic actors, and through them the destruction of the very idea of the market. It is becoming increasingly clear that such turbo-capitalism leads to a growing polarisation between the few 'haves' and the growing numbers of 'have-nots' – not only in terms of North–South relations (Amin, 1997) but also within countries themselves. If traditional development at least had the ideal of raising the living standards of the majority of people, the new turbo-capitalism is satisfied with average numbers demonstrating that trade flows and stocks have increased, yet does not care that the majority of people are actually far worse off than before (Brown, Renner and Flavin, 1997, 1998). Likewise, this global predatory economy now clearly values capital over work – that is, short-term financial benefits resulting from investment in the financial markets over long-term social benefits resulting from work and engagement in the development process (Wolman and Calamosca, 1997). This translates into the fact that the developing countries turn into resource economies – that is, the simple extraction of natural resources without processing them – and that in the North, technologically supported services replace labour-intensive industries, thus redefining work (Castells, 1996; Gorz, 1997; Rifkin, 1995). Finally, free trade also gives rise to a new species of transnational corporations (Korten, 1995), which are increasingly beyond any form of political or community control. Furthermore, there is a process of concentration of these corporations, leading to global cartels or oligopolies; this in turn defies the very notion of the free market. In short – and in purely economic terms – the replacement of development by free trade and a parallel financial market means the end of the aspiration to a good society as a result of development (UNDP, 1997, 1998) and the beginning of a downward spiral, also called the (economic) 'race to the bottom' (Brecher and Costello, 1994). Rather than raising the living standard of the people, which was at least the aspiration of the development ideal, the free-trade model is entirely counterproductive, since it makes the majority of people poorer, and ultimately destroys the very bases of its own success.

Indeed, if one also takes into account the social, cultural, political and ecological consequences of the free-market economy, there is hardly anything positive left. As a matter of fact, free trade pits the 'economy' against society, social aspirations now looking like an impediment to free trade and capital gains (Reich, 1995). Moreover, the consequences for societies of economic globalisation are generally disastrous: poverty, criminalisation, fragmentation, break-up, and so on (UNRISD, 1995). Economic globalisation also erodes communities and cultures, and leads to the phenomenon Knoke calls 'placelessness' (Knoke, 1996) – individuals no longer feel any belonging to a social unit. Consumerism is both a consequence and a cause of this feeling of placelessness. Also, as we will show, the global casino economy has destructive effects on the state, as well as on the natural environment. The point here, however, is not to lament these destructive economic trends but, rather, to show that the very ideal to which adult education was committed – the ideal of humanising development – is being rendered obsolete by the fact that this ideal of development no longer exists. And even if this ideal does still exist, it has been rendered totally irrelevant in the light of the above trends. What is there to be humanised in the global casino? What is there to be promoted by adult education if social development is no longer on the agenda? Rather, given this situation, adult education should rethink its very foundations, and reflect on what needs to be done, given this new context.

In the meantime, adult education practice and even theory are following the mainstream. Indeed, adult education seems to have some useful tips on how to become part of this global race to the bottom. More generally, it offers itself for instrumentalisation and commodification, as we will see in the next chapter. The new global economy, even in the North, is characterised by the precariousness and deskilling of jobs, if not by growing unemployment. As a result, adult education increasingly offers itself as a means for individual survival through retraining for the job market, vocational education, or even so-called 'survival skills'. But this survival scenario even applies to entire organisations or societies. Thus we increasingly see adult education as a means of bringing entire organisations up to speed so that they are competitive again, a process for which the term 'learning organisation' has been created; this in fact is some sort of organisational survival skill. Recently, the term 'learning society', originally coined by UNESCO in a different context and for a different purpose (Faure et al., 1972), has been used by the European Union in this new context of 'societal survival' (Delors et al. 1996; Bélanger, 1998; European Union, 1995; European Commission, 1997; OECD, 1996). Corporations now offer corresponding training and organisational learning skills. And finally, by advocating its services for individuals and organisations trying to cope with the consequences of economic globalisation, adult education itself becomes a commodity to be developed, promoted and marketed for the benefit of turbo-capitalism. In other words, by becoming a servant of the new global casino, adult education turns into an instrument further promoting it and accelerating the race to the bottom, off which it will increasingly live.

The erosion of the welfare state
and the rise of conflicting demands

Adult education had never been as closely associated with the state as conventional education was and still is, since it has never been heavily subsidised and integrated into the administration. Nevertheless, adult education is – and will increasingly be – affected by the transformation of the state, especially the welfare state, whose transformation is a direct result of globalisation. We will present the two main steps of this transformation, and show how it affects the practice of adult education.

The state has preindustrial and even pre-modern origins, as it can be traced back to the institutionalisation of territorial control and military power since the Roman Empire (Poggi, 1978, 1990) and the European medieval city-states (Tilly, 1992). But it was with the French Revolution that the state became synonymous with modernity and acquired a civilising function: the 'citizen-soldier' becomes simultaneously the beneficiary and the defender of the modern state and its *raison d'être*. Education emerged as one of the core civilising functions of the state. However, it is with the Industrial Revolution, and especially as a consequence of it, that the state acquired its key functions, which still legitimise most of its current activities. Indeed, as a result of the negative consequences of industrial development, the state took on the role of rectifying these negative consequences, such as the role of social welfare, and since the 1960s also the role of environmental protection. Since the end of the nineteenth century, and especially since the beginning of the twentieth century, the state has also taken on the role of an industrial development agency, especially in the development of infrastructures. With Keynesian economics, the state finally also added the function of macroeconomic stability to its core functions. This is more generally the function of regulating the market, a function Polanyi traces back to the very origins of the state (Polanyi, 1942). This model of the state was then exported and imposed upon all non-European countries, a process political scientists called 'political development'.

This constant 'growth of the state' comes to a halt with the passage from development to trade: with economic and financial globalisation, accompanied by the neoliberal attack on the state, most of its functions are now being put into question. Financially and commercially attractive activities are increasingly being globalised – privatised, and removed from state control. On the other hand, the economic crisis of the 1970s, accompanied by the overcommitment of the welfare state, led to a structural financial crisis which now makes it difficult for the state to fulfil its welfare, industrial development and macroeconomic stabilisation functions. In other words, with economic and financial globalisation, the benefits of industrial development, and increasingly the benefits of the casino economy, are being privatised, while the social and ecological costs of this same globalisation are being localised, and therefore socialised. For the state, this process of simultaneous globalisation and localisation leads first to financial problems, and these financial problems in turn call for further privatisation and deregulation. Privatisation and deregulation are means of structurally adjusting the state to the new global economy – a process which, in the case of most of the developing countries, is imposed upon them by the multilateral agencies (Caufield, 1996). But a second consequence of this simultaneous process of globalisation and localisation is the erosion of political legitimation and authority, as the state increasingly has to mediate between global pressures on the one hand and local demands on the other. This fundamental contradiction of the welfare state was already recognised during the movement period of the 1960s and 1970s (Habermas, 1973; Offe, 1984), but it has only become more acute with financial and economic globalisation.

Many authors thus conclude that there is an erosion of the state, resulting directly from structural financial problems, and indirectly from financial and economic globalisation (Guéhenno, 1995; Ohmae, 1995; Strange, 1996). In real terms, this means that the main functions of the state – welfare, industrial development and macroeconomic stability – are being undermined, which of course has serious implications for the legitimation of the state. In practice it also means that many activities which traditionally went on at the nation-state level are now being relocated either above or below the state, that the mode of delivery of state services is being transformed – that is, increasingly privatised – and that many state activities are now being delivered by other actors – either commercial or non-governmental actors (Pierson, 1996:

194ff.). All these transformations of the state directly affect adult education. First, the traditional function of providing (adult) education in a social developmental perspective is no longer being assumed by the state, since this activity is being privatised along with many other service functions. Adult education services should be, and increasingly are, ruled by the market, a trend which further strengthens the previously identified slide towards commercialisation and commodification of adult education products. Second, the services which cannot be provided by the market are being handed over to local communities and non-governmental organisations, at times subsidised by the state. This opens up new opportunities for adult education, especially in the area of remedial skills. But it also opens up opportunities at local level, especially in developing countries, where self-help groups and community self-reliance adult educational activities arise in the perspective of local survival. In other words, besides the commodification of adult education, the erosion of the state also offers new possibilities for community-based adult education.

In our view, however, this erosion is only a first stage in the transformation of the state as a result of economic and financial globalisation. In this first stage, the remedial, the industrial development and the macroeconomic stabilisation functions are being privatised, shifted to other public levels, or simply abandoned. This also applies to those functions which were traditionally performed by the state in the area of adult education. Yet there is a second stage, currently announced by the World Bank, in which the state, albeit minimal, is strengthened again (World Bank, 1997). Indeed, even in a world of free trade, certain functions – the functions of facilitating and regulating trade – have to be performed by the state. In particular, the state needs to ensure law and order, trade rules and property rights. These are among the very basic functions of the state, functions which go back to its feudal role. In this second stage, the state is no longer sovereign but has become an instrument in the hands of the multinational corporations, on whose behalf property rights and trade rules are being enforced. In addition, there also remains a function which one can call – with the European Union – 'universal service': maintaining the minimal infrastructure services which are necessary if a society is not to fall apart. One can probably count some of the basic adult education programmes, like literacy or other core skills, among these universal services which the state, if it does not provide, at least subsidises.

In short, the erosion of the state does not necessarily mean the end of adult education, but it certainly means the end of a public adult education agenda as part of a social developmental project. As a result, adult education either takes the commercial route or becomes a subsidised activity in a remedial or universal service perspective. It also means the end of a political adult education, parallel to the decline of traditional politics. Indeed, as the nation-state, which was traditionally the level where political action was defined, is weakened from both the outside (globalisation limiting the state's autonomy) and the inside (legitimation crisis), traditional politics declines. This does not mean that political action is no longer pertinent, but it does mean that both the level and the stakes of traditional political actions are losing their relevance. Consequently, politics has to be reinvented (Beck, 1986), and probably on a level other than that of the state. And there is indeed a search for new political venues, either on the level above the nation-state (global human and ecological rights, global standards), or below it (regional, local and personal politics). However, this is not simply a matter of creating new political institutions, as it also requires a redefinition of politics and the public domain on these levels. Adult education can play an active role in this re-invention of politics, especially on the local level. This role goes beyond remedial training or community self-help activities, and implies a new – socially more responsible – role for adult education as a contributor to redefining politics.

Postmodernism: many roads to nowhere

Adult education as a field of practice and theory is particularly affected by postmodernism, since postmodernism reinforces the individualistic features of the humanistic tradition of adult education. Postmodernism here stands not just for a new fashion in philosophy and cultural theory but, rather, for a sociological phenomenon observable in late capitalist societies, particularly the phenomenon of cultural and social erosion, as well as growing individualism. In this section we will highlight how postmodernism affects the practice and the theory of adult education.

In order to understand the challenge posed by postmodernism to adult education, however, we must recall what postmodernism is opposed to. The development paradigm and the emancipatory role of the state are both held together by an underpinning philosophical framework, which is basically the philosophy of modernity – that is, the philosophy and the project of Enlightenment (Horkheimer and Adorno, 1944). The subject-person and his or her education play a key role, say Enlightenment philosophers, in the realisation of a just, free and equitable society. Indeed, the subject-person's emancipation is considered to be synonymous with societal emancipation, and both are made possible thanks to the progressive and humanising potentials of modern institutions, in particular the state. Also, Enlightenment philosophy assumes the universal validity of modern values such as justice, freedom, human rights and equity (Riedel, 1989). Radical and critical adult education theory, as we saw in Chapter 5, is simply the reaffirmation of this belief in the emancipatory value of (adult) education (Welton, 1995). As for traditional education, there is simply no alternative theoretical foundation available other than the philosophy of Enlightenment. Besides education, the social sciences are also to play a key role in the realisation of such a modern society, mainly though building rational organisations, and through the rationalisation of social behaviour (Caillé, 1986; Giddens, 1984). In other words, until very recently there was a coherent project of modernity which conferred legitimation and direction on the entire enterprise of the social sciences – not to mention the legitimation and direction it provided for the entire endeavour of education, adult education included. It was also this philosophical project of modernity which provided the humanising dimension to the development paradigm, and to the institution and role of the state in modernising societies. This project was based upon the assumption of universal values, the most important of which is the value of Reason, and was to be realised thanks to the emancipation of the subject-person, which simultaneously would mean the emancipation of society (from nature).

Since the 1980s, however, this project of modernity has come under severe attack from within philosophy, cultural theory and sociology. As a result, the project of modernity is fundamentally questioned, the ideal of a rational society with emancipated subject-persons at its core is threatened, and the idea of universal cultural values is about to be abandoned. We here use the term 'postmodernism' in order to summarise these various doubts about the project of modernity in their philosophical, sociological and cultural dimensions. In philosophy, postmodernism did not emerge as a direct attack on Enlightenment philosophy. Rather, it resulted from the relativisation of so-called 'meta-narratives', such as the philosophy of Enlightenment or variations of it, such as Marxism or Critical Theory (Lyotard, 1979; Vattimo, 1985). But this undermining of Enlightenment philosophy had actually started much earlier with an attack on and subsequent relativisation of the endeavour of science, which had always served as the underpinning of philosophy, especially through its reference point of rationality (Feyerabend, 1970; Kuhn, 1962). The Enlightenment project thus appeared, thanks to postmodern philosophers, as only one of many possible narratives. So did 'Reason', the core concept of Enlightenment philosophy (Wood, 1996), as well as its related concepts, such as individual and collective emancipation, democracy, universal justice, freedom, and so forth. Of course, Critical Theorists especially maintained that the Reason one generally referred to was a distorted one to begin with; therefore, the original project of modernity was by no means put into question by postmodernist philosophy (Touraine, 1992). Nevertheless, the damage was – and, by now, is – done, and Enlightenment philosophy has become just one of a myriad of narratives about the good and the desirable. As a result, it is increasingly difficult to distinguish philosophy from cultural theory (see below).

The same thing happened to social theory, and to a certain extent also to social reality. Indeed, over time social theory came to be seen no longer as part of the project of modernity but rather as the task of describing an observed empirical reality with increasingly postmodern features. Postmodern sociologists saw social reality as a world of signs and symbols, disconnected from physical reality yet held together by some underlying principles yet to be discovered (Baudrillard, 1968; Lash and Urry, 1994). This relativistic view, of course, has its conceptual origins in symbolic interactionism, an approach which had already influenced pragmatic adult education. But this disembodied view of social reality is also rooted in the tradition of post-industrialism (Bell, 1973) – in the belief that physical production is being replaced by services and the exchange of information. In other words, the idea in sociology is now that it is communication, symbols and information – and no longer bio-geo-physical constraints – which make up the social world. To a certain extent, this theoretical view concerned rich and developing societies, which increasingly live off the casino economy, while using up resources from developing countries (as well as using developing countries as a dumping ground). This view was then translated into sociological research, to discover a 'postmodern condition', characterised by social complexity 'populated by a great number of agencies, most of them single-purpose' (Bauman, 1992: 192), rootless as they are, engaged in a process of constant self-constitution which makes up for their lack of identity. Currently, it is no longer clear whether postmodern sociology is simply a theoretical construct or actually does describe an existing reality.

At least part of this postmodern social reality is constituted by growing individualism, a characteristic that is particularly relevant to adult education practice and increasingly reflected in adult education theory. Individualism is as much the realisation of the Enlightenment ideal of the autonomous subject-person (Dumont, 1983) – or the distortion of it, as some would argue (Elias, 1987) – as it is the result of the rationalisation of social life, or rather the disaggregation of communities and cultures (Berger et al., 1973; Lasch, 1979; Sennett, 1974). The consequence of this process is not only a 'lonely crowd', as foreseen as early as the 1950s (Riesman et al., 1950) – that is, a mass of individualised atoms looking for meaning and community – but moreover the fragmentation of the individual him- or herself. Thus in the postmodern era we hear about 'life in fragments' (Bauman, 1995), about the 'multiple self' (Elster, 1985), or more generally about the 'damaged life' (Sloan, 1996). As a result, questions of meaning, identity and morality are now disconnected from the public domain, including politics, and interpreted as belonging to the responsibility of the individual alone. The state and traditional politics no longer function as the arena for ethical debates and the search for a common foundation of the 'good society' (Galbraith, 1996).

Instead, one can observe a new 'postmodern politics' character-ised by 'tribalism', 'imagined or virtual communities', desire and the manipulation of it, as well as fear, defensiveness and reaction-ism (Bauman, 1992: 196ff.). This new reality of postmodern indi-viduals also opens up the way for all sorts of religious movements, from fundamentalism to New Age, which offer meaning and iden-tity in a world with essentially no perspectives.

For us, therefore, postmodernism is above all an analytic, not an ideological concept. As such, it describes a social and cultural reality in which individuals are increasingly disconnected from each other, their families, their communities and their nations, yet held together by their shared use of standardised symbols, produced and manipulated by a 'global dream machine' (Cavan-agh and Barnet, 1994). This is the same machine that drives the global shopping mall, and uses the global casino for cash produc-tion. Even though some can certainly take economic advantage of this postmodern world of atomised and manipulable individu-als, the combination of the actors' individualised and thus collec-tively incoherent strategies will ultimately prove fatal (Baudrillard, 1983). The 'minimal self' (Lasch, 1984) is and increasingly will be concerned only with his or her own psychic and physical survival. This is also a disenchanted reality from which religious, moral and ethical values have been expelled in parallel to the supposed rationalisation of the lifeworld (Gauchet, 1985). As Lipo-vetsky has very clearly seen, postmodern individualism goes hand in hand with the new 'era of the void' (Lipovetsky, 1983). This is also a reality in which discontent is becoming increasingly difficult, if not impossible, as this new postmodern disorder, characterised by its lack of consistency and direction, no longer offers any op-portunity for opposition and resistance (Bauman, 1997), a trend which Marcuse had foreseen back in 1964 (Marcuse, 1964). Even if we tend to agree with those critics who consider postmodernism and the corresponding reality to be a luxury of the rich, we never-theless think that postmodernist social and cultural trends are being spread all over the planet, in tandem with the Westernisa-tion being imposed upon the Third World (Mehmet, 1995). And there is no reason why postmodern individualism cannot be com-bined with poverty and the struggle for (increasingly individual) survival.

Adult education, and education more generally, are particularly concerned with postmodernism, as Usher and Edwards (1994) convincingly argue. With the erosion of the project of modernity, education as a whole loses its orientation, if not its *raison d'être*. Admittedly this affects adult education to a lesser degree, as adult education is in part rooted in philosophical schools of thought which can easily survive the end of the project of modernity, or even thrive on it (humanistic and pragmatist adult education). Nevertheless, adult education's underlying ideal of humanising development through individual and collective emancipation is being fundamentally put into question by postmodernism – both because of postmodernist theory and because of postmodernist social and cultural reality. On the other hand, adult education, especially its humanistic strand, will undoubtedly be able to take advantage of postmodernist trends. As a result of postmodernisation, adults increasingly follow their individual projects and (survival) strategies. Adult education can cater to these individuals, helping them to form strategies and develop the necessary skills in order to survive in the postmodern world. Moreover, postmodernism, as we have seen, means a loss of collective and individual meaning. Adult education can – and already does – take advantage of this trend, as adult educators increasingly assist individuals in their search for meaning. Such adult education activities can mostly be found under the auspices of the New Age movement, but are sometimes also related to fundamentalism. Assisting individuals in their search for meaning and in the development of their survival skills contributes to the privatisation of adult education, which is by no means incompatible with its instrumentalisation and marketisation. Yet one could also imagine another project for adult education whereby its function would be to reconstruct communities from atomised individuals, or – even more radically – to question, and contribute to reversing, the forces of postmodernism altogether.

The ecological crisis: the ultimate dead end of industrial society

Adult education is not challenged by the ecological crisis in the same way as it is by the end-of-development paradigm, the erosion of the state, and postmodern reality. We are not talking about the type of challenge whereby adult education should simply take up environmental concerns and translate them into (adult) educational activities, as was done in part with conservationist ecology and, to a lesser extent, with the political ecology of the 1970s. This was the time when adult education became, so to speak, 'instrumentalised' by the ecological crisis, and turned itself into a vehicle for promoting environmental awareness. Rather, we would like to show how the ecological crisis – especially the emerging global ecological crisis, combined with economic and financial globalisation, the erosion of the state, and postmodernism – is becoming a vicious circle, which will ultimately lead industrial civilisation to a dead end. In our view the ecological crisis is the ultimate challenge to adult education, as there is no way out of this vicious circle except through individual and collective learning. Adult education should take up this challenge, if it wants to be true to its original ideal.

The starting point of our argumentation is the bio-geo-physical limits to the pursuit of industrial development and trade. The first discussion about the bio-physical limits to economic growth goes back to the beginning of the 1970s (Meadows et al., 1972). At that time, the talk was mainly about input limits to growth – that is, problems of natural resources and energy. With the political ecology of the 1970s, countries in the North also became preoccupied with problems of pollution and waste. The limits were therefore seen more and more in terms of political will and capacity to act. Since the mid-1980s, and with the emergence of global ecology, we now also have to deal with output limits to industrial development (for example, the hole in the ozone layer and climate change). These limits are in fact much more serious, as they restrict the input limits (negative effects on renewable natural resources such as forests, for example) and limit the capacity for political action. Overall, industrial development, because it uses natural resources and impacts upon the biosphere, restricts rather than expands these limits. Of course, technological progress (ecological efficiency, pollution control, etc.), environmental education (promoting environmentally more responsible behaviour) and environmental politics have, to a certain extent, the capacity to slow down the process of ecological degradation, and thus extend these limits

– at least, this was the original idea behind the concept of 'sustainable development' (World Commission on Environment and Development, 1987). Unfortunately, however, these efficiency gains, as well as all other (political, educational, etc.) efforts, are rapidly offset, mainly because industrial development is expanding more and more rapidly across the entire planet. In other words, industrial development, by its very nature, degrades the biosphere, and thus limits our social and political options. With globalisation, this is becoming a planetary problem which will only get worse. Environmental degradation is no longer simply a temporary local or regional dysfunction, nor is it a problem only for the rich.

In addition to ecological degradation, industrial development also leads to what we like to call sociocultural erosion – in essence, the phenomenon previously described as postmodernism. Until recently, the contribution of industrial development to society and culture was basically considered positive. Industrial development has even been associated with individual and collective emancipation, or even with sociocultural modernisation. The sometimes systematic destruction of communities and cultures (planned by the social sciences and implemented by national administrations and armies), accompanied by the development of the modern individual (the 'modern self'), were not only seen as an active contribution to sociocultural modernisation but constitute still a necessary condition for further industrial development. Today, many elements of our modern societies – for example, individualism, the loss of traditions and lack of responsibility – are both products of industrial development and constitute a necessary condition for its pursuit. But modernisation and sociocultural erosion are in fact simply two faces of the same coin, separated only by perspective. Until recently, it was possible to see this sociocultural modernisation as generally beneficial, mainly because it was never related to industrial development, even though it is industrial development which has made sociocultural modernisation possible. In other words, sociocultural modernisation was, and still is, seen by many as positive, because its bio-physical consequences were, and are, not yet fully visible, thrust as they are on to the developing world, the poorest, or simply future generations. With the expansion and acceleration of industrial development, however, bio-geo-physical limits to growth rapidly emerge, along with the decline of the perspective of unlimited expansion. As a result, the ecological and sociocultural consequences of industrial development become more and more interlinked. Against the background of these global limits, and the subsequent impossibility of pursuing industrial development in the long run, the continuation of sociocultural modernisation becomes counterproductive. This was predicted by Illich (1970c): individualisation, for example, turns into individualism; emancipation turns into lack of responsibility; liberation from traditions turns into loss of roots, and so on. More of the same – that is, more development – not only serves to destroy the foundations of development (ecological degradation), but also distorts what was initially positive (sociocultural modernisation). It turns forces of modernisation into forces of destruction. Today, this process has become a vicious circle where sociocultural erosion promotes ecological destruction, which in turn accelerates sociocultural erosion, and so forth.

In other words, once industrial development, the consumption of Northern countries, and the Western lifestyle have become widespread, ecological degradations on a scale sufficiently large to trigger input and output limits to growth inevitably ensue (Trainer, 1989). As we said above, these global consequences were perceived at the end of the 1980s. At that time, the end of the Cold War, and the acceleration of global commerce through deregulation and liberalisation, gave a new impetus to industrial development (Martin, 1993; Self, 1993). And this has added to the further erosion of communities and of entire countries, especially developing countries and Eastern European countries, opening them up even more to industrial development and to accelerated sociocultural erosion. Thus global ecological degradation has started to reinforce these societal trends, which, in the age of (input and output) limits to industrial development, become increasingly counterproductive. For example, individualism, in addition to being an ecological problem (lifestyle), reinforces societal trends of lack of responsibility and non-participation. This is equally true for population growth, migration and conflicts – all trends which now simultaneously contribute to ecological degradation and sociocultural erosion (Homer-Dixon, 1994; Kaplan, 1996). This erosion of society and culture will in turn accelerate the destruction of the biosphere, and this will happen either directly, via ecologically destructive actions such as wars, conflicts or other ecologically destructive behaviour, or indirectly, because an eroded society will have lost its last (cultural, ethical, social, etc.) resistance to forced further industrial development (global accumulation of capital and power, techno-scientific progress, etc.). Once there is nothing to prevent industrial development from unfolding, as the promoters of globalisation are trying to ensure, the vicious circle will be unhampered.

Without doubt, this vicious circle affects everything: individuals, communities, societies, cultures and the biosphere. Even the nation-states, having actively promoted industrial development, now find themselves on the side of the victims. However, not everybody is a victim of this vicious circle in the same way, and some can actually take advantage of it (Karliner, 1997). The first victims are certainly those who can no longer export the ecological and sociocultural costs of their own 'development' – rural populations (in both South and North), the least mobile peoples (geographically and socially), and more generally the poorest. One can therefore foresee a growing polarisation between the global and the local, between those who promote global industrial development, as they can take advantage of it, and those who have no choice but to resist (locally). The challenge to adult education – at least to an adult education which seeks to promote social responsibility – now becomes very clear: it can help us to 'learn our way out' (Milbrath, 1989) of the dead end towards which this vicious circle is inescapably leading us. We will take up this challenge in Chapter 10, and develop the corresponding perspective for a renewed adult education project in Part III of this book.

In Chapter 8, however, we would first like to show how adult education practice and discourse are already being considerably shaped by the three trends towards turbo-capitalism, the erosion of the state, and postmodernism. As a result, adult education is increasingly privatised, instrumentalised and commercialised.

Chapter 8

The Transformation of Adult Education: Where Adult Education is Going — or Being Driven Towards

The point of departure for this chapter is the current practice and discourse of adult education. Having outlined the new sociocultural context and challenges in Chapter 7, we shall now critically examine adult education reality. In other words, we are going to see to what extent this new context is affecting adult education practice and discourse. Today, the need for permanent education has become an integral part of life. Many societal activities which were previously conceptualised in political or managerial terms are now framed in 'learning language'. Let us just mention here the growing talk about the 'learning society' (European Union, 1995; US Department of Labor, 1991; Okamoto, 1994), and the 'knowledge society' (EU Commission, 1997). This growing prominence of 'learning', even in its fuzziest definitions, in fact makes adult education at least potentially more relevant, but of course also constitutes a danger for it. Without underestimating adult education practices for social change – to which we will turn in Part III – it is probably fair to say that adult education has already significantly adapted to this new context – and become substantially distorted in the process.

As a result, mainstream adult education is no longer pursuing the project of emancipation and social change. Rather, its originally emancipatory practices now become distorted, instrumentalised and counterproductive. On the one hand, as adult learning is becoming a self-evident and universal need, a need in which one participates voluntarily and individually, adult education is being privatised. Learning is becoming a private or purely personal issue, thus abandoning all its collective dimensions. In parallel, this trend is reinforced by the market pressure towards privatisation, as adult education is no longer a responsibility of the public administration but of private bodies (e.g. charitable or for-profit organisations). On the other hand, adult education has become just one among many offerings in the 'cultural market' of society, which also means that adult education is increasingly subjected to the pressures of competition, conditions of supply and demand, and commercialisation. Thus, adult education is also becoming instrumentalised. Privatisation and instrumentalisation of adult education practices are the two issues we would like to address here.

Privatisation 1: me, myself and I

The privatisation of adult education is an inevitable outcome of its individualisation in the context of a 'disenchanted modernity'. The ever-growing importance of lifelong learning coincides both with a pluralisation and diversification of learning needs and opportunities, and with the erosion of the concepts and institutions that once articulated universal ideals and collectively shared responsibilities. As a result, the meaning of learning and education is more and more assessed by the learners themselves, from the perspective of its contribution to self-actualisation and to personal competitiveness on the market. Adult education can no longer afford to offer programmes which represent a universal 'canon' of generally accepted knowledge and values. If it wants to stay in the 'education market', it has to appeal to potential learners by actively responding to their personal learning needs and desires. Adult education therefore increasingly caters to individual goals, both with respect to self-fulfilment and with respect to practical survival skills vis-à-vis the complexity of daily life. More and more, it becomes an instrument that people can use in their personal search for meaning in life, and for their individual empowerment in the competitive struggle for economic, social and cultural life-chances. We will first highlight the individualised practices of adult education, and subsequently show how the adult education discourse has changed accordingly.

Adult education: customised learning for individuals

Both trends towards individual self-fulfilment and trends towards individual competitiveness (training, professional education) are increasingly shaping adult education practices. Let us present some examples which, in our view, are typical for a new type of adult education, catering mainly to individuals.

The Eurodelphi 95 study entitled 'Future Goals and Policies of Adult Education in Europe' (Leirman, 1995), for example, shows that learners want personalised advice on how to survive in the global marketplace:

> Three issues are seen as serious challenges [for individuals]: unemployment, the changing organisation of labour, and time and stress management. Ten problems, from interpersonal relations over insufficient professional knowledge, distrust of politics and lack of meaning to life down to uncertain identity and difficult access to information are regarded by our respondents as fairly serious. (Leirman, 1995: 93)

Adult education, the authors think, should provide the individual learner with answers to these challenges and problems. The same Eurodelphi 95 study also finds that adult educators see themselves as helpers – that is, people who help others to survive. In particular, the authors say, they want to help individuals 'to communicate, to learn how to learn, to develop one's personality, to function as a citizen, and to relate to others' (95–6). Similarly, the key factors underlying adult education areas and practices, as identified by this study, are (1) 'social and political exclusion', a factor which seems to be linked to the development of personal and cultural well-being; (2) 'health and comfort', which seems to be linked to the development of communicative and social abilities; and (3) labour and technology, which seems to be linked to learning how to learn, and to the individual's capacity to cope with the social and political world (64–5).

This trend towards privatisation seems to have invaded even adult literacy, an area traditionally dominated by a social action agenda. Here, the personalisation of practices aimed at being 're-sponsive to individual learners' needs', or 'listening to learners' voices', clearly risks privatising adult literacy altogether, abandoning any collective dimension to learning (e.g. Imel, 1995; Quigley,

1997). More generally, adult education offerings increasingly re-
semble survival kits for individuals. For instance, the proliferation
of 'tools' of adult education – self-help kits, computer-based
materials for self-education, psychological self-improvement materials, self-test, and the like – are illustrations of the direction adult
education is currently taking. Let us also mention the proliferation
of individually customised adult education graduate programmes,
which fit to the individual needs of complex working lives.
Consider, for example, the AEGIS (Adult Education Guided
Independent Study) programme at Columbia University or the
ACE (Adult and Continuing Education) doctoral programme of
National Louis University, which replicates AEGIS. Both programmes stress 'independent learning' as a way of learning which
is particularly suitable to modern adults – and to the individually
packaged higher education programmes.

In the report *Comparative Studies on Lifelong Learning Policies*, edited
by the National Institute for Educational Research of Japan and
the UNESCO Institute for Education in 1997, it is noted that the
issue which is relevant to almost all countries is 'self-education'.
In this report, Bélanger concludes, 'an important transition is the
shift from the policy of provision toward the policy of demand.
Important investment in adult learning is to construct a new infrastructure of self-learning in many ways with a lot of facilities'
(NIER and UNESCO 1997: 290). In fact, as the report shows,
this is a trend in many societies. For example in Germany – and
according to surveys by Kuwan in 1996 – 'terms like "non-
institutionalised", "en passant", "self-directed learning", and others
point to the increasing attention adults pay to these forms of
acquiring knowledge' (177). And in Spain, very significantly, 'research on adult education participation found that people would
participate more if they did not assimilate negative images of
themselves' (215).

Adult education discourse: self-directed learning by individuals

The discourse of adult education is, of course, responding to these
trends towards an ever more individualised practice. To the
practice of independent learning corresponds the theory of – or,
rather, the discourse on – the miracles of 'self-directed learning',

with humanistic adult education philosophy as its centrepiece. Humanistic adult education seems to have invaded most of the US graduate programmes. Consider, for example, the first objective of the University of Minnesota's adult education programme: 'To enhance the intellectual development of individuals as they (a) become more aware of their own life, (b) enjoy the rewards of learning how to learn, (c) critically reflect on their roles as responsible adults, and/or (d) initiate social change' (www.cored.coled. umn.edu:80/Adult-intro.html). Note also that 'self-directed learning' or SDL is now a required topic in 83 per cent of US graduate adult education programmes, according to the Harrison 1995 survey (Harrison, 1995: 206), a number which must be compared with the 22 per cent of 'consciousness theory' required.

Not surprisingly, we also observe within the field of adult education the emergence of a new area called 'adult career counselling in a new age' (1995 ERIC Clearinghouse on Adult, Career and Vocational Education Digest Number 167). This is accompanied by 'one-stop career centres' or 'self-learning centres', which are springing up all over industrialised countries. For several years we have also observed a growing interest in research about the individualisation of biographies and learning, as witnessed by AERC (Adult Education Research Conference) proceedings over the past years (see Proceedings of the 37th Annual AERC, 1996: 49–54, 79–84, 222–7, 258–63, 338–42). This illustrates the fact that for both adult educators and adult learners, learning is increasingly perceived as an entirely private activity.

More generally, and in conclusion, the privatisation of adult learning, both in theory and in practice, fits perfectly into an increasingly individualised social and economic context: adult education offerings and approaches essentially increase one's 'marketable' skills, and this in an increasingly competitive job market. Access to careers is heavily dependent upon the knowledge and skills one can offer. Similarly, position in the job market is highly determinant for one's social status. A 'higher' or 'lower' status is closely linked to the number of appropriate training and education qualifications one has obtained – qualifications that incorporate the rationality which fits the world of labour and professions. Therefore, as Eder rightly observes, 'education, rather than income, marks the barriers between social classes' (Eder, 1993: 92).

Privatisation 2: the erosion of the nation-state and its implications for adult education

But the privatisation of adult education must not be seen only from the perspective of adult learning. In another context, it actually means the end of publicly supported adult education. Growing market liberalisation, deregulation and privatisation lead to, among many other things, the downsizing of government, with important consequences for adult education. There is a general idea that in the current global economic context, the private sector can and should do many of the things that are now done by the state, as the private sector can do them better, and especially more efficiently, than the public sector. The decline in the public funding of social services such as welfare, support of children in poverty, and so on, is a well-known phenomenon. Not so well known is the fact that adult education also is less and less supported by the public sector. Indeed, some remedial adult education activities are being turned over to charitable organisations, or so-called non-governmental organisations (NGOs).

We can highlight many examples of the way adult education is being privatised in the true sense of that word. Let us mention budget cuts in the field of adult education, like the one in Catalonia, where the 1998 adult education budget has been slashed, while at the same time money has been allocated for training unpaid volunteers who will carry out the programmes. One could also mention the growing importance of self-financed continuing education even in universities (Kerka, 1996c), where continuing education becomes a source of profit for both the universities and the professors. More generally, and in a period of cuts in public services, adult education is among the first activities to be out-sourced or privatised. The lucrative portion is being handed over to the private sector, while the non-profitable portion is being 'given' to community organisations, self-help groups, solidarity movements, NGOs, and civil society more generally. As a result, the practice and discourse of an adult education with a social action agenda no longer have an institutional and financial basis. Consequently, community and social change adult education is no longer 'visible' either in graduate programmes (the field from where adult education graduate students came), or in research agendas. It is enough to compare the number of books published by adult education publishing houses on training with those on social action. And where adult educators for social action persist, they are now increasingly being instrumentalised to help solve the problems the state is no longer able or willing to address.

Although Ivan Illich did not anticipate the financial crisis of the state, he nevertheless correctly forecast back in the 1970s that adult education would become an economic commodity that people consume or 'get'. More precisely, he saw 'the conversion of the quality of growing up into the price tag of a professional treatment and the change of the meaning of "knowledge" from a term that designates intimacy, intercourse, and life experience into one that designates professionally packaged products, marketable entitlements, and abstract values' (Illich, 1973a: 39). This is clearly the direction adult education seems to be taking.

Instrumentalisation: learning for earning

The instrumentalisation of adult education is closely connected to the 'economisation' of social life. Learning is seen predominantly in the perspective of its supposed contribution to the economic growth of companies and one's chances to participate in the labour market, or more generally one's ability to survive in the global economy. Because of the pervasiveness of this economic rationality, and the predominance of knowledge and information for the production and distribution of goods and services, the function of adult education is strongly promoted in the fields of labour and vocational education. In workplace training and management development, principles and practices of adult education turn out to be successful means of developing a more skilled workforce, but also for retraining, team-building, collective and collaborative problem-solving, and for all sorts of management development activities. So, from the point of view of the globalised economy, adult education proves an adequate instrument for the purpose of increasing the individual's and the organisation's competitiveness.

There are numerous examples of the way adult education practices have become instrumentalised. Continuing education is increasingly catering to enterprises – a trend illustrated, for example, by the fact that the bulk of EU money for training is channelled through firms and unions, thus turning continuing education into a profitable business. In the USA, government expenditure in the area of workplace literacy, directed at business and industry, amounts to $210 million a year.[1] Moreover, vocational training reforms and schemes are increasingly emphasising the 'competencies, skills, and personal qualities needed to succeed in the high performance workplace' (Lankard, 1995a: 1). Note also that workplace literacy programmes now focus on work/employability skills as advocated by OECD (Ekkehart, 1994; Lichtner, 1992), as well as on vocational performance and accountability.[2]

Adult education discourse changes in exactly the same direction, parallel to the fact that adult education programmes are gradually moving out of educational establishments and becoming more and more part of business schools. More generally, one can observe that business schools now dominate the discourse on learning, as illustrated by the numerous business publications whose titles contain the word 'learning'. But even traditional adult education programmes increasingly use a business-type language to promote themselves. For example, the website of the adult education graduate programmes offered at Teachers College, Columbia University, for the academic year 1997–8 says:

> Adults face new demands for lifelong individual learning in order to flourish in a rapidly changing environment. Leaders in organisations and communities of all types have also taken fresh interest in adult and organisational learning in order to draw effectively on the resources of the entire institution in the search for new solutions to increasingly complex problems. The adult education graduate program, which offered the first degree in this field in the United States, prepares professionals who lead, design, implement, and evaluate programs that are based on principles of Adult and Organisational Learning. (www.tc.columbia.edu/depts)

More generally, one can observe a general shift in European adult education discourse, which now aims to make people fit for the market, like the EU Socrates and Leonardo programmes (see www.eurydice.org/). This trend is particularly evident in Central Europe's so-called 'emerging market societies' (Jelenc, 1995). In the context of the 'information society', adult education also becomes seen as a compensatory activity for the 'information have-nots' (Kerka, 1996a) – not to mention the discourse on the 'learning society' and 'knowledge society' (European Union, 1995; US Department of Labor, 1991; EU Commission, 1997), which implies that everybody has to have some basic knowledge in order to be part of society, and to keep up with its rapidly changing pace. Finally, let us mention the discourse on the so-called 'learning organisation', on the 'new ways of learning in the workplace' (Lankard, 1995b), and on 'workplace literacy' (Imel, 1995), implying that it is now every learner's duty to help the organisation he or she works for to learn.

In this perspective, it is obvious that the instrumental rationality which dominates the market and the organisation of labour has now also become adult education's dominant frame of reference. Knowledge and skills are now measured with respect to their practical usefulness to cope with the 'given' conditions of daily life. Moreover, the concept of qualification is no longer restricted to the area of labour-orientated training and education, but has become a universal paradigm for cultural development as well (Kade, 1988). Finally, note the shift in terminology towards an increasingly instrumental perspective, whereby adult education has become 'client-centred' and 'market-orientated', 'now offering diversified and tailor-made products'.

Conclusion

Where is adult education going? Where is it being driven to? In this chapter we have seen that the 'learning language' has become widespread in society and its organisations. This has contributed significantly to the fact that adult education has folded itself more and more into the practices and discourse of the larger society, a practice and a discourse shaped in particular by the market, competitiveness and survival. But not only has the societal context changed to no longer pursuing an ideal of human development, to which adult education was to contribute; adult education has become reactive as it becomes instrumentalised and privatised. Adult education is now a product of society much more than it is a driving force of its transformation. It is a product, because adult education, like every other institution, is bound to the developments and discourses of the social context in which it is situated.

And in the current context, instrumental and economic rationality is as pervasive as the individualisation of life-courses and the privatised responsibility to construct meaningful biographies.

In short, adult education has substituted the emancipatory discourse of the 'common good' and the politically inspired model of collective welfare with a discourse on individual self-actualisation and the rationality of the market – that is, competitiveness. As a result of its 'successful' evolution, adult education now faces a paradoxical situation. On the one hand, its importance in social and personal life, and thus its potential, are more prominent than ever. On the other, adult education has lost its privileged status as a semi-autonomous social institution responsible for the organisation of adult learning. It has become one among many provisions in the 'cultural market' of society, and is thus subjected to the same competitive pressures and conditions of supply and demand that apply to other provisions in this market.

In Chapter 9 we will sketch out what are – regrettably – the most probable three scenarios of the adult education future. We will challenge these scenarios – true dead end roads in our view – from the perspective of a renewed social responsibility scenario, which we will outline in Part III.

Notes

1. See Cunningham, who also says that adult education has become increasingly complicitous with private industry and business, in *Let's Get Real: A Critical Look at the Practice of Adult Education*. Paper available online at http://www.nlu/nl.edu/ace/Resources/Documents/Cunningham. html.
2. See Commission on the Skills of the American Workforce, *America's Choice: High Skills or Low Wages?* (Rochester, NY: National Center on Education and the Economy, 1990).

Chapter 9

Conclusion: Dead End
or Social Responsibility?

Adult education seems to have accepted, for the most part, the trends towards turbo-capitalism, erosion of the state, and post-modernism, which transform it into a privatised and instru-mentalised activity. In this conclusion, we will briefly outline what the probable outcomes of this evolution will be by highlighting, in particular, three main scenarios for the future of adult education as we see them. However, there is a fourth possible alternative scenario, which we will call the 'social ecological responsibility scenario'; this will be developed in Part III.

On the basis of the societal trends outlined in Chapter 7 and the trends in adult education presented in Chapter 8, we can currently identify three probable scenarios for adult education practice and discourse. These scenarios are not mutually exclu-sive, and might actually occur simultaneously. We call them re-spectively 'the business school scenario', 'the risk group scenario', and 'the leisure society scenario' (see Wildemeersch, Finger and Jansen, 1997).

The *business school scenario* is a very probable outcome of the trends outlined above. As we have said, the privatisation and instrumentalisation of adult education are about to lead to a situ-ation where adult education principles and practices are being incorporated into business training and development efforts. There is already a strong tradition in this area of course, stemming from pragmatic adult education in the case of collective and collabora-tive problem-solving. The newly emerging concept of the learning organisation, for example, allows these various adult education efforts to be integrated into a single coherent framework, so that adult education is now being instrumentalised for the purpose of corporate development and growth. Moreover, at management level one can find more individualistic approaches to adult learning, couched, for example, in terms of 'leadership development'. It is obvious that the business community is about to recuperate the key principles of adult education and incorporate them into an organisational and corporate development framework. Needless to say, in this scenario adult education would lose its very identity, and disappear as a special field and as an institution of social practice and change. Business schools, according to this scenario, will replace adult education programmes in universities.

The *risk group scenario* is another probable outcome of the current evolution in the field of adult education. This scenario might even occur in parallel to the previous one. In this scenario, adult education would be assigned special risk groups of the current turbo-capitalism – those who are unable to fit into the accelerating industrial development process, such as the growing numbers of the unemployed, immigrants, young people, and perhaps women. All these and other risk groups would have to be 'up-skilled' and made fit for turbo-capitalism. Although in this scenario adult education might not actually disappear as a discipline, and might perhaps even benefit from increased finances and institutional support, there would be a ghettoisation of the field. In other words, adult education would become a sort of repair activity to keep turbo-capitalism on track. Also, it is by no means clear whether adult education as such would remain a coherent undertaking. One can easily imagine that adult education – and especially those who offer private adult education – would specialise in particular risk groups, and thus further fragment the field. And this risk group scenario might not be particularly interesting from a theoretical perspective either: it would be unlikely to lead to intellectual innovation in our field, as it would either focus on purely technical skills, or refer to a traditional Marxist vocabulary in order to 'liberate the oppressed'.

The *leisure society scenario* is a third possible outcome of the trends described above. This scenario, which was quite prominent during the 1970s, and gave rise to a whole field of continuing education, might well persist. There are particular groups of people in today's society, even in the current economic crisis, who define learning in terms of leisure – particularly the elderly. Leisure society type activities might also be of interest to particularly privileged social classes, if one considers, for example, adult education leisure-type offerings such as interior decoration, gourmet food preparation, or painting on silk. Although this might constitute a particular niche for adult education, it would never satisfactorily define the field, and would again contribute to its ghettoisation and isolation. Also, from an intellectual point of view, the leisure society scenario would not be particularly challenging – it was not challenging back in the 1970s.

In all three scenarios, adult learning would turn into a simple tool, either promoting turbo-capitalism or repairing its most blatant negative effects. Yet turbo-capitalism will inevitably come to an end, given in particular the ecological limits to economic globalisation, as highlighted in the vicious circle outlined in Chapter 7. An adult education which seeks to reconnect to its original agenda of social action and social change will no longer put adult learning in the service of further industrial development but, rather, in the service of 'learning our way out' of the dead end to which industrial development inevitably leads. In the light of this reality, we propose an alternative '*social ecological responsibility scenario*'. This is obviously the most challenging and intellectually most stimulating scenario, in which adult education will have to redefine its identity in light of today's new societal challenges without abandoning its commitment to social change and social action. In our view, this will be a scenario of participatory democracy, citizens' reassumption of responsibility, community building and empowerment. We can already see trends towards such a social responsibility scenario, especially in developing countries, although there is a constant threat of instrumentalising such adult education practices for the purpose of furthering industrial development. On a conceptual level, we propose the concept of 'Learning Our Way Out' (Finger et al., 1995; Milbrath, 1989) in order to capture this idea of collectively addressing the trends outlined above while simultaneously building sustainable communities and societies in a social action perspective. Learning our way out, both in practice and in theory, will be the subject of Part III.

Part III

Possible Ways Out

In Part II, we saw the challenges of learning our way out, both for industrial civilisation and for adult education. Adult education, in its pursuit of humanising development, seems to have abandoned its original agenda of social action and change. Following the path of development, it appears to have uncoupled itself from a social justice and equity agenda; or, to put it better, social justice and equity can probably no longer be sought within the development path, which, as our evidence shows, has clearly become counterproductive.

So we find adult education, like industrial civilisation, at a crossroads: should it continue to travel the path of development, and accompany the world to a dead end? Or should adult education, rather, abandon the development highways, where it will almost certainly make money yet lose its soul, and go back to its original agenda of social action and change? If the answer to the latter question is yes, as we maintain, adult education has no choice but to face the challenges of learning our way out and building a sustainable society. This would be its social (and ecological) responsibility scenario.

In this last section of our book, we will discuss the theory and praxis of learning our way out. In Chapter 10 we will thus conceptualise learning our way out on a theoretical level, linking it to the original adult education social action agenda. In Chapter 11, we will highlight and discuss what we consider examples of learning our way out – basically, examples of collectively building sustainable communities. This discussion of both the theory and the practice of learning our way out will lead us directly to the Conclusion, where we will assess the challenges of our way out for adult education as a field.

Chapter 10

The Theory of Learning Our Way Out

So far, we have basically argued why there is an urgent need to learn our way out. We have also shown that there is, in fact, no alternative. However, we have not, until now, discussed how such learning can be conceptualised and theorised; that is the purpose of this chapter.

Our theory of learning our way out takes its point of departure in both the historical strengths of adult education and the vicious circle identified above. Each, in our view, defines one of the dimensions of learning our way out. The first dimension – which characterises, so to speak, the essence of adult education thinking – involves *control of the learning process*. It ranges from the extreme of 'no control by the learner' over his or her learning process (top-down instruction) to the other extreme of 'total control by the learner' (bottom-up learning). The second dimension involves the *dynamics of industrial development* itself. This dimension ranges from the extreme of 'unconditional pursuit of industrial development' (thus accelerating the vicious circle) to the other extreme of 'de-industrialisation' (thus slowing down the vicious circle). Learning our way out, consequently, is where de-industrialisation combines with people's control over their own learning processes, as shown in Figure 10.1.

In this chapter we will review each of the two dimensions. We will show how the first dimension is constitutive of adult education's very epistemological identity, then argue why the second dimension gives us a clear sense of direction for slowing down the

Figure 10.1   The territory of learning our way out

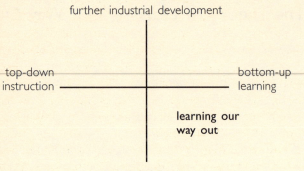

further industrial development

top-down
instruction

bottom-up
learning

learning our
way out

de-industrialisation

vicious circle. Finally, we will discuss the territory of learning our way out, and integrate the two dimensions.

The adult education dimension to learning our way out

The tension between top-down instruction and bottom-up learning is well known to adult educators. One can say that this tension is constitutive of the very essence of the field of adult education. Indeed, this tension – or, rather, this opposition – cuts across all the three schools of thought we presented in Part I. It can be found in the pragmatic school of thought – for example, when Jarvis opposes 'learning from above' to 'learning from below'. Learning from below is, of course, identical to experiential learning. The same opposition is made in the humanistic school of thought – for example by Knowles, when he opposes 'pedagogy' to 'andragogy'. But it is made most obviously by the Marxist school of thought – for example, when Freire opposes 'indoctrination and banking education' to 'conscientisation and liberatory education'. In other words, the very identity of adult education is about learning 'from below' grounded on experience and aiming at liberation. Adult education is about 'learning from and by the people'. Abandoning this credo means abandoning the very identity of the field.

It is probably fair to say, however, that in all three schools of thought, and for most adult educators, this opposition is above all a *political*, not an epistemological one. This can be explained by the fact that the very roots of adult education are in the labour movement, as well as by the fact that adult education has been significantly shaped by the social movement environment of the 1960s and 1970s. The political nature of this opposition is of course most obvious in the Marxist or radical tradition, where the purpose of adult education is the liberation from oppression. But this political agenda also underpins the distinction between pedagogy and andragogy, as well as Jarvis's attempt to redefine experiential learning in political terms. Unfortunately, adult education has not gone much beyond this political definition of its identity; this becomes a problem in the kind of depoliticised environment that exists today, and certainly explains some of adult education's current identity problems.

One therefore has to go back to Ivan Illich to uncover two additional aspects of adult education's defining tension or opposition: an *epistemological* aspect and an *institutional* aspect. Illich defines adult education simultaneously as an epistemological, an institutional, and a political alternative to conventional education. For him, adult education – or rather learning – is the opposite of (expert) knowledge manufactured and crafted *for* the people. Such knowledge is not only exterior to people's experiences and needs, but constitutes a professionally packaged product and a marketable entitlement. Moreover, such knowledge is addictive and manipulative: this type of disembodied knowledge always calls for more of the same – that is, more education as people increasingly become disempowered and incapable of learning by themselves. It also calls for corresponding institutions and technologies in order to sustain a steady supply. And since the means for acquiring knowledge are scarce or are assumed to be scarce – that is, only in the hands and heads of the experts and their institutions – education becomes an economic commodity that one consumes or 'gets' (Illich, 1996).

For Illich, therefore, adult education – or, rather, adult learning – is a tool for understanding the world in which one lives, so that one can make appropriate decisions about how to live in it. Furthermore, it is a tool for understanding how to relate to ourselves, to others and to our environment, and how to act accordingly and responsibly. Such understanding can come only from 'below' – from people's active engagement in their own learning process. Learning is therefore ultimately done *by* the people – and not for them – and it entails free and abundant access to tools for learning. In short, as formulated by Illich, such learning means (1) taking responsibility for one's own learning process (the political dimension); (2) having unrestricted access to learning tools (the institutional dimension); and (3) addressing issues which pertain to people's aspirations and lives (the epistemological dimension). With Illich, adult learning is distinguished from conventional education on all three dimensions, not only on the political dimension. Finally we should also mention the contribution of Participatory Action Research (PAR), which perhaps best summarises all three aspects by opposing the transmission of 'exogenous knowledge' to the creation of 'endogenous knowledge'. Endogenous knowledge creation by and for the people, it is said (and we agree), is the very essence of adult education. Table 10.1 summarises this first dimension to learning our way out.

The developmental dimension to learning our way out

Our theory of learning our way out contains two dimensions: an adult education and a developmental dimension. If the adult education dimension is derived from an analysis of what the field of adult education is all about (see Part I), the developmental dimension results from our analysis of the process of industrial development (see Part II). To recall: in Chapter 7 we identified four different problems resulting from industrial development: the replacement of development by trade; the erosion of the state, which is no longer capable of managing and controlling the development process; postmodernism, or the fragmentation and individualisation of values; and ecological degradation. These problems, however, are simply a manifestation, the last stage of a long-term historical process whose roots can be traced back to the

Table 10.1 The adult education dimension to learning our way out

Exogenous knowledge transmission	Endogenous knowledge creation
1. Education as a tool of the system	Learning as a people's tool (political dimension)
2. Education for all	Learning by all (institutional dimension)
3. Education about the world	Learning from the world (epistemological dimension)

origins of Western civilisation. While these four problems or manifestations in themselves are already overwhelming, especially combined with one another (the 'vicious circle'), many people still believe that they have a technological solution. In other words, many people still believe that they can be addressed without involving a profound social learning process.

It is therefore only when we see these four problems as manifestations of a *long-term historical process* that the idea of learning a way out of such a powerful process becomes inescapable. One can identify several historical stages leading up to today's dead end of industrial civilisation. The most significant are Judaeo-Christianity, colonialism, the Scientific Revolution, the emergence of the state, the Industrial Revolution and, most recently, wars (two world wars plus the Cold War). Judeo-Christianity can be seen as responsible for a certain attitude of domination vis-à-vis nature, which then gave the impetus and the justification for its subservience to human desires (White, 1967; Amery, 1972). Colonialism marks the geographical extension of this Judaeo-Christian world-view to the rest of the planet (Landes, 1969); while the Scientific Revolution puts the idea of conquest and expansion on to rational grounds by replacing God with man-made science (Grinevald, 1975). With the French Revolution arises the modern nation-state, which from then on plays a key role in the expansion of the West, contributing to, among other things, the systematic rationalisation of society with the individual as its centrepiece (Giddens, 1984; Janicaud,

1985). The Industrial Revolution, then, translates the scientific progress achieved, especially in mechanics, into physical power, and thus adds a new power dimension to the conquest of the West, while at the same time opening up a new and unprecedented dimension of ecological destruction (Cottrell, 1955). This process of industrial development is finally significantly accelerated thanks to the two world wars, but also to the Cold War. Thanks to the army and its force, this model of development has by now spread worldwide (Clarke, 1971; Galbraith, 1969; McNeill, 1982), to the point where no alternative is any longer imaginable.

This long-term historical process of industrial development contains a series of at least five underlying components. At each stage of its development each of these components is further strengthened. Table 10.2 lists these components and, by so doing, defines more clearly the developmental dimension to learning our way out.

The theoretical territory of learning our way out

Having defined both dimensions of learning our way out more clearly, we can now locate the theoretical territory where learning our way out is, in our view, to occur: on the endogenous side of the adult education dimension and the de-industrialisation side of the developmental dimension. Let us briefly clarify both sides separately, before linking them.

Striving to create endogenous knowledge is a permanent struggle. There is a constant pressure of 'conversion of the quality of growing up into the price tag of a professional treatment and the change of the meaning of knowledge from a term that designates intimacy, intercourse and life experience into one that designates professionally packaged products, marketable entitlements, and abstract values' (Illich, 1973a: 39). That is why adult education should constantly 'break up and/or transform the present power monopoly of science and culture exercised by elitist, oppressive groups' (Fals-Borda and Rahman, 1991: 30). Against the constant and pressing need for expert knowledge to catch up with the industrial development future, endogenous knowledge proposes to 'celebrate the awareness' of the social construction of knowledge and science, and to take on the responsibility to 'create'

Table 10.2   The developmental dimension to learning our way out

---

The process of industrial development

1. Growing rationalisation, paralleled by growing irrationalism (Freud, 1961).
2. Growing homogenisation of culture and nature (Latouche, 1989; Shiva, 1993).
3. Colonisation and expansion (Trainer, 1989).
4. Bio-physical degradation (Georgescu-Roegen, 1971).
5. Individualisation – that is, sociocultural degradation (Lipovetsky, 1983).

---

alternative futures. Therefore, from a learning-our-way-out perspective, adult education should reject both the 'institutionalisation of adult education needs' and the process of 'professionalisation'. In other words, it should stand up against all sorts of experts and their knowledge, supposedly legitimised by science and rationality.

In contrast, adult education from a learning-our-way-out perspective proposes 'endogenous/people's knowledge' – that is, the activation of diverse and collective learning tools for understanding the world in which people live in order that they can make decisions about how to live in it. These are tools for understanding how we relate to ourselves, to others, and to the environment, and act accordingly and responsibly. The endogenous side of the adult education dimension tells us that knowledge comes from below, is created by people, and entails free and abundant access to tools for learning.

Adult education has long considered that such 'endogenous' learning is sufficient for a definition of the specificity of the field. But given how such learning has been instrumentalised for further industrial development (see Chapter 8), this is, of course, no longer the case. That is precisely why a second dimension – the developmental dimension – is equally important when it comes not only to defining learning our way out but, moreover, to re-creating a social action identity for adult education in the context of the vicious circle of industrial development.

Learning our way out is therefore also located on the *de-industrialisation* side of the developmental dimension. Learning our way out should, by definition, be critical of industrial development, and see it as a root cause of today's ecological and sociocultural crisis – as the source of the dynamics of the vicious circle whose consequences we highlighted in Chapter 7. Consequently, de-industrialisation – the slowing down of the industrial development process in all its five aspects identified above – should constitute the backdrop against which successful learning our way out should be measured. In other words, learning our way out, in its contribution to de-industrialisation, should simultaneously foster de-rationalisation as a remedy for growing rationalisation, and irrationalism, the diversity of culture and nature, de-colonisation, bio-physical rehabilitation, and community development as remedies for growing individualism and sociocultural fragmentation.

From this de-industrialisation perspective, learning our way out uses social ecology as the alternative to industrial development (Bookchin, 1991; Biehl, 1997). Without going into great detail here, let us simply state that learning our way out in its de-industrialisation dimension pertains simultaneously to the reconstruction of human, social and ecological identity and integrity, by fostering a creative biographic adventure that resists administration and institutional arrangements, and by promoting a collectively and permanently self-invented future based on conviviality within nature and among cultures.

Conclusion: towards an integration of the adult education and the developmental dimensions

The territory of learning our way out is thus constituted by the combination of endogenous learning with the perspective of de-industrialisation. In this conclusion, we would like to show how and where these two dimensions are best integrated. In order to do this, we must briefly come back to the industrial development process, and especially to its latest stage, characterised by turbo-capitalism, the erosion of the state, postmodernism and the vicious circle. This last stage can best be captured by a growing tension between the 'global' and the 'local', as illustrated in Figure 10.2.

Indeed, in its latest stage, industrial development seems increasingly to separate the global and the local, while further eroding

Figure 10.2 The growing tension between the global and the local

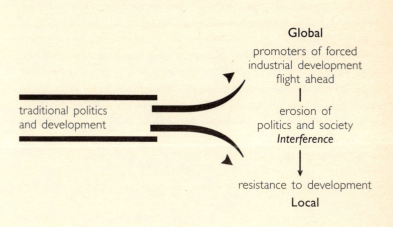

what held them together: the nation-state, and society more generally. Everything that is lucrative and mobile seems to globalise, while on the other hand the negative social and ecological consequences of this flight ahead tend to localise. Promoters of further industrial development, of course, have an interest in its acceleration, while local communities and the majority of people more generally have now clearly become the victims of this process. As a result, they tend to resist globalisation, yet their resistance remains as fragmented as their lives and their communities.

On the basis of this analysis, it is easy to understand that learning our way out, which combines both endogenous knowledge creation and the perspective of de-industrialisation, is above all at the *local* level. Indeed, it is at the local level that resistance to the industrial development process, especially its latest stage of globalised turbo-capitalism, still can be found. Such resistance stems essentially from those who are the direct victims of accelerated industrial development. It is these people who feel the social, the ecological, and the cultural consequences of industrial development most directly and hardest. Finally, as we will show in Chapter 11, it is at this local level that concrete steps and actions towards learning our way out have already been taken, and must be further developed.

This is not to say, however, that the local is the alternative to the global. Rather, learning our way out takes its *point of departure* at the local level, with living people who feel the destructive consequences of industrial development directly. It is these people who, cognisant of the overall dynamics and global dimension of industrial development, and through endogenous knowledge creation, still have the ability to develop alternatives capable of slowing down the vicious circle. At the same time, they can reconstruct some sort of personal, social, cultural and ecological integrity, as we will now show.

Chapter 11

Ways Out: The Practice

This chapter is built around a series of examples of what we consider to be practices of learning our way out – practices where people actively and collectively challenge the entirety, or some aspects, of industrial development, and build alternatives. Generally, these practices relate to the negative consequences industrial development has had on them, on their communities, and on their livelihoods. We focus especially on these practices, which are grounded locally, since we believe that ultimately all alternatives must have local roots. In highlighting and analysing such practices of learning our way out, we will look particularly at where learning plays a role. In other words, we seek to identify how learning, especially collective learning, is organised and practised, who participates in such learning, and its outcomes. Ultimately, our objective is to improve on the theory of learning our way out outlined in Chapter 10.

The structure of this chapter is as follows: we will first recall today's main challenges as we presented them in Chapter 6, and from there derive what these challenges mean for learning. We will therefore distinguish between learning-our-way-out challenges and practices addressing economic, political, cultural and ecological issues. This will lead us to analyse these practices, and so derive the three main steps of learning-our-way-out theory.

Summary of challenges to learning our way out

Adult education's history – at least up to the 1970s – is one of social justice, equity and democracy. But, as we have seen, social justice, equity and democracy are inseparably linked to the project of development. However, Illich, among others, has clearly highlighted how development has become counterproductive and distorted, and in Chapter 7 we examined the different forms such distortions now take in the areas of economics, politics, culture and ecology. Industrial development, rather than leading to human development, has now become distorted into trade and other forms of turbo- and casino capitalism, to such a point that one can no longer expect social and societal benefits from this evolution. The same can be said of ecological issues, where 'development' has basically taken the form of pillage of natural resources on the one hand, and waste production leading to accelerated ecological destruction on the other. And there are also political counterproductivities, as industrial development no longer leads to more democratic political structures but, rather, to the instrumentalisation and hijacking of the state by private interests. And culturally, it has become clear that further development leads to the erosion of any coherent framework, while fostering local and fundamentalist reactions. In short, social justice, equity and democracy can no longer be said to result from further development, but must now be sought outside the project of so-called development.

Learning our way out, in this context, therefore means three things. First, it means becoming *aware* of the fact that development and social justice are no longer connected, or even inversely related – becoming aware of the counterproductivities of the current development track. Second, learning our way out means finding ways and means to slow down this ever-accelerating vicious circle. This is essentially a process of *conceptual clarification*. Third, learning our way out means developing *alternatives* outside this very process, simultaneously on economic, ecological, political and cultural levels. Let us now address each of these four levels separately.

Learning our way out of turbo-capitalism

The first counterproductivity, as identified in Chapter 7, is without doubt the trend, on the economic level, from development to 'free trade' – to what has become called 'turbo-capitalism' and the 'casino economy'. By opening up markets and aspiring to create one single global economy, this trend can best be characterised by the concept of '*de-localisation*'. De-localisation, in fact, means three things: first, the de-localisation of *extraction, production* and *consumption*. What people need in order to live is less and less related to where they actually live. The natural resources required to sustain an increasingly global economy have to be extracted further and further away from where they are needed, often with disastrous environmental consequences, as well as consequences for the indigenous peoples who happen to live in these remote areas. Also, production and consumption of industrial goods are less and less related – not to mention the fact that products, including food, are assembled or processed at numerous places around the globe, and shipped to the consumer, who also has less and less of a relationship with his or her immediate environment.

Second, de-localisation means the creation of a parallel and increasingly *artificial economy*, which goes hand in hand, of course, with the globalisation of extraction, production and consumption. We are thinking here in particular of the creation of financial markets, but also of newly created artefacts such as, for example, 'pollution permits', which are more or less disconnected from the 'real' economy as people experience it in their lives. This parallel and purely artificial economy operates mainly on perception and hearsay, and is therefore essentially speculative in nature, yet it has disastrous consequences for 'real' people with 'real' lives (Strange, 1986).

Finally, de-localisation means *uprooting* – that is, destroying the very roots of these peoples and communities who still have a connection to local reality. Turbo-capitalism does indeed destroy social fabric and livelihoods – not only for people who happen to live on land to be mined or on forests to be cleared, but also for people whose jobs are being moved to lower-wage countries. Moreover, livelihoods are being destroyed because modern consumption patterns no longer relate people to each other, but now relate them instead directly to their supposedly need-fulfilling providers, be they supermarkets or government agencies. Needless to say, this entire process of de-localisation in all three dimensions enhances injustice and inequity both locally and globally.

Learning our way out, in this context, occurs in three separate steps: awareness-raising, conceptual clarification, and the development of alternatives from the bottom up. The very first step in the process of learning our way out implies that individuals and communities become *aware* of the destructive dynamics of turbo-capitalism. Of course, we are not naïve, and therefore do not think that such an awareness can result from studying books and analysing websites prior to and separately from any sort of practice – that is, social action which would seek to change the situation at hand. Nevertheless, it is obvious that without a minimum of awareness such social action will never even get started. Awareness of the destructive impacts of turbo-capitalism on peoples, communities and livelihoods, however, is not enough, and such awareness alone is probably even counterproductive, as it might lead to cynicism, a phenomenon identified elsewhere (Finger, 1994). Therefore, a second step in learning our way out will necessarily have to consist of what we call *conceptual clarification*. In an intellectual context where things are increasingly, and often purposely, confused (see section below, 'Learning our way out of postmodernism'), it is imperative to have a clear understanding of the dynamics and the main underlying and driving forces of turbo-capitalism. Of course, one would have to go beyond a simple analysis of 'de-localisation' as outlined above, yet it is crucial to be fully aware of the causes, driving forces and various dimensions of these trends, which we think will ultimately destroy (local) livelihoods – that is, the very source where an alternative could still emerge. The third step, therefore, in learning our way out is the development of such *alternatives* to turbo-capitalism from the bottom up, and in a participatory way, along adult education lines. Against the background of an overall awareness of the consequences of turbo-capitalism for livelihoods and peoples and with a clear understanding of the dynamics and the different dimensions of turbo-capitalism, the development of such alternatives can take place in a more coherent manner. Indeed, learning our way out, here, means collectively developing alternatives to turbo-capitalism by rebuilding local livelihoods and developing ways and means not only of sustaining them, but of extending them horizontally and vertically. Let us briefly mention here some of the examples of such alternatives to turbo-capitalism as they are currently emerging: the 'fair trade' movement, micro-lending and local currencies.

'Fair trade' is a movement whereby, thanks to new technologies of communication, local and often indigenous producers in developing countries are being linked to consumers in the North, reducing some of the profit-making intermediaries in the process. The movement, which started in the Netherlands in 1959, has now spread worldwide, and today includes over a hundred non-governmental organisations in the United States alone.[1] Micro-lending is based on the assumption that credit, no matter how small, can help poor individuals and collectives who have no access to traditional credit to become self-employed. The original reference here is the so-called Grameen Bank, founded in 1974 in Bangladesh by Muhammad Yunus (Yunus et al., 1997).[2] But micro-lending is part of a larger movement towards alternative – that is, more social and more human – economies, and more sustainable consumption patterns.[3] The development of so-called local, community or ethical currencies, sometimes also called 'green money', goes back to anarchist experiences in the early 1930s (Guillen, 1993); entire communities seek to extract themselves from the dominant currency system and create a true alternative:

> My dream is to create a new global currency, an ethical currency consciously designed to encourage generosity and abundance, build community, restore the Earth, and meet human basic needs. This currency would depend upon the networking of a vibrant local, national, and international local currency movement and the creation of a chaordic organisation, which has no head, and works by cooperative, independent agreement.... 'backed by renewable energy and products ... as opposed to currency backed by gold or silver'. (Brouillet, 1997: 122)

Existing examples of such local currencies are LETS (Local Exchange Trading Systems),[4] BREAD (Berkeley Region Exchange and Development) programme,[5] or the Ithaca NY HOURS.[6] Further along this anarchist road, one finds 'no-money' urban farming systems, such as the 'Community-supported chemical-free agricultural farms' (CSAs),[7] or the Urban Agriculture Network of the New York City Urban Gardens. We think that especially the latter experiences of local currencies and autonomous farming systems have the potential for learning our way out of turbo-capitalism, by breaking the development paradigm and inventing economies outside the current market.

Although adult education is rarely directly involved, as a discipline, in developing alternatives to turbo-capitalism, there are nevertheless some examples where adult education practices do play an active role. Take the Highlander Economics Education Program, whose goal is to bring together individuals from diverse communities so that they can analyse their problems collectively, share ideas, learn from each other's experiences, and develop action plans which can then be implemented in their own communities. Some of these groups have served as catalysts for larger initiatives, such as the Coalition for Jobs and the Environment, which has led to the Clinch Powell Sustainable Development Forum (of south-western Virginia and upper-east Tennessee). The Forum helps communities to meet their needs, establish ecologically responsible businesses, promote sustainable livelihoods, and sustain local resources. Since 1993 it has also created the Highlands Bio-Produce Network, Ecolog, and alternative forestry and wood products companies, several micro-enterprises, and helped in the development of a nature tourism plan (Williams, 1997).

Learning our way out of eroding politics

The second counterproductivity identified in Chapter 7 relates to the erosion of traditional politics. Now, this is not necessarily a bad thing, even though what comes after might be worse. One can distinguish two phases in this process of erosion of traditional politics. First, the *privatisation* of state or public functions. The most lucrative of these functions – such as telecommunications, postal, and many other public services – are being handed over to the private sector, while many non-lucrative functions are being transferred to non-governmental organisations. This process, of course, is paralleled by a loss of democratic control over key political decisions pertaining to these functions. Second, what remains with the state – mainly security, police, judiciary and policy advice functions – is *instrumentalised* by transnational corporations and other global actors (Finger, 1998). So the few democratic mechanisms left are clearly distorted to serve global – that is, commercial – interests. And non-governmental organisations, which have taken over vital repair functions for the state, often at a local level, are equally in danger of being instrumentalised for purposes of social engineering and control of the very people whom they should serve. At the same time, political parties, traditionally a means for articulating citizens' preferences within some sort of coherent ideological framework, are now also becoming instrumentalised by those commercial interests which want to use the state for their own purposes. Finally, in this context of eroding politics, traditional political participation, including voting and electing, has become distorted to such a point that it strengthens precisely those actors whose aim it is to instrumentalise and ultimately do away with 'democracy' and 'participation'. In other words, the erosion of traditional politics requires the development of alternative forms of political and social action.

Learning our way out, in this (political) context, again occurs in three steps: awareness, conceptual clarification, and the development of alternatives. The first step, as in the case of turbo-capitalism, is of course to become aware of the distorted nature of politics and political participation. In most cases, such awareness will result from a critical reflection upon political actions and a corresponding analysis of the failure of such actions. But of course, such awareness will not be enough. Rather, a conceptual clarification will be needed if we are to understand the root causes of the distortion of traditional politics, as well as the dynamics of mainly economic globalisation, which are currently leading to the instrumentalisation of politics for the purpose of further industrial development and profit. Finally, such a conceptual clarification will help us to define what kind of political actions are likely to lead to social change today without being distorted or instrumentalised. On the basis of such conceptual clarification, learning our way out will mean, in a third step, developing concrete alternatives to traditional political action such as voting and electing, and perhaps even to traditional social movements. Such alternatives will necessarily be developed from the bottom up and in a participatory way, and probably also outside the traditional political system (state). In other words, learning our way out means redefining politics in the age of an instrumentalised polity.

Examples of such learning our way out are mainly limited, at the present time, to awareness-raising and conceptual clarification, and many organisations actively contribute to this, especially at the international level. Let us mention here the 'International Forum on Globalization' (IFG),[8] the 'People Centered Development Forum' of David Korten (1984, 1990, 1996, 1997, 1999),[9] the Institute for Policy Studies,[10] the Transnational Institute[11] (George, 1988, 1992, 1994, 1999; George and Sabelli, 1997), the Research Foundation for Science, Technology and Natural Resource Policy[12] (Shiva, 1990, 1991, 1992, 1993, 1997, 1999), the Third World Network,[13] and the teams publishing the *Ecologist*[14] and the *Multinational Monitor*.[15] At the national level, conceptual clarification, let alone alternatives to eroding politics, are even harder to come by. Traditionally, such conceptual and practical alternatives took the form of so-called 'social movements' and corresponding literature (Boggs, 1986; Rammstedt, 1978; Raschke 1985; Touraine, 1982), and later the form of 'new social movements' and corresponding literature (Brand, 1982; Wignaraja, 1993; Riechmann and Fernández-Buey, 1994). This conceptualisation and corresponding practice does have serious flaws, however, as old and new social movements are essentially seen in terms of opposition to an otherwise coherent and unitary state (see the debate in Finger, 1989; Welton, 1993). It is therefore, and not surprisingly, at the local and municipal level that alternative practices to traditional politics, as well as corresponding conceptualisation, are most advanced. We can refer here to the participatory development literature in the case of developing countries (Burkey, 1993), and in the case of industrialised countries to the practical work and the intellectual contributions of the Highlander Research and Education Center[16] (Gaventa, 1988; Gaventa and Lewis, 1991), as well as of the libertarian municipalist movement[17] (Bookchin, 1991; Biehl and Bookchin, 1998). More generally, alternatives to traditional politics are found in the anarchist tradition, rather than in the traditional Left or the New Left, as the Left remains very state-centric. Unfortunately, adult education – with the exception of Illich – has never linked up with anarchism, either in theory or in practice. This alliance, however, will have to be considered if the political dimension of learning our way out is further conceptualised (Goodway, 1989; anarchist websites[18]).

Learning our way out of postmodernism

The third counterproductivity, as we saw in Chapter 7, is the distortion of modernism into postmodernism. Again, the erosion of modernism, with its emphasis on rationality, is not necessarily a bad thing, though what comes after might be worse. Indeed, postmodernism is a trend towards intellectual incoherence and a social trend towards the fragmentation of social and individual life – trends which are not unrelated to economic and cultural globalisation (Featherstone, Lash and Robertson, 1995; Bauman, 1998), new – especially global – communications technologies (Turkle, 1995), and the so-called 'culture industry' (Best and Kellner, 1997). Postmodern *fragmentation* means that social and cultural life splits into innumerable pieces of a puzzle which no longer fit together. As a result, societies and communities are degraded, and processes of turbo-capitalism and political erosion accelerate. Postmodernism even gives rise to a new 'postmodern person' characterised as 'an open system with multiple communities, flowing identities, and movable boundaries' (Anderson, 1997: xii). It is difficult to see how communities and societies can be built with such individuals, let alone social change achieved. On an intellectual level, postmodernism means above all *incoherence*, but also *non-contradiction*. In a postmodern world of intellectuals it is now no longer possible to think in terms of opposition or contradiction, as one can think one thing and its opposite simultaneously. Again, it will be difficult, in such a world, to think in terms of political, social and cultural projects, or in terms of opposing the existing order. Opposition becomes just another cultural expression, an 'acting out' of some of the fragments of an individual's identity.

Learning our way out, in this context of cultural and social fragmentation and intellectual incoherence, again occurs in three steps: awareness, conceptual clarification, and developing alternatives. In the first step, individuals and communities have to become aware of the psychologically, socially and culturally destructive nature of postmodernism. It is obvious that such an awareness cannot result from zapping the televison remote control, nor from navigating on the Web. Rather, such awareness is most probably related to social activism and political engagement with and for real people. The second step consists of conceptual clarification. This step is particularly relevant in postmodernism, where things are deliberately confused and governed by pictures and emotions rather than clear and critical thinking. Conceptual clarification, in this context, therefore means the development of projects and visions which take postmodern reality into account, and do not simply re-actualise past projects, most of which today have become discredited and reduced to 'narratives' anyway. In addition, such visions will have to pertain to social change – that is, ultimately, to a better society. Moreover, according to adult learning principles, such visions and projects will have to be developed by the people in a participatory manner, No longer is it possible to impose such visions upon people from the top down, no matter how good they are. Developing such visions collectively and from the bottom up is an alternative to a fragmented social and individual life. The challenge here, however, is to build such alternatives in a progressive and social change perspective, and not in a regressive perspective, as many individuals today are basically looking for (individual) meaning and collective security.

Examples of learning our way out of postmodernism today relate mainly to conceptual clarification and, at times, to the search for alternatives. Such conceptual clarification can be found especially in some of the new social movement literature. Certain feminist ideas such as 'the personal is political' or 'politics in the first person' capture the new social movements' attempts to democratise everyday life. As Melucci, one of the foremost thinkers of these new developments, says, these are attempts to resist social control and the manipulation of 'dimensions which were regarded as private (body, sexuality) or subjective (cognitive, emotional processes, motives, desires), or even biological (the genetic code, reproductive capacity)' (Melucci, 1994: 101). And this, perhaps, is the most interesting characteristic of the new social movement literature: it focuses on cultural and symbolic aspects of identity, rather than on power or economic grievances, as was the case in traditional social movement theory. The basic idea is that the dichotomy between public and private is an artificial one, and that in abolishing this dichotomy the personal can become political. On the more practical side, we see the emergence of such 'identity politics' (Calhoun, 1994) in certain of the new social movements: environmental, radical feminist, and gay/lesbian movements. Let us mention here, for example, social activists, mainly in the South, who link the defence of human rights with indigenous knowledge and environmental issues (Athanasiou, 1996; Szasz, 1994); radical feminist collectives working on their own identity (e.g. black feminism: hooks, 1993); or gay/lesbian groups opposing sexual normalisation and the patriarchal family.

Linking identity politics with adult education practices, let us mention, for example, the Palmerton Citizens for a Clean Environment, a grassroots group started in 1990 by six women. Hill, who has conducted an in-depth study of this form of social action from an adult education perspective, says: 'Learning for the women – organic intellectuals in the community – was most often embedded in concerns about motherhood and domesticity which became 'generative themes' for community development and community education' (Hill, 1997: iv). The group 'was engaged in a transformative process to ensure that Palmerton, a community at risk, would become a community-at-promise; caring, hope and possibility were its central moments' (v). Another example is the Brenda and Wanda Henson Camp Sister Spirit.[19] The camp, 'whose story is a powerful indictment of homophobia and hate, operates a food and clothing bank, adult literacy programs, always with the spirit of alliance building and community organizing' (Adult Education Research Conference, Gay, Lesbian, Bisexual, and Friends Caucus; see Hill, 1995).

Learning our way out of the ecological crisis

As we saw in Chapter 7, ecological degradation is at the heart of a vicious circle by which the process of industrial development will ultimately lead to a dead end. This also means that ecological degradation can no longer be separated from social, political, economic and cultural problems. This is best illustrated in the case of issues of lifestyle and consumption, as well as the case of the erosion of diversity, both biological and cultural. Both issues capture particularly well the totally interrelated dynamics between sociocultural and ecological degradation. We have also seen that the ecological crisis has now taken on global proportions, making the process of industrial development and the extension of the Western lifestyle totally unsustainable (Lauterburg, 1998). Finally, we have shown that the consequences of this vicious circle are ultimately always local. In other words, the consequences of global ecological degradation affect most those peoples and these species which are least mobile – precisely the ones which are still rooted locally. It is therefore at local levels that the opposition to ecological degradation, and the development of alternatives, must take their point of departure.

Learning our way out, in this context of an accelerating vicious circle, again occurs in the three steps of awareness, conceptual clarification, and the development of alternatives from the bottom up. Environmental – and especially adult environmental – education has focused in the past almost exclusively on such environmental awareness-raising, often in a somewhat naturalistic, scientist and conservationist perspective (Orr, 1992). At times, such environmental awareness-raising has been done in a green political perspective (Claussen, 1997). We have argued that, although it is important to raise awareness, people are already highly aware, and that further awareness-raising might actually be counterproductive (Finger, 1994). A second step in learning our way out relates to conceptual clarification. It is important to understand that current and local ecological problems are historically and anthropologically rooted in a Western industrial techno-scientific civilisation with a dynamic of its own, and that today they are global in nature. This means that techno-fixes are probably not going to be sufficient solutions, and being aware of this fact is an additional argument for developing alternatives from the bottom up – the third step in learning our way out. In this third step there are two quite different approaches: one more political, the other more anthropological.

On the political side, grassroots movements, especially in the South, are particularly relevant. Since the early 1980s, such movements have 'criticise[d], protest[ed], and oppose[d] northern development schemes, promoted by international agencies such as FAO, UNDP, the IFM, and the WB, which are generally implemented with the aid of national and local elites' (Chatterjee and Finger, 1994: 243). More precisely, these movements oppose 'industrial development': that is, large-scale energy constructions, the building of large dams, and all kind of agribusiness schemes, from deforestation to biotechnological piracy and testing. By so doing, they truly resist, and help to develop resistance to, the very process of industrial development and ecological degradation we have highlighted above. On the anthropological side, these and other groups are developing, in a truly Participatory Action Research approach, endogenous and people's knowledge from the bottom up. By so doing, they develop alternative ways of living outside the industrial development paradigm. They are also recovering, creating and fostering indigenous learning tools. In Mies and Shiva's words, when they talk about eco-feminism, these groups 'propagate the need of a new cosmology and a new anthropology which recognise that life in Nature (including human beings) is maintained through co-operation, mutual care, and love. Only in this way will we be able to respect and preserve the diversity of all forms of life, including its cultural expressions, as the true sources of our well-being and our happiness' (Mies and Shiva, 1997: 15). Examples of such groups are the Chipko Movement, as well as other forest-based struggles in India (Shiva, 1988); the Sarvodaya (Ratnapala, 1978) and Navdanya movements (Mies and Shiva, 1998); PAR rural experiences in Nicaragua, Mexico and Colombia (Fals-Borda, 1993); the Green Belt Movement in Kenya, and its successors, such as the 'Women's Gardening Group' in Senegal or the 'Organisation of Rural Association for Peasants' in Zimbawe (Ekins, 1992; Timberlake, 1986); the Forest Action Network in Kenia and the Huitzo Cummunity in Oaxaca (Mexico) as instances of community management of forests (Berkmüller, 1992); experiences of community-based environmental conservation, such as Nepal's Annapurna Conservation Area; initiatives on traditional ecological knowledge such as the Dai people of South-West China, the 'ribeirinhos' river dwellers of the Amazon estuary, or the Mayan peoples in Central America. On a more conceptual level, we could mention bioregionalism (McGinnis, 1999; Sale, 1985), or social ecology (Bookchin, 1991), both of which offer frameworks for relating peoples, communities and the natural world.

Notes

1. For more information, see: http://www.gn.apc.org/fairtrade; http://www.web.net/fairtrade/fair71.html.

2. See http://www.incolor.inetnebr.com/dennis/banking.html.

3. See http://www.incolor.inetnebr.com/dennis/econ.shtml; http://www.eurosur.org/IMAGINA/reas.htm; http://www.eurosur.org/IMAGINA/aeress.htm; www.gn.apc.org/neweconomics.

4. 1660 Embelton Crescent, Courtebay BC, V9N 6N8.

5. PO Box 3973, Berkeley, CA 94703 [jylsafier@aol.com].

6. www.public-com.com./web/ithacahour/.

7. For CSA West and Food First, see: http://www.netspace.org/hungerweb/FoodFirst/index.htm.

8. 1555 Pacific Ave., San Francisco, CA 94109 [ifg@ifg.org][http://www.ifg.org].

9. [http:iisd.ca/pcdf/] Brainbridge (Puget Sound) Seattle, Washington.

10. 1601 Connecticut Ave., Washington, DC 20009 [http://www.ips-dc.org/].

11. Paulus Potterstraat 20, 1071 DA Amsterdam, The Netherlands [http://www.tni.org].

12. A-60 Haus Khas, New Delhi, India 110016 [http://indiaserver.com/betas/vshiva/title.htm].

13. 228 Macalister Road, 10400 Penang, Malaysia [http://www.twnside.org.sg/].

14. http://www.gn.apc.org/ecologist/.

15. http://www.essential.org/monitor/.

16. 1959 Highlander Way, New Market, TN 37820 [hrec@igc.apc.org] [http://www.grass-roots.org/usa/highlander.shtml].

17. For example, Institute of Social Ecology [http://www.tao.ca/¬ise/], bibliography on libertarian municipalism. Libertarian municipalism conference: http://infoshop.org/news3/libmuni.html.

18. Social anarchism [http://www.web.net/¬anarchos/] Institute for Anarchist Studies[http://home.newyorknet.net/ias/].

19. This can be reached through speakout@igc.apc.org.

Chapter 12

Synthesis and Analysis

All our examples of various practices of learning our way out have certain characteristics in common. They all pursue a larger goal of social change, since they all strive to develop alternatives to the current system. Generally, these alternatives relate to sustainable communities in both social and ecological terms. Such communities are somewhat disconnected from the global system, especially from the dynamics of industrial development. Moreover, all these alternatives are grounded in resistance from the bottom up – more precisely resistance to some aspects of the current order which, in all the examples, is being imposed 'from above', generally from the global level, on to local realities. It is resistance to this current order, or aspects of it, which gives people the energy and the motivation to develop alternatives, and it is this resistance which ultimately drives their learning. Finally, almost all the examples involve developing countries, where the process by which such resistance is transformed into sustainable communities is probably best captured in terms of learning as a form of Participatory Action Research. Figure 12.1 translates the objective (sustainable communities), the point of departure (communes of resistance), and the process of learning our way out (praxis) into a graphical form.

Let us briefly comment on Figure 12.1, and recall that resistance is not without its problems. There is a danger that resistance will fall into the trap of fundamentalism, of being reactive, and ultimately of being reactionary. Also, as we have shown, resistance

Figure 12.1   From communes of resistance
to sustainable communities

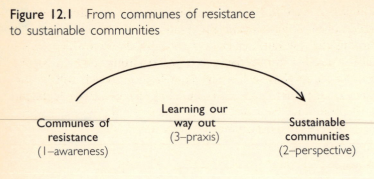

Communes of
resistance
(1–awareness)

Learning our
way out
(3–praxis)

Sustainable
communities
(2–perspective)

often remains somewhat localised, isolated and fragmented; and
since most resistance is local, there is a constant danger that it
will be co-opted or manipulated. Finally, resistance tends to be
fragmented along the lines of the main issues identified above.
Thus one will observe resistance against cultural practices, against
ecological destruction, or against economic marginalisation, without much linkage. While all these different resistances will ultimately contribute to learning our way out, their fragmented nature
makes it difficult to do so in a co-ordinated and coherent way.
Therefore, if these various resistances are ultimately to contribute
to learning our way out, it is necessary to define the three steps
of awareness, conceptual clarification, and praxis. Awareness, as
we have said, is a necessary condition for resistance to develop,
and adult education, historically, has been quite good at contributing to awareness. Conceptual clarification helps to put such
awareness into a social action perspective. We have clarified this
perspective in Part II and again in Chapter 10, and we have shown
that adult education – theoretically, at least – can be related to
such a perspective of learning our way out. Finally, praxis remains
the biggest challenge, as it means bridging the gap between individual and fragmented awareness on the one hand, and building
sustainable communities as alternatives on the other. Today, praxis
is the main challenge for a renewed adult education. If we have

examples of such praxis in developing countries, as outlined above, we do not really have a conceptualisation of the overall process of learning our way out, especially a conceptualisation which would make it possible to transfer such a process from South to North. In order to develop such a conceptualisation, which will be the object of the final chapter of our book, let us briefly highlight each of the three steps involved in learning our way out: awareness, conceptual clarification and praxis.

Awareness

Awareness is a necessary, but not a sufficient, condition for learning our way out. It is necessary to be aware of the destructive dynamics of industrial development, and of its consequences for people and for nature. Our examples show that such awareness exists today among the most direct victims of this process – the poorest and the least mobile people. Many other people are also aware of its destructive dynamics and dead end, but are less able to link their awareness directly with their experiences, since many of these experiences, especially the cultural ones, are being manipulated by the prevailing culture industry. As the destructive dynamics of industrial civilisation accelerates, such awareness will probably grow faster than the overall capacity to manipulate it. So awareness-raising is not the problem, in our opinion.

The real problem is that such awareness can turn into cynicism or reactionary behaviour. This failure is particularly acute in parts of the world – highly industrialised countries – where the link between the awareness and the perspective of what would constitute a way out is more difficult to establish. Awareness needs to be connected to a larger perspective of social change, as well as to concrete actions leading in this direction. More precisely, individual and collective awareness of the destructive dynamics of industrial civilisation needs to be connected to a collective project of what we have called learning our way out – ultimately, a sustainable society made up of sustainable communities. In addition to awareness-raising, therefore, learning our way out also implies defining the perspective, as well as initiating the process, by which such awareness (resistance) can be translated into action that will ultimately lead to a more sustainable society.

Adult education, both in theory and in practice, has been very good at awareness-raising. Be it humanist or cognitivist, the goal of the learning process has always been to help adults become aware of what has shaped their world-views. This can also be said of most of the pragmatic approaches, such as symbolic inter-actionism or 'perspective transformation'. Participatory Action Research is probably the only example of an adult education practice which goes beyond awareness-raising, linking it to concrete social change (see below). This critique applies in particular to Marxist pedagogy, be it Freire's pedagogy of the oppressed or critical pedagogy: in both cases, the link between political awareness and praxis remains quite tenuous – quite apart from the fact that the Marxist social action agenda does not, in our view, constitute a realistic perspective for learning our way out of the destructive dynamics of industrial civilisation (see Part II).

In other words, awareness-raising, no matter how well it is done, and no matter how sophisticated its pedagogy, will be only as good as the perspective (of social change) to which it is connected. Moreover, it will be only as good as the practical steps, actions and processes by which such awareness engenders social action and transformation leading in the direction outlined by the perspective.

Perspective (conceptual clarification)

In the examples above – which, as we have seen, are found mainly in developing countries – the passage from awareness to per-spective is still quite narrow and probably bridgeable, because sustainable communities that are grounded in local and regional agricultural and vocational activities can still be envisioned by the people concerned. In the case of highly industrialised societies, however, it is by no means clear how resistance can be linked to building sustainable communities. There is the perspective of a sustainable society made up of sustainable communities on the one hand, and (communes of) resistance on the other. Let us briefly discuss both separately.

In Chapter 10 we outlined an overall perspective of learning our way out in terms of building sustainable communities, characterised both by participation and by slowed-down (industrial) development: low energy input, low speed and appropriate technology. Consequently, a sustainable society will be made up of such sustainable communities connected to each other. Many of the above examples illustrate the building of such sustainable communities, especially in developing countries. While this perspective of sustainable communities and a sustainable society grounded in both people's participation and the slowing doing down of industrial development still remains nebulous in the North, it is nevertheless possible to offer some theoretically sound perspectives.

In this context, 'social ecology' (Bookchin, 1991, 1993; Biehl, 1997) is, in our opinion, particularly relevant. Social ecology integrates the study of human and natural ecosystems through an understanding of the interrelationships between culture and nature. It suggests that solutions to the ecological crisis will require a new approach to social life, one which is based on human-scale, decentralised and radically democratic communities. As Bookchin says:

> we must go beyond both the natural and the social toward a new synthesis that contains the best of both. Such a synthesis will transcend them in the form of a creative self-conscious, and therefore 'free nature,' in which human beings intervene in natural evolution with their best capacities.... Logistically, 'free nature' is unattainable without the decentralisation of cities into confederally united communities sensitively tailored to the natural areas in which they are located. (Bookchin, 1993: 11)

In other words, the perspective is one of sustainable eco-communities which conferedate into larger networks, in which the citizens participate in a direct and democratic way. These are communities in which 'the collective interest is inseparable from the personal, the public interest from the private, the political interest from the social' (Bookchin, 1993: 12).

But such sustainable communities take their point of departure in resistance, or in what Castells calls 'communes of resistance'. Again, it is possible to refer to the literature to clarify this aspect and, moreover, to show that such resistance is not limited to developing countries, nor is it limited to the most obvious victims of industrial development. Rather, such resistance seems to characterise the 'new social movements', as Castells identifies them (Castells, 1997). Such new social movements in the North, according to Castells and others (Johnston, Laraña and Gusfield, 1994; Melucci, 1994), address precisely some of the core premisses of current turbo-capitalistic industrial development. In so doing, it is said, they oppose 'placelessness' as currently promoted by economic and cultural globalisations. They also oppose 'timelessness', which is being promoted especially through technological development. Resisting both placelessness and timelessness, people seek to re-create community on a human scale by regaining control over technology and market forces.

Praxis

Especially in industrialised countries, where the discrepancy between awareness and perspective is at a maximum, there is a serious danger that such resistance will remain defensive and reactive, and will ultimately fuel reactionary movements rather than change towards a more sustainable society. This danger cannot be separated from political and cultural trends towards fundamentalism, be they of a religious, ecological or political nature. Nor can it be separated from the logic of the market, whose ability to commodify – and thus to instrumentalise – any form of social, political and cultural perspective is unparalleled. And it must, in particular, be related to a more general trend of bureaucratisation and institutionalisation, which cements current unsustainable development patterns, and ultimately means that any social change effort ends in cynicism and despair. In other words – and as we have said above – awareness and resistance, in the light of processes of marketisation and especially institutionalisation, are probably going to be insufficient, and might actually be counterproductive. This is almost certainly going to be the case in the highly institutionalised societies of the North, where the challenge is to connect awareness and resistance by means of a praxis which will specifically address institutional change. In the North, this is the challenge of learning our way out, and it is also the challenge of

adult education as a field and as a discipline. Let us, in conclusion, clarify this challenge, and argue why adult education theory
(and practice) is insufficient when it comes to addressing it.

Conclusion

As Illich shows, industrial development goes hand in hand with a
process of institutionalisation and bureaucratisation. Institutions
interpose themselves not only between nature and society but also
between resistance and perspective (Illich, 1970a, 1973a, 1974a,
1975). The more developed a society, the more disconnected
people's lives will be from what their resistance actually aspires to,
and this distance is more or less proportional to the degree of
institutionalisation. Connecting resistance to perspective thus
means addressing institutions and organisations as a problem that
impedes sustainable communities and, ultimately, a sustainable
society. Connecting resistance to perspective thus means engaging
in substantial institutional and organisational change and transformation.

   This in turn means that, especially in highly industrialised
societies, learning our way out – the passage from awareness/
resistance to sustainable communities/society – has to address the
issue of organisational and institutional change, if it does not want
to end up in cynicism and despair. This, we think, is both adult
education's weakness and its most important challenge today, at
least when it comes to highly industrialised countries. If adult
education wants to connect back to its social action agenda and
become relevant again, it has to clarify not only the perspective
of what social change means today, but – even more so – the
(learning) process of getting there. And this process will entail
linking resistance and awareness to organisational change and
learning, with the ultimate perspective developing sustainable
communities and a sustainable society. In other words, the practice
of learning our way out is contingent upon the ability to relate
individual and collective learning to institutional and organisational transformation, and the future of adult education is contingent upon the ability to make this link on a conceptual and
theoretical level. While – as we will show in Chapter 13 – Partici-

patory Action Research constitutes a first step in this direction, it remains somewhat limited in the case of highly industrialised societies, where institutionalisation is at its 'best'.

Chapter 13

Adult Education, De-institutionalisation, and the Theory of Learning Our Way Out

So far we have identified both the still quite abstract goal of learning our way out – sustainable communities and a sustainable society – and the dynamics running contrary to this goal – turbo-capitalism, the erosion of politics, postmodernism and ecological degradation, all linked in an accelerating and increasingly vicious circle. Furthermore, we have seen that there are practices of learning our way out which – through awareness-raising, conceptual clarification and praxis – move communes of resistance towards more sustainable communities. Adult education, we have claimed, should – and to some extent already does – play a role in this process. This is especially true of Participatory Action Research (PAR).

PAR, however, applies essentially in the context of (some) developing countries – environments – which are not yet fully institutionalised. In highly institutionalised (i.e. bureaucratised) environments – that is, generally in highly industrialised societies – this process of learning our way out is significantly hampered by institutions (i.e. bureaucracies) and their interest in maintaining the status quo. So the theory and practice of learning our way out in the context of highly industrialised, and thus highly institutionalised, societies faces an additional and quite particular challenge: the challenge of 'overcoming' institutional interests and organisational resistance – in other words, the challenge of actively promoting 'de-institutionalisation' through learning.

The purpose of this concluding chapter is therefore twofold: on the one hand, we would like to identify as precisely as possible where the intellectual and practical challenges lie if adult education wants to contribute actively to learning our way out, especially in the context of highly industrialised societies. On the other hand, we would also like to outline a future social action perspective for adult education as a field of thinking and practice – the only perspective possible if adult education is to have such a future. In order to do so, we will proceed in three stages: first, we will recall, with Ivan Illich, that the process of institutionalisation is not only parallel to but, moreover, an integral and central part of the vicious circle of industrial development. In so doing, we will argue that (de-)institutionalisation is a central – if not *the* central – challenge for the praxis of learning our way out, at least in the case of highly industrialised environments. So far, however, adult education, even adult education for social action, has not addressed the challenge of de-institutionalisation, either intellectually or in practice. We will therefore go on to outline an intellectual and research agenda for adult education for doing precisely that, by reflecting critically on the link between adult learning and de-institutionalisation. Finally, we will locate this reflection within the larger context of learning our way out of the dead end of industrial civilisation, which is, we think, the only worthwhile perspective for the field of adult education, if it is to have a future at all. This challenge of learning our way out in the context of highly industrialised and thus highly institutionalised societies is represented graphically in Figure 13.1.

Illich and the critique of institutionalisation

In Chapter 11 we concluded that the main obstacles in trying to link awareness with practice – that is, trying to move from communes of resistance to sustainable communities – are institutions. If it is the case that this obstacle can in part be overcome in less 'developed' – thus less institutionalised – societies by means of PAR, such institutional obstacles to learning our way out are nevertheless much more pervasive in highly industrialised societies. We must therefore conclude that – at least in such societies – institutions and institutionalisation are the core challenge to learning our way out. If adult education wants to contribute to learning our way out, institutions and institutionalisation thus also

Figure 13.1   The challenge of learning our way out

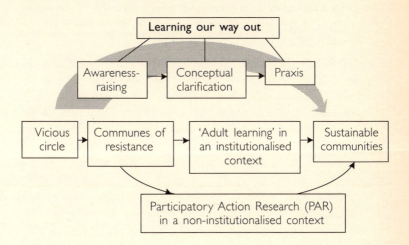

become the core challenge to its theory and practice. In this section, we want to stress this point by coming back to Ivan Illich (see Chapter 1): by recalling his arguments (1) that the process of institutionalisation goes hand in hand with industrial development; (2) that institutionalisation is destructive of conviviality; and (3) that institutionalisation is ultimately a counterproductive process – a key, if not *the* key, impediment to learning our way out.

In the process of institutionalisation, Illich argues, industrial development is cementing the myth that this is the only possible way to live. He says:

> modern institutions are ceremonies creating myths, social liturgies celebrating certainties. In this spirit I have examined the school, transport, and housing in order to understand their hidden and inevitable functions: what they proclaim rather than what they produce: the myth of '*Homo educandus*', the myth of '*Homo transportandus*', at the end the myth of entrapped man.... I have chosen medicine as the example whereby one can illustrate the various levels of counterproductivity which characterise all postwar institutions, their technical, social and cultural paradoxes: on a technical level the therapeutic synergies which

produce new sicknesses, on the social level the uprooting created by a diagnosis, which will follow the sick, the idiot, the elderly and even the one who is going slowly. And above all, on the cultural level, the promise of progress which leads to the refusal of the human condition and to the disgust of the art of suffering. (Illich, 1999: 28)

In other words, industrial development is institutionalising, in tandem with its destructive dynamics, the idea that there is no alternative. Institutionalisation, for Illich, is therefore above all a mental process, as well as a process of physical and social dependency, by which people ultimately come to believe that there is no alternative to the way they currently live. Institutionalisation, therefore, is the highest stage, the ultimate incarnation, of industrial development.

Needless to say, for Illich, development and institutionalisation are fundamentally counterproductive processes. Let us quote his argumentation here in detail:

First, undesired externalities exceed benefits – the tax burden of schools and hospitals is more than any economy can support; the ghost towns produced by highways impoverish the urban and rural landscape. Plastic buckets from São Paulo are lighter and cheaper than those made of scrap by the local tinsmith in Western Brazil. But first cheap plastic puts the tinsmith out of existence, and then the fumes of plastic leave a special trace on the environment – a new kind of ghost. The destruction of age-old competence as well as these poisons are inevitable byproducts and will resist all exorcisms for a long time. Cemeteries for industrial wastes simply cost too much, more than the buckets are worth. In economic jargon, the 'external costs' exceed not only the profit made from plastic bucket production, but also the very salaries paid in the manufacturing process. These rising externalities, however, are only one side of the bill which development has exacted. Counterproductivity is its reverse side. Externalities represent costs that are 'outside' the price paid by the consumer for what he wants – costs that he, others or future generations will at some point be charged. Counterproductivity, however, is a new kind of disappointment which arises 'within' the very use of the good purchased. This internal counterproductivity, an inevitable component of modern institutions, has become the constant frustration of the poorer majority of each institution's clients: intensely experienced but rarely defined. Each major sector of the economy produces its own unique and paradoxical contradictions. Each necessarily effects the opposite of that for which it was structured. Economists, who are increasingly competent to put price-tags on externalities, are unable to deal with negative internalities, and cannot measure the inherent frustration of captive clients which is something other than a cost. For most people, schooling twists genetic differences into certified degradation; the medicalisation of health increases demand for services far beyond the possible and useful, and undermines that organic coping ability which common sense calls health; transportation, for the great majority bound to the rush hour, increases the time spent in the servitude to traffic, reducing both freely chosen mobility and mutual access. The development of educational, medical and other welfare agencies has actually removed most clients from the obvious purpose for which these projects were designed and financed. This institutionalised frustration, resulting from compulsory consumption, combines with the new externalities. It demands an increase in the production of scavenging and repair services to impoverish and even destroy individuals and communities, affecting them in a class-specific manner. In effect, the peculiarly modern forms of frustration and paralysis and destruction totally discredit the description of the desirable society in terms of installed production capacity. (Illich, 1980: 101)

In short, Illich argues, development is a fundamentally counter-productive process, and the institutionalisation of development helps it to hide this very fact. This, in turn, helps the vested interests to keep their privileges and ultimately to stay in power. Thus institutionalisation is basically a means to preserve and increase the power of those who benefit from industrial development and its destructive dynamics. In other words, institutionalisation, in addition to being the highest form of development, is also its best protection against any form of criticism or attack. Therefore institutionalisation relates fundamentally to political interests and power relations. The more advanced – and thus the more absurd – the development process, the stronger its institutional dimension and the political interests behind it. This institutionalisation, however, is exactly what is needed in order to hide both the absurdity of the development process and the vested interests therein.

If one follows Illich, it will be totally illusory to criticise and seek alternatives to development without simultaneously criticising and overcoming its corollary process of institutionalisation. Furthermore, the very strength of the development process lies in the power of its institutions and its parallel process of institutionalisation.

Institutionalisation not only legitimises development; it also ensures that development is never even questioned. Attacking development without attacking its parallel institutionalisation is thus illusory and most probably counterproductive, since the strength of the institutionalisation process will always be capable of neutralizing any form of criticism. In other words, seeking to overcome development without seeking to overcome its parallel institutionalisation will lead only to despair and frustration, if not simply to neutralisation. Or, to put it another way, learning our way out cannot be satisfied with the critique and elaboration of alternatives to industrial development. Rather, it must also address the issue of institutionalisation: parallel to the development of such alternatives, the 'development institutions' must also be deconstructed, and alternatives to them must be elaborated. 'Sustainable communities' thus not only have an economic, an ecological, a social, and a political dimension, they also – and perhaps above all – have an institutional dimension, and this is the dimension learning our way out theory has not yet sufficiently addressed.

To sum up: Illich has helped us to clarify the intrinsic relationship between development and institutionalisation. Furthermore, he has helped us to understand that only a radical critique of institutionalisation – and subsequent 'de-institutionalisation' – will ultimately allow us to find a way out of the vicious circle of industrial development. However, Illich, in his critique of institutions and institutionalisation, still remains very much on an ideological and intellectual level, and does not really address their structural and organisational components; nor does he really say anything about the actual practice of de-institutionalisation.

Remaining on that intellectual and ideological level, it is easy to understand why, for Illich, adult education, in its awareness-raising approach, can be considered an answer. Illich's conceptualisation of how to overcome institutionalisation, development, and their counterproductivities – as highlighted in Chapter 1 – rests very solidly on critical adult education, albeit with a more radical dimension than that of his followers. For him it is a critical adult education which looks at institutionalisation as a form of (mental) oppression. While we do embrace Illich's overall conceptual framework – his critique of development, his critique of institutionalisation, and his conceptualisation of institutionalisation as a central impediment to learning our way out – we do not think that he really addresses the practical nature of institutions and organisations. In other words, while we think that his understanding of adult education as a means of overcoming institutionalisation is unique and crucial, we do not think that his conceptualisation of the link between adult learning and the critique of institutionalisation is sufficient. He is interested mainly in the intellectual critique of institutions, not in their concrete transformation. Still, to his credit, Illich goes much further here than any other adult education thinker. In the next section, we want to build on his legacy and overall conceptual framework as we further conceptualise the link between adult learning and de-institutionalisation.

Adult learning and de-institutionalisation: a research agenda

According to Illich – and we agree – de-institutionalisation constitutes *the* challenge for learning our way out. Going beyond Illich, however, we think that awareness-raising is certainly a first step, yet by no means a sufficient one, in transforming institutions and organisations. With the exception of some organisational learning theories, adult education has not addressed the issue of organisational change and transformation at all. In Chapter 8 we discussed these theories and showed that they are particularly illustrative of the instrumentalisation of adult learning for purposes of profit, organisational survival and economic competitiveness – that is to say, the pursuit of industrial development as we know it.

If, therefore, adult education is to make a contribution to learning our way out – at least in the context of highly industrialised societies – it has to clarify its relationship with organisations and instititutions, and their change and transformation. In this section we would like to outline a three-step research agenda for doing precisely that. In other words, adult education, both conceptually and in practice, has to rethink the relationship between learning and organisations; it has to gain a better understanding of the dynamics of institutions and power (interests and actor strategies); and it has to develop ways and means of overcoming vested interests and power in organisations and institutions by (adult) learning. Let us briefly explain each of these points, which constitute as many research agendas.

To begin with, adult education must critically examine one of the new trends in the field: the instrumentalisation of adult education theory and practice for purposes of organisational competitiveness, as discussed in Chapter 8. As we described there, all three main schools of adult learning – cognitivism, humanism and pragmatism – are currently actively contributing to making organisations more efficient, more flexible, and thus more competitive. Many adult educators have found in the areas of organisational learning and the learning organisation a renewed field of practice. We must examine this evolution critically, and try to understand in particular what it is in adult learning theory that makes it particularly vulnerable to such instrumentalisation. Only such a critical understanding will allow us to build on the tradition of adult education, and recover its emancipatory and social action potentials.

Simultaneously, adult education has to go beyond Illich and try to gain a better understanding of the relationships between power, interest and actors' strategies on the one hand, and organisations and institutions on the other. Let us recall: institutions, in Illich's view, are part and parcel of the process of industrial development; furthermore, they help to hide the fact that this process is basically counterproductive and ultimately destructive of people's lives and livelihoods. Thus institutions reflect the interests of those who ultimately profit from industrial development's destructive dynamics. Moreover, the process of institutionalisation serves to co-opt some into the institutions' power structures and blind others by making them believe that development is unavoidable. Illich, unfortunately, has not gone much further in his analysis of how institutions work and ultimately manage to exert such power over people and their lives. We think that it is neccesary, therefore, to go back to the classics in organisational sociology if we are to gain a better understanding of the relationship between people, power and organisations. We are thinking here in particular of authors such as Blau (1963), Crozier (1964), Etzioni (1964, 1975), March (1999) and Simon (1945). In our view, such an understanding is necessary if adult education wants to conceptualise deinstitutionalisation in terms of (adult) learning.

Building on both the critical analysis of adult learning's instrumentalisation for the purposes of organisational competitiveness, and on a better understanding of the relationships between power, interests, actor strategies and institutionalisation, we can say that *adult education's main future research agenda will be concerned with the linkages between learning, power and organisational change.* In a social action perspective – and within the larger framework of contributing to learning our way out – the next frontier in adult education's theory and practice will have to address the question of how (adult) learning can contribute to organisational change and transformation, taking into account the vested interests and power structures that maintain the status quo. Obviously, the instrumentalisation of adult education theory and practice by the business literature and management schools was precisely at the price of evacuating the issues of power and institutionalisation. Strengthened by a better understanding of how power relates to institutionalisation, adult education should, thanks to this research agenda, recover its social action potential and put it into the larger framework of de-institutionalisation. In so doing, however, adult education should never lose sight of the fact that even de-institutionalisation is only a means within the larger perspective of learning our way out.

Future challenges to adult education

We have tried to show that, in a less institutionalised context, characterised by a less advanced industrial development process, Participatory Action Research (PAR) is a significant contribution to learning our way out. PAR allows communes of resistance to reappropriate their destiny and become more sustainable communities, thus uncoupling, to a certain extent, from the industrial development process. PAR, however, does not address institutions, and even less so de-institutionalisation, and is therefore quite limited in its contribution to learning our way out in the context of highly institutionalised and highly industrialised societies. This is why we claim that a solid research endeavour is necessary, so that adult education will be much more resolute when it comes to linking learning to the process of de-institutionalisation.

In Part II we argued that, even more generally, adult education, from being a means of social change and emancipation until the late 1970s, has become a means of furthering industrial development and its vicious circle. If adult education wants once more to become a meaningful project and praxis, and if adult education theory wants once more to offer something other than helping business learn to compete better and faster, then it will itself have to learn its way out. To begin with, adult education will have to become aware of where its current dynamics is leading it – in essence, to become an appendage of management development. Then adult education will have to re-create a perspective for itself which, we think, should redefine social action in the context of the dead end of industrial development – both in developing, but also and especially in highly industrialised, societies. And finally, it will have to conceptualise the praxis of such adult education in terms of learning our way out of both industrial development and its corollary process of institutionalisation. Such praxis, as we have seen, must address the process of institutionalisation and, more precisely, the question of power and vested interests in institutions and organisations. It is these institutionalised interests and power relations which not only perpetuate (and accelerate) the destructive dynamics of industrial development but, moreover, hide its very counterproductivity and destructiveness. We claim that such a praxis, on an adult education conceptual level, will combine concepts of pragmatic organisational learning within the larger framework of Participatory Action Research. And this is what we see as the new frontier of adult education thinking: *how do we combine adult learning with organisational change and de-institutionalisation, thus putting adult education back into the perspective of social action and change, albeit now in a context of highly institutionalised societies and an ever more destructive industrial development process?*

Bibliography

Adorno, T.W. (1970). *Erziehung zur Mündigkeit.* Frankfurt am Main: Suhrkamp.

Adorno, T.W. and Horkheimer, M. (1944). *Dialectic of Enlightenment.* New York: Social Studies Association.

Alsina, O. and Sunyer, R. (1998). *Informe sobre la banca ètica a Europa.* Barcelona: FUS.

Amery, C. (1972). *Das Ende der Vorsehung; die gnadenlosen Folgen der Christentums.* Reinbek bei Hamburg: Rowohlt.

Amin, S. (1997). *Capitalism in the Age of Globalization: The Management of Contemporary Society.* London and New Jersey: Zed Books.

Anderson, W.T. (1997). *The Future of the Self: Exploring the Post-identity Society.* New York: Tarcher/Putnam.

Apple, M. (1996). *Cultural Politics and Education.* New York: Teachers College Press.

Argyris, C. (1983). *Reasoning, Learning and Action: Individual and Organizational.* San Francisco: Jossey-Bass.

Argyris, C. (1992). *On Organizational Learning.* Oxford: Blackwell.

Argyris, C., Putnam, R. and Smith, D.M. (1985). *Action Science: Concepts, Methods, and Skills for Research and Intervention.* San Francisco: Jossey-Bass.

Argyris, C. and Schön, D.A. (1974). *Theory in Practice: Increasing Professional Effectiveness.* San Francisco: Jossey-Bass.

Argyris, C. and Schön, D.A. (1978). *Organizational Learning: A Theory of Action Perspective.* Reading, MA: Addison-Wesley.

Arnove, R. and Graff, H. (1987). *National Literacy Campaigns: Historical and Comparative Perspectives.* New York: Plenum.

Aronowitz, S. and Giroux, H. (1993). *Education Still Under Siege.* Westport, CT: Bergin & Garvey.

Athanasiou, T. (1996). *Divided Planet: The Ecology of Rich and Poor.* Boston: Little, Brown.

Atweh, B., Kemmis, S. and Weeks, P. (1998). *Action Research in Practice: Partnerships for Social Justice*. New York: Routledge.

Baudrillard, J. (1968). *Le système des objets: La consommation des signes*. Paris: Gallimard.

Baudrillard, J. (1983). *Les stratégies fatales*. Paris: Grasset.

Bauman, Z. (1992). *Intimations of Posmodernity*. London and New York: Routledge.

Bauman, Z. (1995). *Life in Fragments: Essays in Postmodern Morality*. Oxford and Cambridge, MA: Blackwell.

Bauman, Z. (1997). *Postmodernity and its Discontents*. Cambridge: Polity Press.

Bauman, Z. (1998). *Globalization: The Human Consequences*. Cambridge: Polity Press.

Beck, U. (1986). *Risikogesellschaft: Auf dem Weg in eine andere Moderne*. Frankfurt am Main: Suhrkamp.

Beetson, J. (1996). 'Adult Education and the Rights of Indigenous Peoples'. Address to the General Assembly of the Asia South Pacific Bureau of Adult Education. Darwin, Australia, December.

Bélanger, P. (1995). 'The Historical Roles of UNESCO and of the UN Family'. In B. Cassara (ed.), *Adult Education through World Collaboration*. Malabar, FL: Krieger.

Bélanger, P. (1998). 'El sorprendente retorno de la educación a lo largo de la vida'. In G. Janer (ed.), *Sectores emergentes en el campo de la educación permanente*. Palma de Mallorca: Universitat de les Illes Balears.

Bélanger, P. and Gelpi, E. (eds) (1994). *Lifelong Education*. Amsterdam: Kluwer.

Bell, D. (1973). *The Coming of Post-industrial Society: A Venture in Social Forecasting*. New York: Basic Books.

Berger, P., Berger, B., and Kellner, H. (1973). *The Homeless Mind: Modernization and Consciousness*. New York: Vintage.

Berkmüller, K. (1992). *Environmental Education about the Rain Forest*, revised edn. Cambridge: IUCN–The World Conservation Union.

Bernstein, R.J. (ed.) (1985). *Habermas and Modernity*. Cambridge, MA: MIT Press.

Bertolami, S. (1995). 'Turbokapitalismus'. *Die Weltwoche*, 31 August, p. 23.

Best, S. and Kellner, D. (1997). *The Postmodern Turn*. London: Guildford Press.

Bhola, H. (1982). *Campaigning for Literacy: A Critical Analysis of Some Selected Literacy Campaigns of the 20th Century with a Memorandum to Decision Makers*. Paris: UNESCO/ICAE Study.

Biehl, J. (ed.) (1997). *The Murray Bookchin Reader*. London: Cassell.

Biehl, J. and Bookchin, M. (1998). *The Politics of Social Ecology: Libertarian Municipalism*: Black Rose.

Blau, P. (1963). *The Dynamics of Bureaucracy. A Study of Interpersonal Relations in Two Government Agencies*. Chicago: University of Chicago Press.

Blumer, H. (1969) *Symbolic Interactionism: Perspective and Method*. Englewood Cliffs, NJ: Prentice-Hall.

Boff, L. (1974). *Jesucristo el liberador*. Buenos Aires: Latinoamericana Libros.

Bogard, G. (1994). *L'éducation des adultes: Un pari progressiste du Conseil de l'Europe*. Strasbourg Cedex: Les éditions du Conseil de l'Europe.

Boggs, C. (1986). *Social Movements and Political Power: Emerging Forms of Radicalism in the West*. Philadelphia: Temple University Press.

Bookchin, M. (1991). 'Libertarian Municipalism: An Overview'. *Green Perspectives* 24, 41–54.

Bookchin, M. (1993). 'What is Social Ecology?' In M. Zimmerman (ed.), *Environmental Philosophy: From Animal Rights to Radical Ecology*. Englewood Cliffs, N.J.: Prentice-Hall.

Borremans, V. (1979). *Guide to convivial tools*. New York: R.R. Bowker.

Boud, D., Coher, R. and Walker, D. (eds) (1993). *Using Experience for Learning*. Bristol, PA: The Society for Research into Higher Education and Open University Press.

Bourdieu, P. and Passeron, J.C. (1977). *Reproduction in Education, Society and Culture*. Beverly Hills, CA: Sage.

Bowles, S. and Gintis, H. (1976). *Schooling in Capitalist America*. London: Routledge & Kegan Paul.

Brand, K.-W. (1982). *Neue soziale Bewegungen: Entstehung, Funktion und Perspektive neuer Protestpotentiale: eine Zwischenbilanz*. Opladen: Westdeutscher Verlag.

Brecher, J. and Costello, T. (1994). *Global Village or Global Pillage: Economic Reconstruction from the Bottom Up*. Boston: South End Press.

Brookfield, S. (1983). 'Adult Education and the Democratic Imperative: The Vision of Eduard Lindeman as a Contemporary Charter for Adult Education'. *Studies in Adult Education* 15, 36–46.

Brookfield, S. (1984a). 'The Contribution of Eduard Lindeman to the Development of Theory and Philosophy in Adult Education. *Adult Education Quarterly*, 34 (4), 185–96.

Brookfield, S. (1984b). 'The Meaning of Adult Education: The Contemporary relevance of Eduard Lindeman'. *Teachers College Record*, 85 (3), 513–24.

Brookfield, S. (1987). 'Eduard Lindeman'. In P. Jarvis (ed.), *Twentieth Century Thinkers in Adult Education*. London: Routledge.

Brookfield, S. (1990). *The Skillful Teacher: On Technique, Trust, and Responsiveness in the Classroom*. San Francisco: Jossey-Bass.

Brookfield, S. (1995). *Becoming a Critically Reflective Teacher*. San Francisco: Jossey-Bass.

Brookfield, S. and Preskill, S. (1999). *Discussions as a Way of Teaching: Tools and Techniques for Democratic Classrooms*. San Francisco: Jossey-Bass.

Brown, L.R., Renner, M. and Flavin, C. (1997). *Vital Signs 1997*. New York and London: W.W. Norton.

Brown, L.R., Renner, M. and Flavin, C. (1998). *Vital Signs 1998*. New York and London: W.W. Norton.

Bühner, B. and Birnmeyer, A. (1982). *Ideologie und Diskurs: Zur Theorie von Jürgen Habermas und ihrer Rezeption in der Pädagogik*. Frankfurt: Haag & Herchen.

Bulmer, M. (1984). *The Chicago School of Sociology: Institutionalization, Diversity, and the Rise of Sociological Research*. Chicago: University of Chicago Press.

Caffarella, R. and J. O'Donnell (1989). 'Research in Self-directed Learning: Past, Present and Future Trends'. In: H. Long et al., *Self-directed Learning: Application and Theory*. Athens, GA: University of Georgia Press.

Caillé, A. (1986). *Splendeurs et misères des sciences sociales: Esquisses d'une mythologie*. Geneva: Librairie Droz.

Calhoun, C. (ed.) (1994). *Social Theory and the Politics of Identity*. Oxford: Blackwell.

Cárceles, G. (1990). 'World Literacy Prospects at the Turn of the Century: Is the Objective of Literacy for All by the Year 2000 Statistically Plausible? *Comparative Education Review*, 34 (1), 4–20.

Cardoso, F.H. and Faletto, E. (1979). *Dependency and Development in Latin America*, trans. M. Mattingly Urquidi. Berkeley and Los Angeles: University of California Press.

Carr, W. and Kemmis, S. (1986). *Becoming Critical: Education, Knowledge and Action Research*. London: Taylor & Francis.

Castells, M. (1996). *The Information Age: Economy, Society and Culture*. Cambridge, MA: Blackwell.

Castells, M. (1997). *The Information Age: Economy, Society and Culture. Volume II: The Power of Identity*. Cambridge, MA: Blackwell.

Castells, M. (1998). *The Information Age: Economy, Society and Culture. Volume III: End of Millennium*. Cambridge, MA: Blackwell.

Caufield, C. (1996). *Masters of Illusion*. London: Macmillan.

Cavanagh, J. (1997). 'Globalization'. *International Herald Tribune*, January 24.

Cavanagh, J. and Barnet, R.J. (1994). *Global Dreams: Imperial Corporations and the New World Order*. New York: Simon & Schuster.

Cell, E. (1984). *Learning to Learn from Experience*. Albany, NY: State University of New York Press.

Center for Dewey Studies (1990). *The Collected Work of John Dewey 1882–1953*. Carbondale, IL: Southern Illinois University Press.

Chamoux, M.N. and Contreras, J. (eds) (1996). *La gestión comunal de recursos: Economía y poder en las sociedades locales de España y América Latina*. Barcelona: Icaria and Institut Català d'Antropologia.

Charters, A.N. and Siddiqui, D.A. (1989). *Comparative Adult Education: State of the Art with Annotated Resource Guide*. Vancouver: University of British Columbia.

Chatterjee, P. and Finger, M. (1994). *The Earth Brokers: Power, Politics, and Development*. London: Routledge, 1994.

Chesnais, F. (1994). *La mondalisation du capital*. Paris: Syros.

Chousssudovsky, M. (1997). *The Globalisation of Poverty: Impacts of IMF and World Bank Reforms*. London and Penang: Zed Books and Third World Network.

Cicourel, A. (1964). *Method and Measure in Sociology*. New York: Free Press of Glencoe.

Clarke, R. (1971). *The Science of War and Peace*. London: Jonathan Cape.

Claussen, B. (1997). *Politische Bildung. Lernen für die ökologische Demokratie*. Darmstadt: Primus Verlag.

Collard, S. and M. Law (1989). 'The Limits of Perspective Transformation: A Critique of Mezirow's Theory', *Adult Education Quarterly* 39.

Collins, M. (1991). *Adult Education as Vocation: A Critical Role for the Adult Educator*. New York: Routledge.

Cottrell, F. (1955). *Energy and Society: The Relation between Energy, Social Change, and Economic Development*, Wesport, CT: Greenwood Press.

Cremin, L.A. (1970). *American Education: The Colonial Experience, 1607–1783*. New York: Harper & Row.

Cross-Durrant, A. (1987). 'John Dewey and Lifelong Education'. In P. Jarvis (ed.), *Twentieth Century Thinkers in Adult Education*. London: Routledge.

Crozier, M. (1963). *Le phénomène bureaucratique*. Paris: Seuil.

Cummings, T. and Worley, C. (1993). *Organizational Development and Change*. Minneapolis, MN: West Publishing.

Cunningham, P. (1993). 'Let's Get Real: A Critical Look at the Practice of Adult Education'. *Journal of Adult Education*, 1 (22), 3–15.

Dag Hammarskjöld Foundation. (1975). *What Now? Another Development*. Uppsala: DHT.

Darcy de Oliveira, R. and Dominicé, P. (1975). *Freire–Illich*. Geneva: IDAC.

Dave, R.H. (1976). *Foundations of Lifelong Education*. Paris: UNESCO.

Delgado, G. (1993). *Beyond the Politics of Place: New Directions in Community Organizing in the 1990s*. Ford Foundation.

Delors, J., Mufti, I.A., Amagi, I., Carneiro, R., Chung, F., Geremek, B., Gorham, W., Kornhauser, A., Manley, M. and Padrón, M. (1996). *Learning: The Treasure Within. Report to UNESCO of the International Commission on Education for the Twenty-first Century*. Paris: UNESCO.

Development Assistance Committee. (1997). *Final Report of the ad hoc Working Group on Participatory Development and Good Governance*. Paris: OECD.

Dewey, J. (1964). *Democracy and Education*. London: Macmillan.

Dewey, J. (1971). *Experience and Education*. London: Collier–Macmillan.

Dixon, N. (1994). *The Organizational Learning Cycle: How We Can Learn Collectively*. London: McGraw-Hill.

Dominicé, P. (1982). 'La biographie éducative, instrument de recherche pour l'éducation des adultes'. *Education et Recherche* 3.

Dumont, L. (1983). *Essais sur l'individualisme: Une perspective anthropologique sur l'idéologie moderne*. Paris: Seuil.

Ekins, P. (1992). *A New World Order: Grassroots Movements for Global Change*. London: Routledge.

Ekkehard, N. (1994). 'The Increasing Importance of Adult Education in Europe'. *Adults Learning*, 6 (1), 31–4.

Elias, N. (1987). *Die Gesellschaft der Individuen*. Frankfurt am Main: Suhrkamp.

Ellacurria, I. (1973). *Teología política*. San Salvador: Secretariado Social Interdiocesano.

Elster, J. (ed.) (1985). *The Multiple Self*. Cambridge: Cambridge University Press.

Escobar, A. (1995). *Encountering Development: The Making and Unmaking of the Third World*. Princeton, NJ: Princeton University Press.

Etzioni, A. (1964). *Modern Organizations*. Englewood Cliffs, NJ: Prentice-Hall.

Etzioni, A. (1975). *A Comparative Analysis of Complex Organizations*. New York: The Free Press.

European Commission. (1997). *Towards a Europe of Knowledge*. Brussels: EU.

European Union. (1995). *White Paper on Education and Training*. Brussels: EU.

Evans, A., Evans, R., and Kennedy, W. (1987). *Pedagogies for the Non-poor*. Maryknoll, NY: Orbis.

Fals-Borda, O. (1993). 'Countervailing Power in Nicaragua, Mexico and Colombia'. In P. Wignaraja (ed.), *New Social Movements in the South: Empowering the People*. London: Zed Books.

Fals-Borda, O. and Rahman, M.A. (1991). *Action and Knowledge: Breaking the Monopoly with Participatory Action Research*. New York and London: Apex Press and Intermediate Technology Publications.

Faure, E., Herrera, F., Kaddoura, A.-R., Lopes, H., Petrovsky, A.V., Rahnema, M., and Ward, F.C. (1972). *Learning to Be: The World of Education Today and Tomorrow*. Paris: UNESCO.

Fay, B. (1987). *Critical Social Science*. Ithaca, NY: Cornell University Press.

Featherstone, M., Lash, S. and Robertson, R. (1995). *Global Modernities*. London: Sage.

Fernandes, W. and R. Tandon (eds) (1981). *Participatory Research and Evaluation: Experiments in Research as a Process of Liberation*. New Delhi: Indian Social Institute.

Ferriss, S., Sandoval, R. and Hembree, D. (1997). *The Fight in the Fields: Cesar Chavez and the Farmworkers Movement*. New York: Harcourt Brace.

Feyerabend, P. (1970). *Against Method: Outlines of an Anarchistic Method of Knowledge*. London: New Left Books.

Feyerabend, P. (1987). *Farewell to Reason*. London: Verso.

Finger, M. (1989). 'New Social Movements and their Implications for Adult

Education'. *Adult Education Quarterly*, 40 (1), 15–22.

Finger, M. (1990). 'The Subject-person of Adult Education in the Crisis of Modernity'. *Studies in Continuing Education*, 12(1), 24–30.

Finger, M. (1991). 'Can Critical Theory Save Adult Education from Post-Modernism?' *Canadian Journal for the Study of Adult Education*, Special Issue, IV(1).

Finger, M. (1992). 'The Changing Green Movement – A Clarification'. *Research in Social Movements, Conflict and Change, 1992* (Supplement 2), 229–46.

Finger, M. (1994). 'From knowledge to Action? Exploring the Relationship between Environmental Experiences, Learning and Behavior'. *Journal of Social Issues*, 50 (3), 141–60.

Finger, M. (1998). Néoliberalisme conre nouvelle gestion publique. *Nouveau Cahiers de l'IUED* 8, 57–76.

Finger, M., Asún, J.M., and Volpe, M. (1995). 'Learning Our Way Out: Theoretical implications for Adult Education'. Paper presented at Adult Learning and Social Participation, Ströbl, Austria.

Finger, M. and Ruchat, B. (eds) (1997). *Pour une nouvelle approche du management public*. Paris: Seli Arslan.

Flecha, R. (1997). *Compartiendo palabras: El aprendizaje de las personas adultas a través del diálogo*. Barcelona: Paidós.

Flecha, R. (1999). 'New Educational Inequalities'. In M. Castells, P. Freire, R. Flecha, H. Giroux, D. Macedo and P. McLaren (eds), *Critical Education in the New Information Age*. Lanham, MD, Boulder, CO, New York and Oxford: Rowan & Littlefield.

Foley, G. (ed.) (1995). *Understanding Adult Education and Training*. St Leonards, Australia: Allen & Unwin.

Foley, G. and Flowers, R. (1990). *Strategies for Self-determination: Aboriginal Adult Education, Training and Community Development in New South Wales*. Sydney: Faculty of Education, University of Technology.

Foley, G. and Flowers, R. (1992). 'Knowledge and Power in Aboriginal Adult Education'. *Convergence*, XXV (1), 61–73.

Follen, S., Clover, D. and Hall, B. (1997). *The Nature of Transformation: Environmental Adult and Popular Education*. Toronto: OISE/UT Press.

Freinet, C. (1972). *Por una escuela del pueblo*. Barcelona: Fontanella.

Freire, P. (1971). *Pedagogy of the Oppressed*. New York: Herder & Herder.

Freire, P. (1980). Acción cultural liberadora. In C.A. Torres (ed.), *Paulo Freire: Educación y concientización*. Salamanca: Sígueme.

Freire, P. (1994). *Pedagogy of Hope*. New York: Continuum.

Freire, P. (1998a). *Pedagogy of the Heart*. New York: Continuum.

Freire, P. (1998b). *Pedagogy of Freedom: Ethics, Democracy and Civic Courage*. Lanham, MD, Boulder, CO, New York and Oxford: Rowan & Littlefield.

Freire, P. and Betto, F. (1985) *E esta escola chamada vida*. São Paulo: Atica.

Freire, P. and Faundez, A. (1989). *Learning to Question: A Pedagogy of Liberation*. New York: Continuum.

Freire, P., Illich, I. and Furter, P. (1974). *Educación para el cambio social*. Buenos Aires: Tierra Nueva.

Freire, P. and Macedo, D. (1987). *Literacy: Reading the Word and the World*. South Hadley, MA: Bergin & Garvey.

Freud, S. (1961). *Civilization and its Discontents*. New York: W.W. Norton.

Friesenhahn, G. (1985). *Kritische Theorie und Pädagogik*. Berlin: Express Edition.

Fromm, E. (1941). *Escape from Freedom*. New York: Farrar & Rinehart.

Gabbard, D.A. (1993). *Silencing Ivan Illich: A Foucauldian Analysis of intellectual Exclsuion*. San Francisco: Austin & Winfield.

Galbraith, J. et al. (1993). *Organizing for the Future: The New Logic for Managing Complex Organizations*. San Francisco: Jossey-Bass.

Galbraith, J.K. (1969). *The New Industrial State*. Harmondsworth: Penguin.

Galbraith, J.K. (1996). *The Good Society*. Boston: Houghton-Mifflin.

Galilea, S. (1976). *Teología de la liberación: Ensayo de síntesis*. Bogotá: Indo-American Press Service.

Garfinkel, H. (1967). *Studies in Ethnomethodology*. Englewood Cliffs, NJ: Prentice-Hall.

Gauchet, M. (1985). *Le désenchantement du monde: Une histoire politique de la religion*. Paris: Gallimard.

Gaventa, J. (1988). 'Participatory Research in North America'. *Convergence*, XXI (2/3), 19–27.

Gaventa, J. and Lewis, H. (1991). *Participatory Education and Grassroots Development: The Case of Rural Appalachia*. London: International Institute for Environment and Development.

George, S. (1988). *A Fate Worse than Debt*. Harmondsworth: Penguin.

George, S. (1992). *The Debt Boomerang*. London: Transnational Institute/Pluto Press.

George, S. (1994). *Faith and Credit: The World Bank's Secular Empire*. Harmondsworth: Penguin.

George, S. (1999). *The Lugano Report: On Preserving Capitalism in the Twenty-first Century*. London: Pluto Press.

George, S. and Sabelli, F. (1997). *La Suisse aux enchères: Répliques à la pensée unique*. Geneva: Editions Zoé.

Georgescu-Roegen, N. (1971). *The Entropy Law and the Economic Process*. Cambridge, MA: Harvard University Press.

Giddens, A. (1984). *The Constitution of Society: Outline of the Theory of Structuration*. Cambridge: Polity Press.

Giddens, A. (1990). *The Consequences of Modernity*. Stanford, CA: Stanford University Press.

Giroux, H. (1997). *Pedagogy and the Politics of Hope: Theory, Culture, and Schooling. A Critical Reader*. Boulder, CO: Westview Press.

Glaser, E. and Strauss, A. (1967). *Discovery of Grounded Theory: Strategies for Qualitative Research*. Chicago: Aldine.

Goodway, D. (ed.) (1989). *For Anarchism: History, Theory and Practice*. London and New York: Routledge.

Gore, J. (1993). *The Struggle for Pedagogies: Critical and Feminist Discourses as Regimes of Truth*. New York: Routledge.

Gorz, A. (1988). *Metamorphoses du travail – Quête du sens*. Paris: Galilée.

Gorz, A. (1997). *Misères du présent, richesse du possible*. Paris: Galilée.

Gould, R.L. (1978). *Transformation: Growth and Change in Adult Life*. New York: Simon & Schuster.

Greider, W. (1997). *One World, Ready or Not: The Manic Logic of Global Capitalism*. New York: Simon & Schuster.

Grinevald, J. (1975). 'Science et développment: Esquisse d'une approche socio-épistémologique'. In *La pluralité des mondes/Cahiers de l'IED*. Paris and Geneva: PUF.

Griswold del Castillo, R., García, R. and Chavez, C. (1995). *Cesar Chavez: A Triumph of the Spirit*. Norman: University of Oklahoma Press.

Guéhenno, J.-M. (1995). *The End of the Nation State*. Minneapolis, MN: University of Minnesota Press.

Guevara, J.R.Q. (1996). 'Learning through Participatory Action Research for Community Ecotourism Planning.' *Convergence*, XXIX (3), 24–39.

Guillen, A. (1993). 'Principles of Libertarian Economy.' *Libertarian Labor Review*, 14 (Winter 1992–93), 20–25.

Gutiérrez, G. (1974). *Praxis of Liberation and Christian Faith*. S. Antonio, TX: MACC.

Habermas, J. (1971). *Knowledge and Human Interests*. Boston and London: Beacon Press.

Habermas, J. (1973). *Legitimationsprobleme im Spätkapitalismus*. Frankfurt am Main: Suhrkamp.

Habermas, J. (1984). *The Theory of Communicative Action, Vol. 1. Reason and Rationalization of Society* (trans. Thomas McCarthy). Boston: Beacon Press.

Habermas, J. (1987). *The Theory of Communicative Action, Vol. 2. Lifeworld and System: A Critique of Functionalist Reason* (trans. Thomas McCarthy). Boston: Beacon Press.

Hajnal, P.I. (1983). *Guide to UNESCO*. London: Oceana Publications.

Hall, B. (1998). 'Reflections on the Origins of the International Participatory Action Research Network and the Participatory Research Group in Toronto'. Paper presented at the Participatory Research Strategies for Empowerment Workshop. New Delhi, 16–18 April.

Harmon, J.B. (1998). 'The Sisters Take on the Rednecks: Harassment against a Lesbian Community. *New Statesman*, 127 (4400), 28–32.

Harrison, C. (1995). 'A Survey of Graduate Programs and the Adult Learning and Development Curriculum. *Adult Education Quarterly*, 45 (4), 197–212.

Hart, M.U. (1992). *Working and Educating for Life: Feminist and International Perspective on Adult Education*. New York: Routledge.

Hayes, E. and Colin, S.A.J. (eds) (1994). *Confronting Racism and Sexism*. San Francisco: Jossey-Bass.

Haymes, S.N. (1995). *Race, Culture and the City: A Pedagogy for Black Urban Struggle*. New York: SUNY Press.

Héber-Suffrin, C.A.M. (1981). *L'école éclatée*. Paris: Stock.

Henwood, D. (1997). *Wall Street: How it Works and for Whom*. London and New York: Verso.

Herman, E.S. (1995). *Triumph of the Market: Essays on Economics, Politics and the Media*. Boston: South End Press.

Hern, M. (ed.) (1996). *Deschooling our Lives*. Gabriola Island, BC and Philadelphia, PA: New Society Publishers.

Hill, R. (1995). 'Gay Discourse in Adult Education: A Critical Review'. *Adult Education Quarterly*, 45 (3), 142–58.

Hill, R. (1997). 'Growing Grassroots: Environmental Conflict, Adult Education and the Quest for Cultural Authority'. Unpublished doctoral thesis, Pennsylvania State University.

Hoffman, D. (1978). *Kritische Erziehungswissenschaft*. Stuttgart: Kohlhammer.

Homer-Dixon, T. (1994). 'Environmental Scarcities and Violent Conflict: Evidence from Cases'. *International Security*, 19 (1), 5–40.

hooks, b. (1993). *Sisters of the Yaw: Black Women and Self-recovery*. Boston: South End Press.

Horton, A. (1989). *The Highlander Folk School: A History of its Major Programs 1932–1961*. Brooklyn, NY: Carlson.

Horton, M. and Freire, P. (1990) *We Make the Road by Walking: Conversations on Education and Social Change*. Philadelphia: Temple University Press.

Horton, M. with Kohl, J. and H. (1990). *The Long Haul: An Autobiography*. New York: Doubleday.

Huxley, J. (1947). *Unesco: Its Purpose and its Philosophy*. Washington: Public Affairs Press.

Illich, I. (1970a). *Deschooling Society*. New York: Harper & Row.

Illich, I. (1970b). *The Dawn of Epimethean Man, and Other Essays*. Cuernavaca: CIDOC.

Illich, I. (1970c). *Celebration of Awareness: A Call for Institutional Revolution*. Garden City, NY: Doubleday.

Illich, I. (1970d). *The Church, Change and Development*. Chicago: Urban Training Center Press.

Illich, I. (1973a). *Tools for Conviviality*. New York: Harper & Row.

Illich, I. (1973b). *After Deschooling, What?* London: Writers & Readers.

Illich, I. (1974a). *Energy and Equity*. London: Calder & Boyars.

Illich, I. (1974b). *Alternativas*. Mexico, DF: J. Mortiz.

Illich, I. (1975). *Medical Nemesis: The Expropiation of Health*. New York: Pantheon.

Illich, I. (1978a). *Towards a History of Needs*. New York: Pantheon.

Illich, I. (1978b). *Fortschrittsmythen*. Hamburg: Rowohlt.

Illich, I. (1978c). *The Right to Useful Employment and its Professional Enemies*. London: M. Boyers.

Illich, I. (1979). 'Preface'. In V. Borremans (ed.), *Guide to Convivial Tools*. New York: R.R. Browker.

Illich, I. (1980). 'The Three Dimensions of Social Choice'. *CoEvolution Quarterly*, 100–125.

Illich, I. (1981). *Shadow Work*. Boston and London: M. Boyars.

Illich, I. (1983). *Gender*. London and New York: M. Boyars.

Illich, I. (1985). *H_2O and the Waters of Forgetfulness: Reflections on the Historicity of 'Stuff'*. Dallas: Dallas Institute of Humanities and Culture.

Illich, I. (1987). 'Un alegato en favor de la investigación sobre el alfabetismo laico'. *Revista de Educación* 288, 45–61.

Illich, I. (1991). *In the Mirror of the Past: Lectures and Addresses 1978–1990*. New York: M. Boyars.

Illich, I. (1993a). 'Needs'. In W. Sachs (ed.), *The Development Dictionary: A Guide to Knowledge as Power*. London and New Jersey: Zed Books.

Illich, I. (1993b). *In the Vineyard of the Text: A Commentary to Hugh's Didascalion*. Chicago: University of Chicago Press.

Illich, I. (1996). 'Foreword'. In M. Hern (ed.), *Deschooling Our Lives*. Gabriola Island, BC and Philadelphia, PA: New Society Publishers.

Illich, I. (1999). 'La obsesión por la salud perfecta'. *Le Monde Diplomatique* (March), 28.

Illich, I. et al. (1977). *Disabling Professions*. London: M. Boyers.

Illich, I. and Sanders, B. (1988). *A B C: The Alphabetization of the Popular Mind*. San Francisco: North Point Press.

Illich, I. and Verne, E. (1976). *Imprisoned in a Global Classroom*. London: Writers & Readers.

Imel, S. (1995). *Workplace Literacy: Trends in the Literature*. Chicago: ERIC Clearinghouse on Adult, Career, and Vocational Education.

Jackson, R.G.A. (1969). *A Study of the Capacity of the United Nations Development System*. Geneva: United Nations.

Janicaud, D. (1985). *La Puissance du rationnel*. Paris: PUF.

Jarvis, P. (1985). *The Sociology of Adult and Continuing Education*. London: Croom Helm.

Jarvis, P. (1987a). *Adult Learning in the Social Context*. London: Croom Helm.

Jarvis, P. (ed.) (1987b) *Twentieth-century Thinkers in Adult Education*. London: Croom Helm.

Jarvis, P. (1990). *An International Dictionary of Adult and Continuing Education*. London: Routledge.

Jarvis, P. and A. Chadwick (eds) (1991). *Training Adult Educators in Western Europe*. London: Routledge.

Jarvis, P. with A. Stannett (1992). *Perspectives on Adult Education and Training in Europe.* Leicester: National Institute of Adult Continuing Education.

Jarvis, P. and N. Walters (1993). *Adult Education and Theological Interpretations.* Malabar, FL: Krieger.

Jay, M. (1973). *The Dialectical Imagination: The History of the Institute of Social Research and the Frankfurt School 1923–1950.* Boston: Little, Brown.

Jelenc, Z. (1995). *Adult Education Research Trends in Central and Eastern European Countries* (Research Project Report), Ljubljana: Slovene Adult Education Center.

Johnston, H., Laraña, E. and Gusfield, J.R. (1994). 'Identities, Grievances and New Social Movements'. In E. Laraña, H. Johnston and J. Gusfield (eds), *New Social Movements: From Ideology to Identity.* Philadelphia: Temple University Press.

Joint Research Team and UIE and NIER (1996). *Comparative Studies on Lifelong Learning Policies* (Report). Tokyo and Hamburg: National Institute for Educational Research and UNESCO Institute for Education.

Jones, P. (1988). *International Policies for Third World Education: UNESCO, Literacy and Development.* London and New York: Routledge.

Kade, J. (1988). *Erwachsenenbildung und Identität: Eine empirische Studie zur Aneignung von Bildungsangeboten.* Weinheim: Deutscher Studien Verlag.

Kaplan, R. (1996). *The Ends of the Earth: A Journey at the Dawn of the 21st Century.* New York: Random House.

Kaplan, R.D. (1994). 'The Coming Anarchy'. *Athlantic Monthly* (February), 44–76.

Karliner, J. (1007). *The Corporate Planet: Ecology and Politics in the Age of Globalization.* San Francisco: Sierra Club Books.

Kassam, Y. and Mustafa, K. (1982). *Participatory Research: An Emerging Alternative Methodology in Social Science Research.* New Delhi: Society for Participatory Research in Asia.

Kerka, S. (1995a). *Adult Career Counseling in a New Age* (Digest EDO-CE-95–167): ERIC Clearinghouse on Adult, Career, and Vocational Education.

Kerka, S. (1995b). *The Learning Organization* (Myths and Realities). Chicago: ERIC Clearinghouse on Adult, Career, and Vocational Education.

Kerka, S. (1996a). *Acces to Information; To Have and Have Not* (Trends and Issues Alert). Chicago: ERIC Clearinghouse on Adult, Career, and Vocational Education.

Kerka, S. (1996b). *Adult Education: Social Change or Status Quo?* (Digest 176). Chicago: ERIC Clearinghouse on Adult, Career, and Vocactional Education.

Kerka, S. (1996c). *Continuing Education: Market Driven or Student Centered?* (Myths and Realities). Chicago: ERIC Clearinghouse on Adult, Career, and Vocational Education.

Kerka, S. (1996d). *Postmodernism and Adult Education* (Trends and Issues Alert). Chicago: ERIC Clearinghouse on Adult, Career, and Vocational Education.

Kett, J.F. (1994). *The Pursuit of Knowledge under Difficulties: From Self-improvement to Adult Education in America, 1750–1990.* Stanford, CA: Stanford University Press.

Ki-Zerbo, J. (1990). *Educate or Perish: Africa's Impasse and Prospects.* Dakar and Abdijan: UNESCO BREDA and UNICEF WCARO.

Knoke, W. (1996). *Bold New World: The Essential Road Map to the Twenty-first Century.* New York: Kodansha International.

Knowles, M. (1968). 'Andragogy not Pedagogy'. *Adult Leadership* 16.

Knowles, M. (1970). *The Modern Practice of Adult Education: Andragogy versus Pedagogy.* New York: Association Press.

Knowles, M. (1973). *The Adult Learner: A Neglected Species.* Houston, TX: Gulf Publishing.

Knowles, M. et al. (1984). *Andragogy in Action: Applying Modern Principles of Adult Education.* San Francisco: Jossey-Bass.

Kolb, D. (1984). *Experiential Learning: Experience as the Source of Learning and Development.* Englewood Cliffs, NJ: Prentice-Hall.

Korten, D. (1990). *Getting to the 21st Century: Voluntary Action and the Global Agenda.* West Hartford, CT: Kumarian Press.

Korten, D. (1995). *When Corporations Rule the World.* San Francisco and West Hartford, CT: Berret-Koehler and Kumarian Press.

Korten, D. (1996) *When Corporations Rule the World.* London: Earthscan.

Korten, D. (1997). *Globalizing Civil Society: Reclaiming our Right to Power.* Seven Stories Press.

Korten, D. (1999). *The Post-corporate World: Life after Capitalism*: Berret-Koehler.

Korten, D. and Klauss, R. (eds) (1984). *People-centered Development: Contributions toward Theory and Planning Frameworks.* West Hartford, CT: Kumarian Press.

Kothari, R. (1989). *State against Democracy: In Search of Humane Governance.* Delhi: Ajanta Publications.

Kothari, R. (1993). *Growing Amnesia: An Essay on Poverty and the Human Consciousness.* New Delhi and New York: Viking.

Kozol, J. (1978). *Children of Revolution.* New York: Delacorte.

Kuhn, T. (1962). *The Structure of Scientific Revolutions.* Chicago: University of Chicago Press.

Landes, D. (1969). *The Unbound Prometheus: Technological Change and Industrial Development in Western Europe from 1750 to the Present.* Cambridge: Cambridge University Press.

Lankard, B.A. (1995a). *Business/Industry Standards and Vocational Program Accountability* (Digest EDO-CE-95–157). Chicago: ERIC Clearinghouse on Adult, Career, and Vocational Education.

Lankard, B.A. (1995b). *SCANS and the New Vocationalism* (Digest EDO-CE-95–165). Chicago: ERIC Clearinghouse on Adult, Career, and Vocational Education.

Lankard, B.A. (1995c). *New Ways of Learning in the Workplace* (Digest EDO-CE-95–161). Chicago: ERIC Clearinghouse on Adult, Career, and Vocational Education.

Lasch, C. (1979). *The Culture of Narcissism: American Life in an Age of Diminishing Expectations.* New York: Warner Books.

Lasch, C. (1984). *The Minimal Self: Psychic Survival in Troubled Times.* London: Picador.

Lash, S. and Urry, J. (1994). *Economies of Signs and Space.* London: Sage Publications.

Latouche, S. (1989). *L'occidentalisation du monde: essai sur la signification, la portée et les limites de l'uniformisation planétaire.* Paris: La Découverte.

Lauterburg, C. (1998). *Fünf nach Zwölf. Der globale Crash und die Zukunft des Lebens.* Frankfurt: Campus.

Leirman, W. (1995). 'Eurodelphi 95: Future Goals and Policies of Adult Education in Europe'. *Questions de formation/Issues in Adult Education*, VI (11/12), 15–107.

Lengrand, P. (1975). *An Introduction to Lifelong Education.* Paris: UNESCO.

Lengrand, P. (1989). 'Lifelong Education: Growth of the Concept'. In C.J. Titmus (ed.), *Lifelong Education for Adults. An International Handbook.* Oxford: Pergamon Press.

Levine, B. (ed.) (1996). *Works about John Dewey 1886–1995.* Carbondale, IL: Southern Illinois University Press.

Lichtner, M. (1991). 'Labor Market Strategies and Adult Education in Europe'. *Studies in the Education of Adults*, 23, 2145–53.

Lindeman, E. (1929). 'The Meaning of Adult Education'. In S. Brookfield (ed.), *Learning Democracy: Eduard Lindeman on Adult Education and Social Change.* London: Croom Helm.

Lindeman, E. (1945). 'The Sociology of Adult Education'. In S. Brookfield (ed.), *Learning Democracy: Eduard Lindeman on Adult Education and Social Change.* London: Croom Helm.

Lindeman, E. (1947). 'Methods of Democratic Adult Education'. In S. Brookfield (ed.), *Learning Democracy: Eduard Lindeman on Adult Education and Social Change.* London: Croom Helm.

Lindeman, E.C. (1925). 'What is Adult Education?' Unpublished manuscript. Columbia University, Butler Library Lindeman Archive.

Lipovetsky, G. (1983). *L'ère du vide: Essais sur l'individualisme contemporain.* Paris: Gallimard.

Luttwak, E. (1995). 'Turbo-charged Capitalism is the Enemy of Family Values (America's Post-liberal Paradigm Shift)'. *New Perspectives Quarterly*, 12 (2), 10–13.

Luttwak, E. (1999). *Turbo-capitalism: Winners and Losers in the Global Economy.* New York: HarperCollins.

Lyotard, J.-F. (1979). *La condition postmoderne: Rapport sur le savoir.* Paris: Editions de Minuit.

McCarthy, T. (1978). *The Critical Theory of Jürgen Habermas*. Cambridge, MA and London: MIT Press.

McGinnis, M.V. (ed.) (1999). *Bioregionalism*. London and New York: Routledge.

McKibben, B. (1989). *The End of Nature*. New York: Random House.

McLaren, P. and Lanskshear, C. (eds) (1993). *Critical Literacy: Politics, Praxis, and the Postmodern*. Albany: State University of New York Press.

McNeill, W. (1982). *The Pursuit of Power: Technology, Armed Force and Society since A.D. 1000*. Chicago: University of Chicago Press.

McTaggart, R. (1991). 'Principles for Participatory Action Research'. *Adult Education Quarterly*, 41 (3), 168–87.

March, J. (1999). *The Pursuit of Organizational Intelligence*. Oxford: Blackwell.

Marcuse, H. (1964). *One-dimensional Man: Studies in the Ideology of Advanced Industrial Society*. Boston: Beacon Press.

Märja, T. (1997). 'The Role of Adult Education in Restoring Democratic Society'. *Convergence*, XXX (2/3), 84–91.

Martin, B. (1993). *In the Public Interest? Privatization and Public Sector Reform*. London: Zed Books.

Martin, H.P. and Schumann, H. (1997). *The Global Trap: Globalization and the Assault on Prosperity and Democracy*. London: Zed Books.

Maslow, A.H. (1954). *Motivation and Personality*. New York: Harper & Row.

Masood, E. (1997). 'La ciencia que hay detrás de Kioto'. *El País* (in collaboration with *Nature* and *Le Monde*), December 3, 28.

Mathen, K. (1997). 'The Burden of Literacy: A Letter from India'. *The Ecologist*, 27 (5), 175–7.

Mayo, P. (1997). 'Paulo Freire 1921–1997: An Appreciation'. *Convergence*, XXX (1), 4–8.

Mead, G.H. (1934). *Mind, Self, & Society from the Standpoint of a Social Behaviorist*. Chicago and London: Chicago University Press.

Meadows, D.H., Zahn, E. and Milling, P. (1972). *Limits to Growth*. New York: Basic Books.

Mehmet, O. (1995). *Westernizing the Third World: The Eurocentricity of Economic Development Theories*. London and New York: Routledge.

Melucci, A. (1989). *Nomads of the Present: Social Movements and Individual Needs in Contemporary Society*. London: Hutchinson Radius.

Melucci, A. (1994). 'A Strange Kind of Newness: What's "New" in New Social Movements?' In E. Laraña, H. Johnston and J.R. Gusfield (eds), *New Social Movements: From Ideology to Identity*. Philadelphia: Temple University Press.

Merriam, S. (ed.) (1983). *Themes of Adulthood through Literature*. New York: Teachers College Press.

Merriam, S.B. and Caffarella, R.S. (1991). *Learning in Adulthood: A Comprehensive Guide*. San Francisco: Jossey-Bass.

Metz, J.B. (1970). *Teología del mundo*. Salamanca: Sígueme.

Mezirow, J. (1991a). *Transformative Dimensions of Adult Learning*. San Francisco: Jossey-Bass.

Mezirow, J. (1991b). 'Faded Visions and Fresh Commitments. Adult Education's Social Goals. Policy paper prepared for AAAE.

Mezirow, J. (1995). 'Being Close to Home'. In M. Welton (ed.), *In Defense of the Lifeworld: Critical Perspectives on Adult Learning*. Albany: State University of New York Press.

Mezirow, J. and Associates (eds) (1990). *Fostering Critical Reflection in Adulthood: A Guide to Transformative and Emancipatory Learning*. San Francisco: Jossey-Bass.

Mies, M. and Shiva, V. (1997). *Ecofeminismo: Teoría, crítica y perspectivas*. Barcelona: Icaria Antrazyt.

Mies, M. and Shiva, V. (1998). *La praxis del ecofeminismo: Biotecnología, consumo, reproducción*. Barcelona: Icaria.

Milbrath, L. (1989). *Envisioning a Sustainable Society: Learning Our Way Out*. Albany: State University of New York Press.

Mohrmann, A.M. et al. (eds) (1989). *Large-scale Organizational Change*. San Francisco: Jossey-Bass.

Moltmann, J. (1971). *Teología de la esperanza*. Salamanca: Sígueme.

Moore, D.P. and Poppino, M.A. (1983). *Successful Tutoring: A Practical Guide to Adult Learning Processes*. Springfield, IL: Thomas.

Moser, H. (1975). *Aktionsforschung als kritische Theorie der Sozialwissenschaften*. Munich.

National Institute for Educational Research of Japan and UNESCO Institute for Education. (1997). *Comparative Studies on Lifelong Learning Policies*. NIER and UIE.

Norberg-Hodge, H. (1991). *Ancient Futures: Learning from Ladakh*. San Francisco: Sierra Club Books.

Newman, M. (1994). *Defining the Enemy: Adult Education in Social Action*. Sydney: Stewart Victor.

OECD (1996). *Lifelong Learning for All*. Paris: OECD.

Oelkers, J. (1983). Pädagogische anmerkungen zu Habermas' theorie kommunikativen handelns. *Zeitschrift fur Pädagogik*, 29(2), 271–96.

Offe, C. (1984). *Contradictions of the Welfare State*. London: Hutchinson.

Ohliger, J. (1991). 'Alternative Images of the Future in Adult Education'. In S. Merriam and P. Cunningham (eds), *Handbook of Adult and Continuing Education*. San Francisco: Jossey-Bass.

Ohliger, J. and McCarthy, C. (1971). 'Lifelong Learning or Lifelong Schooling: A Tentative View of the Ideas of Ivan Illich with a Quotational Bibliography'. Syracuse: Syracuse University Publications in Continuing Education and ERIC Clearinghouse on Adult Education.

Ohmae, K. (1995). *The End of the Nation State*. New York: The Free Press.

Okamoto, K. (1994). *Lifelong Learning Movement in Japan: Strategy, Practices and Challenges*. Tokyo: Ministry of Education, Science and Culture.

Orr, D.W. (1992). *Ecological Literacy: Education and the Transition to a Post-modern World*. Albany: State University of New York Press.

Osborn, T. (1997). *Coming Home to America: A Roadmap to Gay and Lesbian Empowerment*. New York: St. Martin's Press.

Paffrath, F.H. (ed.) (1987). *Kritische Theorie und Pädagogik der Gegenwart*. Weinheim: Deutscher Studien.

Panikkar, R. (1993). *Paz y desarme cultural*. Santander: Sal Terrae.

Parlant, F. (1982). *La fin du développement*. Paris: François Maspéro.

Pearson, L., et al. (1969). *Partners in Development: Report of the Commission on International Development*. Washington: Praeger.

Pedler, M., Burgoyne, J. and Boydell, T. (1991). *The Learning Company: A Strategy for Sustainable Development*. London: McGraw-Hill.

Peterson, E. (1996). *Freedom Road: Adult Education of African Americans*. Malabar: Krieger.

Pierson, C. (1996). *The Modern State*. London and New York: Routledge.

Pineau, G. (1977). *Éducation ou aliénation permanente?* Montreal: Dunod.

Pineau, G. (1983). *Produire sa vie: autoformation et autobiographie*. Montreal: Saint-Martin.

Poggi, G. (1978). *The Development of the Modern State: A Sociological Introduction*. London: Hutchinson.

Poggi, G. (1990). *The State: Its Nature, Development and Prospects*. Cambridge: Polity Press.

Polanyi, K. (1942). *The Great Transformation: The Political and Economic Origins of Our Time*. Boston: Beacon Press.

Probst, G. and Büchel, B. (1994). *Organisationales Lernens*. Herrsching: Barbara Kirsch.

Puekart, H. (1983). 'Kritische Theorie und Pädagogik'. *Zeitschrift fur Pädagogik*, 29 (2), 195–218.

Quigley, B.A. (1997). *Rethinking Literacy Education: The Critical Need for Practice-based Change*. San Francisco: Jossey-Bass.

Raghavan, C. (1990). *Recolonization: GATT, the Uruguay round and the Third World*. London and Penang: Zed Books and Third World Network.

Rahman, M.A. (1993). *People's Self-development: Perspectives on Participatory Action Research*. London and Dhaka: Zed Books and University Press Limited.

Ramdas, L. (1997). 'The Tao of Mangoes, Adult Education and Freire: The Continuing Challenges and Dilemmas. *Convergence*, XXX (2/3), 17–26.

Rammstedt, O. (1978). *Soziale Bewegung*. Frankfurt am Main: Suhrkamp Verlag.

Raschke, J. (1985). *Soziale Bewegungen – Ein historisch-systematischer Grundriss*. Frankfurt: Campus Verlag.

Ratnapala, N. (ed.) (1978). *The Sarvodaya movement: Self-help Rural Develop-*

ment in Sri Lanka. Connecticut.

Reich, C. (1995). *Opposing the System*. London: Little, Brown.

Reifner, U. (1992). *Banking for People*. New York: de Gruyter.

Reimer, E. (1971). *School is Dead*. Harmondsworth: Penguin.

Riechmann, J. and Fernández Buey, F. (1994). *Redes que dan libertad: Introducción a los nuevos movimientos sociales*. Barcelona: Paidós.

Riedel, C. (1989). *Subjekt und Individuum: Zur Geschichte des philosophischen Ich-Begriffes*. Darmstadt: Wissenschaftliche Buchgesellschaft.

Riesman, D., Glazer, N. and Denney, R. (1950). *The Lonely Crowd*. New Haven, CT and London: Yale University Press.

Rifkin, J. (1995). *The End of Work*. New York: Putnam.

Riggs, R.E. and Plano, J.C. (1994). *The United Nations*. Belmont, CA: Wadsworth.

Rist, G. (1997). *The History of Development: From the Western Origins to Global Faith*. London and New Jersey: Zed Books.

Rogers, C. (1951). *Client-Centered Therapy: Its Current Practice, Implications and Theory*. Boston, MA: Houghton-Mifflin.

Rogers, C. (1969). *Freedom to Learn: A View of What Education Might Become*. Columbus, OH: Merrill.

Rogers, C. (1980). *A Way of Being*. Boston, MA: Houghton-Mifflin.

Rohmoser, G. (1983). 'Darf man Erziehungstheorie aus Gesellschafts-theorie reduzieren? *Zeitschrift fur Pädagogik*, 29 (2), 255–70.

Ross, D. (1991). *The Origins of American Social Science*. Cambridge: Cambridge University Press.

Roszak, T. (1994). *The Cult of Information: A Neo-luddite Treatise on High-tech, Artificial Intelligence, and the True Art of Thinking*. Berkeley: University of California Press.

Sachs, I. (1994). *L'ecodevelopment. Strategies de transition vers le XXe siècle*. Paris: Les Editions Ouvrières.

Sachs, W. (ed.) (1992). *The Development Dictionary: A Guide to Knowledge as Power*. London: Zed Books.

Sachs, W. (ed.) (1993). *Global Ecology: A New Arena of Political Conflict*. London: Zed Books.

Sale, K. (1985). *Dwellers in the Land: The Bioregional Vision*. San Francisco: Sierra Club Books.

Schapiro, R.M. (1995). 'Liberatory Pedagogy and the Development Paradox. *Convergence*, 28 (2), 28–48.

Schied, F. (1993). *Learning in Social Context: Workers and Adult Education in Nineteenth-Century Chicago*. DeKalb, IL: LEPS Press.

Schön, D.A. (1983). *The Reflective Practitioner: How Professionals Think in Action*. New York: Basic Books.

Schön, D.A. (1987). *Educating the Reflective Practitioner: Toward a New Design for Teaching and Learning in the Professions*. San Francisco: Jossey-Bass.

Schumacher, E.F. (1974). *Small is Beautiful*. New York: Harper Torchbooks.

Schweickart, D. (1997). *Más allá del capitalismo*. Santander: Sal Terrae.

Segundo, J.L. (1975). *Liberación de la teología*. Buenos Aires: Carlos Lohlé.

Senge, P. (1991). *The Fifth Discipline: The Art and Practice of the Learning Organization*. San Francisco: Jossey-Bass.

Sennett, R. (1987). *Verfall und Ende des öffentlichen Lebens: Die Tyrannei des Intimität*. Frankfurt am Main: Fischer Wissenschaft.

Sennett, W. (1974). *The Rise and Fall of Public Man*. Los Angeles: University of California Press.

Setem. (1997). *Café amargo: Por un comercio Norte-Sur más justo*. Barcelona: Icaria.

Sewell, J.P. (1975). *UNESCO and World Politics: Engaging in International Politics*. Princeton: Princeton University Press.

Shepherd, G. (1992). 'Managing Africa's Tropical Dry Forests: A Review of Indigenous Methods' (Agricultural Ocasional Paper). London: Overseas Development Institute.

Shiva, V. (1988). *Staying Alive: Women, Ecology, and Development*. London: Zed Books.

Shiva, V. (1991). *Biodiversity: Social and Ecological Consequences*. New York: St. Martin's Press.

Shiva, V. (1992). *The Violence of the Green Revolution: Third World Agriculture, Ecology and Politics*. London: Zed Books.

Shiva, V. (1993). *Monocultures of the Mind: Perspectives on Biodiversity and Biotechnology*. New York: St. Martin's Press.

Shiva, V. (1997). *Biopiracy: The Plunder of Nature and Knowledge*. Boston: South End Press.

Shiva, V. (1999). *Stolen Harvest: The Hijacking of the Global Food Supply*. Boston: South End Press.

Shor, I. (1992). *Empowering Education: Critical Teaching for Social Change*. Chicago: University of Chicago Press.

Shor, I. and Freire, P. (1987). *A Pedagogy for Liberation: Dialogues on Transforming Education*. Massachusetts: Bergin & Garvey.

Simon, H. (1945). *Administrative Behavior: A Study of Decision-making Processes in Administrative Organizations*. New York: The Free Press.

Sims, R.R. and S.J. (eds) (1995). *The Importance of Learning Styles: Understanding the Implications for Learning, Course Design, and Education*. Westport, CT: Greenwood Press.

Sloan, T. (1996). *Damaged Life: The Crisis of the Modern Psyche*. London and New York: Routledge.

Smith, R. (1982). *Learning How to Learn: Applied Theory for Adults*. New York: Cambridge University Press.

Sobrino, J. (1976). *Cristología desde América Latina*. Mexico.

Stein, G. (ed.) (1979). *Kritische Pädagogik: Positionen und Kontroversen*. Hamburg: Hoffman & Campe.

Sternberg, R.J. (1997). *Thinking Styles*. Cambridge and New York:

Cambridge University Press.

Stiefel, M. and Wolfe, M. (1994). *A Voice for the Excluded. Popular Participation in Development: Utopia or Necesity*. London and Atlantic Highlands, NJ: Zed Books in association with UNRISD.

Strange, S. (1986). *Casino Capitalism*. Manchester: Manchester University Press.

Strange, S. (1996). *The Retreat of the State: The Diffusion of Power in the World Economy*. Cambridge: Cambridge University Press.

Stubblefield, H.W. and Keane, P. (1994). *Adult Education in the American Experience*. San Francisco: Jossey-Bass.

Suchodolsky, B. (1966). *Fundamentos de la pedagogía socialista*. Barcelona: Laia.

Szasz, A. (1994). *Ecopopulism: Toxic Easte and the Movement for Environmental Justice*. Minneapolis: University of Minnesota Press.

Tarrow, S. (1994). *Power in Movement: Social Movements, Collective Action and Mass Politics in the Modern State*. New York: Cambridge University Press.

Thomas, A.M. (1987). 'Roby Kidd: Intellectual Voyageur'. In P. Jarvis (ed.), *Twentieth-century Thinkers in Adult Education*. New York: Routledge.

Thomas, W. and Znaniecki, F. (1927). *The Polish Peasant in Europe and America*. New York: Octagon Books.

Thompson, J. (1980). *Learning Liberation: Women's Response to Men's Education*. London: Croom Helm.

Thorndike, E.L., Bregman, E.O., Tilton, J.W. and Woodyard, E. (1928). *Adult Learning*, New York: Macmillan.

Tilly, C. (1992). *Coercion, Capital, and European States AD 990–1992*. Oxford and Cambridge, MA: Blackwell.

Timberlake, L. (1986). *Africa in Crisis: The Causes, the Cures of Environmental Bankrupcy*. Philadelphia: New Society.

Torres, C. (ed.) (1997). *Education, Power and Personal Biographies: Introduction to Dialogues with Critical Educators*. New York: Routledge.

Touraine, A. (1978). *La voix et le regard*. Paris: Seuil.

Touraine, A. (1982). *Mouvements sociaux d'aujourd'hui. Acteurs et analystes*. Paris: Fayard.

Touraine, A. (1992). *Critique de la modernité*. Paris: Fayard.

Trainer, T. (1989). *Developed to Death: Rethinking Third World Development*. London: Green Print.

Tuijman, A. (ed.) (1996). *International Encyclopaedia of Adult Education and Training*. Oxford: Pergamon.

Turkle, S. (1995). *Life on the Screen*. New York: Simon & Schuster.

US Department of Labor (1991). *What Work Requires of Schools: A SCAN Report for America 2000*. The Secretary Commission on Achieving Necessary Skills, US Department of Labor.

UNCED. (1991). *In Our Hands*. Geneva: Earth Summit '92.

UNDP. (1997). *Human Development Report 1997*. New York and Oxford: UNDP and Oxford University Press.

UNDP. (1998). *Human Development Report 1998*. New York and Oxford: UNDP and Oxford University Press.

UNESCO. (1979). *Documents from the Experimental World Literacy Programme*. Paris: UNESCO.

UNESCO. (1993). *World Education Report 1993*. Paris: UNESCO.

UNESCO. (1995). *Programmes and Priorities 1994–1995*. Paris: UNESCO.

UNESCO/UNDP. (1976). *The Experimental World Literacy Programme: A Critical Assessment*. Paris and New York: UNESCO and UNDP.

UNRISD. (1994). *Environmental Degradation and Social Integration*. Geneva: United Nations Research Institute for Social Development.

UNRISD. (1995). *States of Disarray: The Social Effects of Globalization*. Geneva: UNRISD.

Usher, R., Bryant, I. and Johnston, R. (1997). *Adult Education and the Postmodern Challenge: Learning Beyond the Limits*. New York: Routledge.

Usher, R. and Edwards, R. (1994). *Postmodernism and Education*. London and New York: Routledge.

van Krogh, G. and Ross, J. (eds) (1996). *Managing Knowledge. Perspectives in Cooperation and Competition*. London: Sage.

Vattimo, G. (1985). *La fine della modernità: Nichilismo ed ermeneutica nella cultura post-moderna*. Milano: Garzanti Editore.

Watkins, K. and Marsick, V. (1993). *Sculpting the Learning Organization: The Art of Systemic Change*. San Francisco: Jossey-Bass.

WCED. (1987). *Our Common Future*. World Commission on Environment and Development. Oxford: Oxford University Press.

WCEFA. (1990). World Conference on Education for All and Framework for Action to Meet Basic Learning Needs. New York: Interagency Commission.

We The People Organization, K. (1996). *Ivan Illich with Jerry Brown*. Los Angeles: Green Plan Archives Radio University.

Weiss, T.G., Forsythe, D.P. and Coate, R.A. (1994). *The United Nations and Changing World Politics*. Boulder, CO: Westview Press.

Welton, M. (1993). 'Social Revolutionary Learning: The New Social Movements as Learning Sites. *Adult Education Quarterly*, 43 (3), 152–64.

Welton, M. (ed.) (1995). *In Defense of the Lifeworld: Critical Perspectives on Adult Learning*. Albany, NY: State University of New York Press.

West, C. (1989). *The American Evasion of Philosophy: A Genealogy of Pragmatism*. Madison: University of Wisconsin Press.

Whalley, J. and Hamilton, C. (1996). *The Trading System after the Uruguay Round*. Washington, DC: Institute for International Economics.

White, L. (1967). 'The Historical Roots of Our Ecological Crisis'. *Science* 155.

Wignaraja, P. (ed.) (1993). *New Social Movements in the South: Empowering the People*. London: Zed Books.

Wignaraja, P., Hussain, A., Sethi, H. and Wignaraja, G. (1990). *Participa-*

tory Development: Learning from South Asia. Karachi and Oxford: Oxford University Press.

Wildemeersch, D., Finger, M. and Jansen, T. (eds) (1997). *Adult Education and Social Responsibility*. Frankfurt am Main: Peter Lang.

Witschel, G. (1983). *Die Erziehungslehre der kritischen Theorie*. Bonn.

Wolman, W. and Calamosca, A. (1997). *The Judas Economy: The Triumph of Capital and the Betrayal of Work*. Reading, MA: Addison-Wesley.

Wood, D.N. (1996). *Post-intellectualism and the Decline of Democracy: The Failure of Reason and Responsibility in the Twentieth Century*. Westport, CT and London: Praeger.

Woods, P. (1992). 'Symbolic Interactionism: Theory and Method'. In *The Handbook of Qualitative Research Education*. Orlando, FL: Academic Press.

World Bank (1997). *World Development Report 1997: The State in a Changing World*. New York: World Bank and Oxford University Press.

Yergin, D. (1991). *The Prize: The Epic Quest for Oil, Money and Power*. New York: Simon & Schuster.

Yunus, M. et al. (1997). *Vers un monde sans pauvreté*. Paris.

Zacharakis-Jutz, J. (1988). Post-Freirean Adult Education: A Question of Empowerment and Power. *Adult Education Quarterly* 39.

Index